THE LEGENDARY TALES
AND HISTORICAL TRUTHS OF THE
MOST NOTORIOUS

WARRIORS

THE LEGENDARY TALES
AND HISTORICAL TRUTHS OF THE
MOST NOTORIOUS

Daniel Mersey

CONWAY

*To Mum and Dad – who showed me that history could be fun
from an early stage in my life.*

*Thanks to Symmie Tyson for patiently allowing me to work on my manuscript,
and to John Lee and Caroline Bolton for commissioning my book and helping
me through the writing process.*

© Daniel Mersey, 2002

First published in Great Britain in 2002 by Brassey's

This paperback edition first published in Great Britain 2007
by Conway An imprint of Anova Books Company Ltd
151 Freston Road
London W10 6TH
www.anovabooks.com

British Cataloguing in Publication Data
A catalogue record for this book is available from the British Library.

ISBN 10: 1857533704
ISBN 13: 9781857533705

Edited by Alison Moss

Typesetting by SX Composing Ltd, Rayleigh, Essex
Printed and bound by CPD Ltd, Ebbw Vale, Wales

Contents

Daniel Mersey was born in Edmonton, London in 1974. Educated as an archaeologist at the University of York, he now works as an editor and writer in Sussex, specialising in British early medieval military history. His book, *Arthur, King of the Britons* (Summersdale, 2004), was runner up in the Longman–History Today Awards in 2006, in the 'New Generation' category.

INTRODUCTION

To every age, and to every nation, there is a peculiar
ideal of heroism, and in the popular legends of each age
this ideal may be found. Again, these legends give not
only the hero as he seemed to his age; they also show
the social life, the virtues and vices, the superstitions
and beliefs, of earlier ages embedded in the tradition, as
fossils are found in the uplifted strata of some ancient
ocean-bed. (M I Ebbutt, *The British*, 1910)

Among the most enduring stories passed down through
generations are those which celebrate the feats of
great warriors in battle. Indeed, all the warriors
described in this book are most likely to be familiar by name
to the casual reader, even if not by deed. The truth behind
such legends is often as interesting as the mythical tale. Many
mythical characters have bridged the historical and
mythological chasm by their real life actions being
memorable to following generations, and the historical
figure being outstanding in his or her own way before being
cast into the realm of folklore.

But what constitutes myth and what constitutes history?

Warriors

Lewis Spence eloquently assessed the thin dividing line between fact and fiction in history: '…myth is the ivy that binds all historical ruins and makes them picturesque to the eye;' (1914: 223). As will be seen throughout the chapters of this book, myth and historical fact become entwined over the decades and centuries following the death of a great leader. In the case of some, such as Dracula, their original deeds are all but lost in the fantastic legends that build up around their name. Other figures are luckier in as much as their original deeds are remembered – to some extent this includes Robin Hood and William Wallace.

How would these famous warriors actually have fought – if indeed they did exist? This is often misrepresented by myth, the warriors and battles being transported from their own time into using the weapons and tactics current at the time of the legend's most popular epoch. By looking at the military history of a period, combined with the known history of each figure and their legend, I hope to present a glimpse of the truth behind some of the world's greatest fighters.

As will be seen in the following chapters, not all myths surrounding these legendary heroes are ancient in origin. Our twenty-first-century version of bards and folklore is undoubtedly the cinema, and film-makers in the twentieth century and beyond have not been afraid of rewriting history, or of plucking a poorly known tale from obscurity for millions of watchers to enjoy world-wide. In turn, the information presented in these cinematic spectacles has passed into folklore – perhaps the two most significant

Introduction

examples in this book are Robin Hood and William Wallace. No longer are the feats of arms of these heroes just recited orally within their own insular culture as the bards of old had. Now, folklore and mythology must be able to leave their mark on a global audience. This undoubtedly explains the introduction of a Moorish warrior to the Robin Hood cycle, an (American-influenced) Irish warrior at the side of William *Braveheart* Wallace, and a variety of knights in King Arthur's court foreign to the British Isles – from Connecticut Yankees and spacemen to yet another Moorish warrior.

I have tried to place a dividing line between myth and history throughout the book. The historical sections have been based on archaeological interpretation (which is seldom perfect but so often enlightening) and on events interpreted either at the time or by modern historians as having taken place. Certain mythological elements, such as Beowulf's Grendel, and the various dragons and giants that characters such as Arthur and Roland pitted themselves against, are certainly fictitious, and I have chosen to interpret the superhuman feats often undertaken in a similar light, given the slim possibility of their enactment.

One author's historical fact may be debated by another writer as dubious or absolute myth; I have tried to stand in the middle ground wherever possible, ascribing only to 'history' the events that seem certain to have occurred; the more contentious historical issues have been termed 'myth' unless otherwise noted. Few of the folktales presented here have remained unchanged since their first telling. Such is the

nature of myth and folklore that each new generation of
storytellers add their own twists to the tale – incorporating
aspects relevant to their own times and lives, and often
bringing unrelated tales into the overall cycle. Many of the
warriors featured in this book have developed into such epic
tales over the centuries that a writer could not hope to
encompass every single story about them in a book of this
type. For these mighty giants of folklore, I have tried
to present an overall, rounded retelling of their
story, presenting some of the most significant and
interesting aspects of their legendary lives.

In the same way that many of the
warriors in this book have drawn on
diverse sources of history and
folklore over the centuries, I have
tried to present a broad
range of illustrative
material to support the
text. These vary from
archaeological artefacts
and interpretations of
carvings or drawings several
hundred years old, to modern
artworks. I have intended the imagery of this
book to help represent and describe both myth and
history from as many aspects as possible.

Two of the earliest warriors who undertook deeds on an epic scale – David and Goliath,
shown here in mid twelfth-century armour. (From Hewitt's *Ancient Armour and
Weapons in Europe*, 1855)

Introduction

Similarly, I have attempted to look to a number of sources for quotations about each legend contained within this book. To present all of the characters from just one version of the tale would not accurately reflect a point which I feel is key to a book of this type – that each warrior has changed over time, the stories about him being altered to appeal to each new audience of each new age. This is perhaps slightly unusual in a book of this type, where an author may feel that he or she should stick doggedly to one translation for authenticity; this ignores the fact that the stories have changed over time, and I therefore make no apologies for using different storyteller's words to recount the same tales.

Given the common occurrence of warriors in mythology and folklore world-wide, it has been quite a task selecting which heroes were worthy of inclusion in this book. The majority that I chose come from Western Europe, for the simple reason that such warriors display the virtues common in English-speaking thought as typifying the skills and honour of such figures. Hiawatha is an exception from such warrior ethics, as he was a bringer of peace; the background to Hiawatha's appearance was one of violent warfare, however, and he is historically portrayed as a leader, and would have probably led his own people in battle before achieving his long-lasting peace.

I have not included warriors from what we now consider to be the Classical myths of Greek and Rome – Achilles and his fellow warriors from the Trojan Wars are often placed alongside heroes such as Bellerophon, Perseus, and Hercules, but actually come from a different mythological cycle. The simple reason for the exclusion of the traditional Greek and Roman heroes is that there is little good evidence to place them at any point on a historical timeline, as they are from a world clearly created by and overseen by groups of gods, instead of having been superimposed on a specific historical period. Similarly, it may seem strange that well-known and historically attested to characters such as Spain's El Cid and the ex-gladiator Spartacus are absent; however, these are better thought of as purely historical figures, where only a small amount of myth or exaggeration has crept into the tale that we know of them now.

Duelling knights, attired in late twelfth- or thirteenth-century armour. (From Hewitt's *Ancient Armour and Weapons in Europe*, 1855)

Introduction

Some of the warriors included have become eponymous and famous as figures of valour – Achilles and King Arthur spring immediately to mind, although Roland and Cuchulain should lay equal claim. Others, such as Dracula, Robin Hood and Hiawatha have become famous due to their non-historical and non-martial deeds of legend.

I have tried to present a rounded picture of each warrior – their fictitious deeds, historical precedents, and their way of plying violent trade in their own historical sense is described. Even so, the diversity of information available for most of the characters (especially King Arthur and Robin Hood – the stories of each I have only had space to cover in the briefest detail) has not allowed me to delve into the deepest depths of every aspect of legend, history and battle. One or two others included within are known to us from more limited sources (notably Beowulf and Roland), so their stories are allowed enough space to be described in more detail. Despite this, I hope that I have managed to convey some of the finest glories of the greatest warriors known in legend, and to explain the armament and tactics of some of the most intriguing military forces known in ancient and medieval history.

ARTHUR
King of the Britons

Arthur, renowned as the 'once and future king of Britain', is probably the world's most famous fictional king. The legend of Arthur has two distinct strands – Arthur as a Celtic hero, and Arthur as an Anglo-Norman hero. The Celtic Arthur is portrayed in many lights, variable in character – he is sometimes shown as a battle hero, sometimes as a thief. In Anglo-Norman eyes, Arthur was one of the three great heroes of medieval romance (along with Alexander the Great and Charlemagne). Arthur has suffered less through modern cinema history than most other folk heroes have; the few cinema releases about these legends stick, for the most part, to the writings of Malory. Perhaps the finest rendering of Arthurian legend on film came in 1981 with John Boorman's *Excalibur.*

Welsh folklore presents a sometimes confusing image of Arthur. He appears sometimes as a fool, sometimes as a trickster, occasionally as a rapist, but most often as an accomplished warrior. The reason for this rather unappealing portrayal of the most famous Celtic hero is uncertain; it is conceivable that the Welsh bards wished to disown Arthur

after the development of Anglo-Norman legends about him
– or perhaps they reflect the true man as opposed to the
chivalric myth. Probably the earliest surviving tale of the
mythical Celtic Arthur is his appearance in the tale of
Culhwch and Olwen, where Arthur is curiously portrayed as a
cross between a barbaric Celtic chieftain and a courtly
medieval king.

In contrast to Welsh tradition, the English folklore tales of
Arthur are classified as the 'Arthurian Romances'. As early as
1136, Geoffrey of Monmouth's *Historia Regnum Britanniae* (A
History of the Kings of Britain) mentions Arthur as a king.
Wace translated Geoffrey of Monmouth's ideas into verse in
1155, and his *Brut d'Angleterre* includes the first mention of the
infamous Round Table. Layamon built further on these ideas in
1205, transporting Arthur to the mystical island of Avalon for
his death. Around this time, when Arthurian tales were also
becoming popular in France, Robert de Borron introduced
the Grail Quest and Merlin became more prominent in his
version. Characters from other legends became knights of
Arthur (some Arthurian characters may even trace their
ancestry back to pagan Celtic gods). Many other Welsh and
Breton ideas were incorporated into the legend of Arthur and
Sir Thomas Malory contributed his famed prose *Le Morte
d'Arthur*, printed by Caxton, in 1485. In the Victorian era,
Tennyson took the legends further with his poetry.

The tales that we commonly tell as the legends of Arthur
and the Round Table are a combination of stories from the
above writers. The entirety of Arthurian myth would be far too
complex to relate in full in a book twice this length, let alone

this chapter, so I retell what I consider to be the most important aspects of the cycle below. The most common aspects used in the modern tales come from Malory's work – but the Arthurian legend stands as a firm reminder that such folktales grow into epic tales over decades, with new generations adding touches important to their own culture and life.

Gawain and the Green Knight

Many aspects of Arthurian legend have their origin in pre-Christian symbolism and folklore. One such story is that of Sir Gawain and the Green Knight.

Gawain accepted the challenge of 'an appalling figure… garbed all in green' with green hair and green skin, carrying a holly cluster (a Christian symbol of good luck – the beginnings of which lay in pagan mythology), who rode into Arthur's court at Christmas, daring the 'good sport' of a beheading game. The essence of his challenge was that any one of Arthur's knights brave enough to try could deliver an undefended blow at the Green Knight's neck; if the Green Knight survived, the blow would be returned.

Silence followed the speech, nobody wishing to accept the mystical looking knight's request, but to save Arthur from having to accept the challenge, Gawain stepped forward. He beheaded the giant Green Knight with a mighty blow, yet the Green Knight stood, picked his head up by the hair and commanded Gawain to arrive at the Green Chapel in a year's time, to receive the return blow.

For much of the year, Gawain spent his time searching for the chapel – his chivalric duty did not allow him to decline the demand – and was told by a knight named Sir Bercilak in the Wirral where he might find it. Gawain stayed at the knight's castle for several nights before undertaking the final part of his fateful journey (as was the chivalric custom). Sir Bercilak's wife came to Gawain each night, exchanging kisses (but nothing more) and finally giving him a green baldric with magical powers of protection. Scared of his coming appointment with the Green Knight, Gawain accepted this.

Arriving at the Green Chapel, the Green Knight twice made to deliver blows, stopping short at Gawain's neck on both occasions – claiming that the knight of the Round Table was shaking with fear. He hafted the axe for a third time, and delivered a blow so skilfully that it did no more than nick Gawain's skin.

Leaping to his feet, Gawain confronted the Green Knight, who turned out to be Sir Bercilak – enchanted by Morgan le Fay to test the honour of the Round Table. The first blow, Bercilak explained, was withheld as Gawain had honourably kept his appointment with certain death; the second he withheld as Gawain honourably spurned his wife's advances; yet the third was delivered, but gently, for the unworthy act of accepting the magical green baldric.

From that time on, Arthur decreed that Gawain's shield device would be a green baldric, so that all may know how he upheld the honour of the Round Table at the Green Chapel.

The poem – often described as one of the most masterly pieces of fourteenth-century literature – bears many similarities to the Irish epic of Cuchulain (see Chapter Nine), where the Hound of Ulster agrees to play the beheading game with Uath mac Imomai.

Warriors

Arthur was born into a time of strife – the Britons and their enemies were fighting bloody wars, and Arthur's father, Uther, was at the forefront of the fighting. Arthur, born illegitimately to Uther with the help of the powerful and mysterious sorcerer Merlin, was brought up in secret by a worthy knight named Sir Ector, as Merlin had desired.

With Uther's death, the British nobles fell further into civil war. Merlin announced that the leader of the Britons would become evident through a challenge – he summoned the nobility to a site where a beautiful sword lay embedded in a stone; whoever drew the sword, Merlin proclaimed, would rule the country:

> . . . letters there were written in gold about the sword that saiden thus:– WHOSO PULLETH OUT THIS SWORD OF THIS STONE AND ANVIL, IS RIGHTWISE KING BORN OF ALL ENGLAND. Then the people marvelled, and told it to the Archbishop. (Malory, translated in Cowen, 1969, 16)

Many tried but all failed; Arthur, unknown to all to be the son of Uther, succeeded. The majority of the nobility were appalled that Merlin was prepared to support Arthur, and for a while it seemed that the civil strife would continue. However, fear of Merlin, respect for the memory of Uther, and the support of a few nobles loyal to Arthur saw him rise to become king.

Although Arthur had led his early life as the lowly squire of a good knight, his charisma and leadership qualities

Arthur: King of the Britons

evidently shone through – the enemies of the Britons were expelled and Arthur set about restoring order to his realm, aided by the now united British nobility.

As Arthur grew in power, knights flocked to join his retinue; as the numbers expanded, Arthur founded his famous round table – where no knight would sit more prominently at the table than his fellows, not even Arthur himself. Some legends have Arthur travelling far and wide, fighting Roman armies on the continent, giants, dragons, a variety of other mystical beasts, and undertaking military campaigns in France, Ireland and further afield.

In one, Arthur finds and marries Guinevere, the daughter of a giant – who Arthur must outwit and overpower before he may reach her; Guinevere held Arthur in high regard once she set eyes upon him:

> As for the princess, she no sooner saw Arthur than she thought him the bravest and most splendid king in the world. (Guerber, 1919: 290)

Merlin continued to advise and protect Arthur, and many mystical elements are introduced into the essentially Christian mythos of medieval writers such as Malory. One such event, overtly pagan in origin, is the story of how Arthur acquired his magical sword, Excalibur. It came to Arthur's attention that a foreign knight had made camp at a bridge in Arthur's realm. The knight would only let a traveller pass if they could defeat him in a duel; as yet, no one had been successful. Arthur journeyed to the site, saw a number of his retinue defeated by this faultless fighter, and then challenged the mysterious knight himself. In the ensuing duel, Arthur and the knight wounded each other many times, and Arthur eventually overpowered his opponent, but only after breaking his sword. The knight, at the end of the duel, was revealed to be not any ordinary knight,

> But one Sir Lancelot du Lake,
> Who was approved well,
> He for his deeds and feats of armes
> All others did excell.
> (*Sir Lancelot du Lake*, an old ballad quoted in Guerber, 1919: 293)

Lancelot swore allegiance to Arthur, and Merlin then led the king to a mysterious lake, where a feminine arm emerged from the water to hand Arthur a new, shining sword. This Lady of the Lake, who presented Arthur with Excalibur, draws directly on pagan Celtic myth, where weapons were sacrificed into watery depths to honour distant gods. Excalibur, it should be noted, was a different weapon to the sword drawn from the stone, which broke in the fight with Lancelot; Excalibur, the Lady of the Lake told Arthur, 'was gifted with magic powers, and that as long as the scabbard remained in his possession he would suffer neither wound nor defeat.' (Guerber, 1919: 289)

When the kingdom had settled as Arthur and Merlin desired, Arthur had a vision and turned his attention to

Arthur: King of the Britons

finding a most Christian of artefacts – the Holy Grail. The Grail chalice had been used to collect blood pouring from Jesus's wound on the cross, and locating it appealed to Arthur's sense of Christian pride. Arthur's knights set out to find the Grail, each undertaking a number of difficult tasks, often highly symbolic in their nature. The vast majority of Arthur's knights died, yet Galahad and Percivale succeeded in finding the Grail (or at least a vision of it) – although they failed to bring it to Arthur.

Lancelot became Arthur's champion, and defender of his wife Guinevere. Eventually, the king's wife and champion fell in love, and Lancelot left to live in exile. Guinevere was later to do the same.

The affair between Lancelot and Guinevere, and the waste of Arthur's men's lives on the Grail Quest was indicative of the decline in Arthur's kingdom after the initial long period of success. Worse was to come, however, as Arthur's illegitimate son Modred made his lineage known throughout the kingdom. Whilst Arthur was engaged in a military campaign overseas, Modred seized power, usurping Arthur's throne and stealing Excalibur's scabbard, which granted protection from injury to its wearer.

Arthur returned and gathered his loyal forces to oppose Modred. The two armies, meeting in civil war as the Britons had before the glorious stability of Arthur's reign, clashed at the battle of Camlann. By the end of a long and gruelling fight, the majority of warriors on either side had perished or fled; Arthur, with his few remaining knights, spotted Modred and his retinue across the battlefield. Arthur and his son met, and delivered fatal blows to each other. Modred died outright, and Arthur, lying mortally wounded, thought he was the last warrior left alive:

> The mist aside, and with that wind the tide
> Rose, and the pale King glanced across the field
> Of battle: but no man was moving there;
> Nor any cry of Christian heard thereon,
> Nor yet of heathen; only the wan wave
> Brake in among dead faces, to and fro
> (Tennyson, *The Passing of Arthur*, 1869, LL: 125–130)

However, Bedevere, 'first made and latest left of all the knights,' (Tennyson, *The Passing of Arthur*, 1869: LL 2) also remained, and drew close to Arthur; the mortally wounded king asked his loyal warrior Bedevere to cast Excalibur into the lake. Twice Bedevere went to cast Excalibur into the depths of the lake, but could not bring himself to lightly discard Arthur's symbol of authority and the symbol of British stability; both times he lied to Arthur and told him that he saw nothing when the sword entered the water. Arthur forced Bedevere to return each time, and finally Bedevere threw Excalibur into the lake, watching the Lady of the Lake's arm rise and take the sword back to the depths of the water. Once Arthur knew this, he was placed on to a boat and sailed away to the mysterious island of Avalon, where he was laid to rest. The legend of Arthur ends with the prediction that whenever the island of Britain was in true danger, Arthur and his knights would rise from their slumber, and ride to protect the island's inhabitants.

Many other characters feature in Arthurian myth. Balin and Balan, the brothers who almost kill each other in a duel; Gawain, and his tormentor the Green Knight – who challenges Gawain to a beheading competition; Culhwch and Olwen, and Tristam and Iseult, both with their archetypal tragic love stories. Many of these figures were imported from other myths, which have long been forgotten outside of the Arthurian cycle; some seem to derive from pagan gods, and others – such as King Mark – appear to have actually existed in a historical sense.

In History

Despite the fame of the legendary Arthur, his historical precedent is a great mystery. Under the latinized version of his name, Artorius, he is first mentioned by the ninth-century British historian Nennius (although it seems that Nennius's sources may have been written as early as the seventh century AD). Here, Arthur is mentioned not as a king but as a warrior fighting alongside the British kings, who fought twelve great battles against the Saxons, including his most famous victory at 'Mons Badonicus'. It seems likely that this historical Arthur lived towards the end of the fifth century or in the sixth century AD. A second early reference exists in the northern British war poem *Y Gododdin*; Arthur is mentioned in just one line, and the possibility that it is a later interpolation is strong:

Warriors

> He glutted black ravens on the wall
> of the fort although he was no Arthur

This line should be interpreted as evidence of Arthur as a great warrior: another warrior had slain many enemies (feeding the ravens that picked on the corpses), yet even so, he was not as great a warrior as Arthur was renowned to be. Arthur was the paragon of a great warrior.

To understand the likelihood and role of a historical writer, the background to his lifetime must be explained. Around the year AD 400, Roman rule in Britain was drawing to a close after almost 400 years. After some initial 'teething problems', the Britons took to the Roman way of life with enthusiasm, and by the middle of the third century AD, the average Briton living in or around a Romanized city would consider himself as Roman as a native of Rome itself.

Of course, when the legions gradually withdrew to mainland Europe at the start of the fifth century AD, it was a cause of concern for the Romanized inhabitants of Britain. The legions departed to defend the continental empire from incursions from the east by Huns, Goths and Franks; others had departed earlier to fight in the power struggles amongst competing emperors. The later years of the fourth century and the early years of the fifth century AD had seen barbarian raiders and settlers overrunning the imperial border; this happened in Britain as well as on the continent. Raids from the Irish and Picts to the north and west, and from continental Saxons and Franks to the south and east beset the Romanized Britons.

Arthur: King of the Britons

An Arthurian Inscription?

Tintagel, precariously sited on the edge of a western Cornish cliff, has long been associated with Arthurian legend. Over the years hundreds of thousands of visitors have flocked to see the supposed birthplace of the legendary Arthur. The ruins which stand on the site today are not, as many imagine, the ruins of an Arthurian, High Medieval castle, but the remains of a medieval monastic site. Beneath these ruins, however, lie the remains of an early medieval high status site – one in which an historical Arthur or one of his rival warlords would have lived.

In August 1998, an English Heritage excavation team, continuing a long series of revealing excavations at Tintagel, uncovered an artefact that reopened the long dead debate as to whether Tintagel was indeed the home of an historical Arthur. A broken piece of slate with an inscription stating that Artognov or Artognou had built it ('it' presumably being a building with this slate plaque mounted on it).

The archaeological layer that this slate was found in suggested a sixth-century date – plausible for a late Arthurian date – although the slate may well have been reused in the sixth century and been inscribed at an earlier date.

Is this artefact good evidence for locating an historical Arthur? It may have been inscribed for an entirely unrelated person, especially as the many name variations from which 'Arthur' may be derived has never included the name Artognou or Artognov until the discovery at Tintagel. We have no evidence as to the mysterious Artognou or Artognov's place in history, although the inscription describes him as a descendant of Col; possibly this is the semi-historic Coel Hen from whom many early medieval British royal families claimed to be descended, and who we now remember through the modern nursery rhyme Old King Cole. For the foreseeable future, we will never know for sure.

The Roman way of life did not disappear with the legions; the Romanized Britons continued with town life and Roman governmental systems. What they did lack, however, was a strong imperial army to defend the country from the ever increasing raids. The period from the withdrawal of Roman military support to the formation of the early Anglo-Saxon kingdoms is the true 'Dark Age' of British history. The evidence often passed down to us as 'history' may just as easily be legend. The overall picture, constructed from archaeological evidence and this myth-history, is that the Britons continued their enfeebled, sub-Roman way of life until the early years of the sixth century AD. The fifth century AD saw the gradual loss of land to invading tribes such as the Saxons, Frisians, Irish and Picts, and the British army (supported by Irish and Germanic Saxon mercenaries – following a precedent set by the late Roman army) suffered a series of humiliating defeats. It seems likely that the gradual degeneration of the Roman governmental system saw the British dividing into rival factions or kingdoms, which presented a disunited front to the enemy and effectively sealed the fate of the Britons. The years before the final decline of the Britons seem to have been the historical background to the real King Arthur, judging from the available British sources.

Arthur: King of the Britons

One of our key sources for history during this time is
the *Anglo-Saxon Chronicle*, which gives only very terse
entries for these early years. It makes no mention of
Arthur – perhaps this is understandable, as a historical
Arthur would have been one of the main tormentors of
Saxon power, and the *Chronicle* chooses to give the
impression that Anglo-Saxon kingdoms quickly
overpowered their rival Britons (the *Chronicle* only really
covers British defeats, conveniently excluding any battles
which the Britons may have won). However, it was not
until the mid sixth century AD, when the Britons seem to
have weakened themselves through endemic civil war,
that the Germanic invaders expanded into being the
dominant culture.

A few names survive through the mists of time, presenting
themselves as important leaders in the confused years after
the Roman withdrawal. Vortigern has entered history as the
sub-Roman ruler who invited the Saxons to settle as
mercenaries; although Vortigern may actually have existed,
and even if he didn't, others like him almost definitely did,
his name is a corruption of 'High King', and his feats are
rooted firmly in the beginning of Arthurian literature rather
than on any sound evidence. Vortigern's son, Vortimer, also
fought the invaders, as did Ambrosius (often portrayed as
Vortigern's enemy). In reality, we know virtually nothing of
these characters beyond their names and a few of their
supposed deeds.

Post-medieval authors and historians have probably spent
more time in an attempt to discover information about

Arthur than on examining every other aspect of British history between the withdrawal of the Romans and the arrival of the Normans. This interest has been fuelled by the fascinating fictional writings of medieval authors such as Sir Thomas Malory, and also by medieval transcriptions of Welsh oral tradition (which often portray Arthur in purely legendary terms, but also occasionally may offer tantalizing glimpses of the historical man).

Before the tales of Arthur became entwined with folklore and began to incorporate other figures from British and Celtic myth, only a few references to a purely historical Arthur were written down. *Historia Brittonum* records the most complete 'biography', listing twelve battles that Arthur fought and won; the *Annales Cambriae* tersely record that Arthur and Medraut died at Camlann; there is a passing reference to Arthur in *Y Gododdin*; and Gildas mentions the battle of Badon, later attributed to Arthur. Most of these references probably first existed between fifty and three hundred years after Arthur's supposed death, but some were not recorded in writing until the twelfth century AD – which brings in the possibility that the texts were corrupted at some point. Gildas, writing in the mid sixth century AD, remembered that the battle of Badon, Arthur's supposed last great victory, had taken place in the year of his (Gildas's) birth – presumably in the very early sixth century AD. After Arthur's victory at Badon, Gildas tells us, there was peace for a generation; this would seem to place Arthur as having led his men at the end of the fifth and start of the sixth centuries AD.

Arthur: King of the Britons

However, as Arthur was so poorly recorded, at least in the documentation surviving in modern times, we should consider the possibilities that may have led to this:

i)   Arthur did not actually exist beyond folklore.
ii) Arthur (meaning 'Bear') was the battle name or nickname of another documented person.
iii) Arthur was so well known and renowned among the Britons in the period shortly after his death that there was no need to record him in writing at that time, and that these oral stories have since been forgotten (or incorporated into folklore).
iv) Arthur was frequently recorded in written documentation, but that many of these have since been lost, to make him now seem ill documented.
v)   Arthur existed in an area beyond the knowledge of the British chroniclers of his time – it is possible that the writers may have known little of events outside of their own kingdoms, and that only later did stories of his exploits filter through.

At one time or another, various authors and historians have examined all of these theories. A great deal of what has been written about the historical Arthur should be filed, at best, as historical fiction. Of the modern writers on the historical Arthur, Leslie Alcock and Peter Beresford Ellis achieve the most credence: both believe that Arthur was a real person, but discuss the evidence in a way acceptable as historical research, showing that there is no clear cut case. Gerald of

Wales mentions an account of Arthur's absence from the historical record, as told to him in his twelfth-century journey through Wales. He claimed that:

> The Britons maintain that, when Gildas criticized his own people so bitterly, he wrote as he did because he was so infuriated by the fact that King Arthur had killed his own brother, who was a Scottish chieftain. When he (Gildas) heard of his brother's death, or so the Britons say, he threw into the sea a number of outstanding books which he had written in their praise and about Arthur's achievements. As a result you will find no book which gives an authentic account of that great prince. (1978: 259)

As far as Arthur's geographical locale is concerned, we cannot rely on place name evidence. Although this is useful for certain other historical leaders, the mythical Arthur has been attributed to many areas. Place name evidence is not conclusive, as an 'Arthur's Seat' or an 'Arthur's Cave' may be so named in the same way as a 'Nelson Mandela House' in London – just because the name exists, we cannot necessarily accept any direct relationship or close geographical ties between the two, only an acknowledgement of a person's success.

Tintagel in Cornwall has long been considered as the birthplace of Arthur. Beneath the current ruins (a medieval monastery), traces of an early medieval fortress have been found. Excavations in the late 1990s uncovered an inscription bearing a name similar to Arthur, but this cannot be firmly dated, and may well remember an unrelated person or be a later hoax.

Many researchers have attempted to locate the sites of Arthur's attributed twelve battles: most theories place them in modern Lincolnshire and northern England, or on the Welsh borders. In the nineteenth century, Skene bravely identified all of the battles as having taken place in southern Scotland. Therefore, despite the tradition of Arthur in western Britain (especially Cornwall), and if the *Historia Brittonum* is to be believed, Arthur was more likely to have been from a northern kingdom. Even so, a fact overlooked by, to my knowledge, all researchers apart from Professor Nitze in 1937, is that a River Camlad flows as a tributary of the River Caebitra near to Churchstoke, Shropshire. Several sites for the battle of Camlann have been put forward by authors, yet the Camlad is geographically close to another supposed Arthurian site, the old Roman fort at Rhyd-y-Groes near to Forden, which is a location in the twelfth-century Welsh Arthurian tale *The Dream of Rhonabwy*. Nitze also tells us that the Camlad was known by the names Camalet, Camlet and Kemelet in earlier times.

Another trend that has emerged in twentieth-century studies is that Arthur was not actually a king in his own right, but a 'leader of battles'. The suggestion for this comes from the wording of early sources. Most modern authors now see Arthur as have being a warlord employed by the British kingdoms to do battle with the invading Germanic peoples. There is a danger of over-examining the scanty documentary evidence for hidden or suggested meanings, but this idea does seem to at least be credible. Whether he was a king, or just a battle leader, is less significant from a military point of view; what is more important is that a British leader's name became synonymous with glory and success in warfare, suggesting that he held his opponents in the balance (be they British, Germanic, Pictish, or Irish).

Arthur's later association with western Britain probably came about as an attempt by the last true British kingdoms to remember their most glorious leader (the northern kingdoms had by the tenth century become amalgamated into Scotland – also a Celtic area, but no longer British – and English Northumbria). In an attempt to do so, they moved the historical Arthur from his real geographical setting to one that their audience could readily identify with – their own kingdoms in Cornwall and the West Country.

The British early medieval period is not the only one to which a historical Arthur has been ascribed. Arguments have existed for Arthur as a British (Breton) warlord at a similar time in western France – emigration from Britain to the continent did occur at this time, and it is conceivable that the French Arthur would have been an ex-pat Briton, fighting the Franks and Goths. Other suggestions have Arthur as a Pict, a Scot, or a Bronze Age leader (sometimes linked with an unlikely plan by Merlin to build Stonehenge).

Arthur: King of the Britons

In Battle

The popular image of Arthur as a medieval king sees him fighting in plate armour, on a caparisoned horse, and with a lance. The reality of Arthur – or, if his historical existence is doubted, his contemporary British warlords – is very different. The style of the fighting man in the Arthurian period can be broadly defined by his degree of Romanization, and the continuation of an Imperial style of culture and government after the Roman withdrawal. Areas of Britain falling into this kind of category would have been the most fertile agricultural areas.

Clothing and arms would have been like those of Roman armies on the continent, at least for the period before AD 500. Contemporary sources suggest that the Romans gave the Britons patterns to manufacture arms and armour from, which implies that as long as some degree of order was maintained, these could have been produced. However, civil order seemed to decline with the onset of plague and Germanic revolts in the mid fifth century AD.

The impression given by early sources was that the Britons were weak in warfare; they pleaded with Rome for help, hired mercenaries to fight their wars, and were overwhelmed with Irish, Pictish and German raiders. However, the Saxon historian Bede stated that the Britons in the period straight after independence were still well organized and fought their enemies until peace was achieved, but when this generation died out, those left had never known anything but peace, and were militarily weak.

It should also be realized that the Britons held back
Germanic conquests until the sixth century (when the
Britons, according to Bede, were weaker than before),
limited Irish invasions so that the Picts bore the brunt of
Irish aggression, and that the northern Britons kept the Picts
confined to modern Scotland so much so that the Picts are
now viewed as a mysterious culture.

Civil wars seemed to be the main threat to stability in
Britain before the Germanic expansions of the sixth century
AD – it appears that as the centralized Roman government
collapsed, quarrelling successor states sprang up, each being
ruled by a 'tyrant' or king. This idea is very persuasive, being
supported by similar but better documented events in north-
west Europe at the same time. Such quarrelling states would
have presented a weak front to external enemies, so it would
seem likely that this was the case in Britain.

The later Celtic Britons, in the time when Roman rule
had been almost forgotten, would have fought as a warband
– a loyal bodyguard *comitatus* or *teulu* (as opposed to a paid
army), which existed as an elite retained by their chieftain.
Typically, they would occupy a hill fort and its hall, feasting
and 'earning their mead'. It is probable that most British
warbands would have developed into this kind of
organisation the further removed both spatially and
chronologically they were from Imperial rule. When
discussing how widespread the ideas of Romanization were
in Britain at the end of the Empire, the words of Nigel Saul
(1994: 81) sum the situation up well:

Arthur: King of the Britons

> One may well doubt whether these [Roman]
> aspirations had penetrated far into the notions of the
> Romano-British of the countryside, especially of
> the western uplands and the northern frontiers.

Instead of receiving monetary payment like his Roman
forebears, the warband warrior would have received rewards
and gifts for his service; mead was drunk in *Y Gododdin* as a
metaphor for the lord's obligations, and Martin Welch (1992:
50), speaks of the Anglo-Saxon contemporaries:

> One way a king could reward the warriors who served
> him, apart from giving them gold and other treasures,
> or weapons, armour and horses, was to grant them
> land.

As the British warriors of this period were paid with goods
as opposed to straight currency, it is reasonable to assume
that they would have been fairly well equipped and armed.
Certainly the British were well enough equipped and skilled
to limit Germanic expansion into the Midlands until the
sixth century AD, and later Wales and Scotland were forged
from the strong highland kingdoms of the Britons in later
centuries.

Before the Roman army left in the early fifth century
AD, a large number of Germanic soldiers were posted in
Britain as part of the field army. Some of these would
undoubtedly have remained in Britain when the army left, as
they had made their homes in Britain, and they may have

The traditional view of the legendary King Arthur is as a medieval monarch, armoured in chainmail and charging forth on a heavy warhorse. (Author's collection)

been used as mercenaries or as a continuation of the standing army. The use of barbarian troops was well attested to in the later Roman Empire; large numbers of Germanic warriors had been recruited in preference to untrained civilians, and it should be no surprise that the rulers of sub-Roman Britain copied this. Legend states that the early sub-Roman British leader Vortigern invited German warriors into Britain, to defend the civilians against Pictish and Irish raiders. It is also recorded that the northern British Votadini tribe were moved into north Wales either shortly before or shortly after the Roman withdrawal to guard against or expel Irish settlers. Some authors have claimed that Visigothic warriors and ships were hired or settled in the sixth century AD, but there does not appear to be any archaeological evidence for this.

The size of the forces engaged in warfare at this time is one of the major areas of disagreement among historians studying this period. The seventh century *Laws of Ine* decreed that an 'army' consisted of anything over thirty-five men, and indeed Cyneheard tried to overthrow the kingdom of Wessex in AD 786 with just eighty-five men – and almost succeeded. It was recorded that the British king Ecdicus fought the Goths in Gaul with just eighteen horsemen and was successful. *Y Gododdin* recorded that the army marched from Din Eidyn (Edinburgh) with 300, or possibly the more poetic figure of 363. Similarly, re-occupied hill forts, assumed to be the strongholds of British kings and their elite warbands, were small – usually only an acre or two in size and incapable of housing a force much over one hundred. Evans reiterates Leslie Alcock's view of small armies, stating that as the late Roman field army in Britain probably did not number more than about 6000, it is inconceivable that any of the successor kingdoms could raise over 1000 warriors each; Alcock also offers the opinion that a king's personal warband was organized on a 'highly personal basis' (1989: 336–337), and included many members of his extended family. Holmes (1996: 84) asserts that engagements of this period involved 'such numbers...small enough to be fed by raids on the surrounding countryside'. Evans re-affirms the idea of small warbands, stating:

> ...in no uncertain terms that the number of warriors who comprised these warbands could not have exceeded a few hundred at the most, and in most cases numbered far less (1997: 135)

However, the case is not that simple: the *Anglo-Saxon Chronicle* states that 4000 Britons were slain at Crecanford in AD 456; 5000 were killed with Natanleod in AD 508; and 2000 at Beandun in AD 614. A similar comparison in army size can be drawn from armies involved in the struggle on the continent – Belisarius's *bucellarii* numbered 7000 in the sixth century AD; late Roman legions consisted of 1000 to 1200 men, and their auxiliaries were grouped into bodies of 500 men. Professor Jackson, writing about *Y Gododdin*, has expressed the opinion that in all probability they (the 300 of *Y Gododdin*) were accompanied by a large body of footmen. In reality there is little to support this statement beyond a modern prejudice that so small a force of men could be termed 'an army'. It is fairly hard for the modern layman to believe that so small an army as eighty-five or even three hundred could defeat a powerful early medieval rival kingdom; however, it must be remembered that the population at this time was considerably smaller (probably around about six million – although it is very difficult to give an accurate estimate). Therefore armies may have been proportionately smaller.

Alcock's suggestion that none of the British successor kingdoms could have raised over 1000 men (one sixth of the late Roman field army in the country) provides a reasonable guide to the size of early armies. But what of the *Anglo-Saxon Chronicle*'s claim that British casualties numbered by the thousand? Like the image of the British being militarily weak, these figures were merely Germanic propaganda. Conversely, Ecdicius' eighteen triumphant horsemen were probably also propaganda, designed to show the leaders' success without the need of a huge force. Oswald was reported to have slaughtered Cadwallon in the seventh century AD with a far smaller force – but with the divine justice of God on his side. Eighth-century Irish armies had, on average, a *tuatha* of around 700 men, and a British poem lamenting the death of the seventh century king of Powys, Cynddylan, claims that his warband consisted of 700 men too. By the medieval period, a Welsh *teulu* would have consisted of 120 warriors on average, although Llywelyn ap Gruffydd raised 30,000 foot and 500 cavalry to support Simon de Montfort in 1265 – but Llywelyn had united several Welsh regions for this. The Welsh, a century before in 1136, had raised 6000 foot and 2000 cavalry at the battle of Crug Mawr. However, it must be remembered that this was 400 hundred years after the end of our period, and the population of Britain had increased.

Compared to Roman and later continental battles, British warfare of this period seems to have been a rather unsophisticated and backward affair. Maybe this was because the warriors of the British Isles were more limited in influence (they had not suffered the ravaging of eastern tribes such as the Huns, or had military contact with the eastern Romans). However, there does appear to be enough evidence to broadly define some strategic and tactical concepts used in warfare in Britain during the period AD 400 to AD 700.

Strategic tactics are largely defined through historical guesswork by modern authors. Of this work, more effort has been put into uncovering historical evidence for Arthur than any other topic. No clear picture of the strategy of warfare in Britain between about AD 400 and AD 600 can be defined. Many of the battle sites cannot be identified by modern research, due to changes in place names and the uncertainty of the location of early medieval kingdoms. Leslie Alcock has suggested that many battles during this early period were fought on or near the borders of a ruler's kingdom, and that campaigns were not waged far afield. For example the battles fought by Wessex in the AD 570s all seem to have been fought within a 90-mile radius.

Arthur: King of the Britons

By the seventh century AD, better documentation
provides a clearer picture of distances involved in
campaigning: the Dal Riadans travelled 120 miles (at least)
to the site of the battle of Degastan in AD 603;
Aethelfrith's army journeyed 175 miles in AD 615 from
Bamburgh to fight a victorious battle at Chester; although
Edwin's army travelled only 35 miles from his capital to
his defeat in AD 632, his respective enemies had travelled
75 miles from the capital of Mercia, and 145 miles from
that of Gwynedd; when Penda of Mercia and his British
allies travelled north to give battle to Oswy, they were 250
miles from Penda's capital and 280 from that of Gwynedd.
Roads and rivers were probably used in military
campaigns; roads could be either well built Roman ones,
or ancient causeways – often well trodden paths over harsh
terrain.

Battles were usually fought at the frontier of a kingdom,
and two main types of campaign existed: the raid and the
conquest. Raids, famed in Irish myth, may have been carried
out to gain cattle or horses, or to collect other forms of
tribute, from a weaker neighbour. The conquest of land was
probably a political conquest initiated by military victory as
opposed to a large-scale migration. Cemetery evidence
suggests that Britons and Anglo-Saxons lived alongside each
other, and therefore control of an area was politically as
opposed to racially defined. Wholesale slaughter of an area's
non-military populace seems to have been less common
than the picture sometimes painted, although Bede noted
that Aethelfrith killed off or subjugated the natives.

However, Cadwallon's butchery of Germanic men, women, and children during his conquest of Northumbria was seen as pagan and evil.

Using a variety of sources, it is possible to piece together a fairly good picture of battle tactics in Britain between AD 400 and AD 700.

Night or dawn attack: This form of attack was mentioned repeatedly in *Y Gododdin*, and was also spoken of with regard to the battle of Strathcarron in AD 642. Also in the middle of the seventh century AD, Oswald marched to defeat Cadwallon of Gwynedd 'as dawn was breaking'. Such tactics would have made sense, especially if attempting to catch a numerically stronger opponent off guard (as was the case with the attacks made by Oswald and the warriors of *Y Gododdin*).

Defence of river or ford: Many early battles of our period are recorded as having been fought at rivers. This may be due to the fact that river crossings were easy to keep watch over (and many old Roman forts could have been reconstructed to help in this), and used in a similar fashion to the dykes described previously.

Ian Heath claims that 'the expansion of Wessex…is a history of battles at fords' (1980: 40), and it should also be noted that of the twelve battles of Arthur noted in the *Historia Brittonum*, seven are located on rivers. Many authors have claimed that mounted British troops would have an advantage in a clash of arms by a river, due to their extra height; despite this, many of the early battles are described as Germanic victories.

Heroic British Poetry

The most famous early medieval British war poem is *Y Gododdin*. It is an epic, heroic elegy describing the valiant yet failed attempt by the army of the northern British kingdom of Gododdin to defeat their powerful Anglo-Saxon neighbours to the south. Often described as 'the earliest Scottish literature', *Y Gododdin* is actually a Cymric piece, told by the northern ancestors of the later Welsh. Three hundred mounted warriors set out to do battle with the Saxons, hoping to inflict a decisive defeat upon their Germanic enemies. Instead, they met with a spectacular defeat, all except one of the Gododdin warriors being slain in battle. The poet described the pick of British warriors in their full battle glory:

> The men who went to
> Catraeth with a battle-cry
> in their army had
> the strength of stallions, steel-blue
> armour, shields; their shafts
> were held aloft & their spears
> were keen: their mail-coats
> were shining as were their swords.
> (trans. Short, 1994: 55)

Another, less well-known battle commemorated by an early medieval British poet, was the victory of the men of Gododdin at Wensleydale in Yorkshire; this appears to have been a bloody, hard fought combat at a ford, where the enemies of the Gododdin were battered into submission:

Warriors

On the entrance of the ford
I saw bloodstained warriors,
their weapons abandoned
before a grizzly lord.
A truce they want
since they became ensnared,
their arms crossed,
trembling for fear of death,
palefaced.
Dead drunk are their leaders
on Idon's bloody binge.
(trans. Pennar, 1988: 51–52)

Finally, the poem *Geraint son of Erbin* describes the battle of Llongborth, and the earliest version that we now have was probably written in the mid ninth century. Geraint appears in the poem as a prince in southern Britain, who led his Britons to defeat in this battle against the Saxons (sometimes identified as having taken place at Portsmouth in Hampshire). This poem is one of the key accounts in acknowledging that British warriors fought from horseback in battle in the early medieval period, and also contains one of the earlier, non-legendary, references to Arthur himself:

At Llongborth I saw Arthur's
brave men, they hewed with steel,
emperor, leader in toil.

At Llongborth were slain Geraint's
brave men from the lowlands of Devon,

and before they were slain, they slew.
(Coe & Young, 1995: 119)

Unlike modern war poetry, the composer of *Y Gododdin* and other
similar poems celebrated the feats of men in battle. The tragedy of
poems such as *Y Gododdin* for their original audience lay not in the
fact that men's lives were lost in war, but that the Britons were
defeated; if the battle had been won, it would have been considered a
victory song (Short, 1994: 11). This reflects a different social attitude to
that of the modern world – perhaps this should be considered
alongside the idea that early medieval warfare was the pursuit of small
bands of professional warriors, for whom warfare was a way of life,
compared to the carnage of the First World War, which stripped the
twentieth century of a whole generation of men.

The '*Gododdin* contains enough references to infantry
being drawn up into ranks or squares . . . [to] allow the
conclusion that this was a common tactic' (Evans, 1997: 38).
We should not be surprised to hear of close formations
being used so much on the early medieval British battlefield.
This type of formation had been proved to be the most
effective for spear and shield armed troops – the Romans
and Greeks used such formations, and later the Anglo-Saxons
and other Germans were recorded as employing a shield wall.
Late Roman infantry used the *cunesus* (wedge), the *fulcum*
(better known as the 'tortoise'), and the shield wall against
mounted opposition. The Britons at the battle of Beran-birig

in AD 556 fought in three lines – the first being spear-armed infantry, the middle being archers, and the rear line cavalry. This may have been misrepresented by later chroniclers superimposing their own medieval tactics on the battle, although the document also refers to the Anglo-Saxons as fighting in a shield wall. Analysis of the language used in the British war poem Y Gododdin shows us that terms for closed ranks of troops (including 'wall of battle' and 'battle pen') are used six times in the poem.

Beyond documentation, archaeological evidence may suggest that close formations were prevalent amongst foot soldiers. The Sutton Hoo helmet has an enclosed face that impairs vision; this would be too dangerous for a warrior to wear in anything but a close formation. This again infers that close ranks were used for mutual protection.

Both the Roman and Celtic predecessors of the Britons used horses in war, and several passages of Y Gododdin only make sense if speaking of a mounted man. Ian Heath (1980: 40) suggests that the 'few' cavalry fought around the closed ranks of British infantry, and Evans says that horses would have been of limited use. However, neither author appears to have considered the late Roman army's extensive use of cavalry, nor the literary evidence of the Britons fully.

It would appear that British cavalrymen rode in loose formations and harried their enemies with javelins, ready to follow up and exploit any advantage that occurred. Late Roman light cavalry made constant sallies to exhaust their enemies, and served numerous other scouting and policing functions too.

Arthur: King of the Britons

Some authors believe the Britons used heavy cavalry,
claiming that this is where the idea of Arthur's knights
originated – it is more likely that medieval writers
anachronistically, and incorrectly, referred to such 'knights'.
Evans believes that the horses used in Britain at this time
were too small to be of any military use. However, as we
shall see, horses were not used in Britain as heavy cavalry
chargers, but were used as mobile missile platforms – their
size therefore being of less importance. An interesting
analogy has been brought to light by Southern and Dixon:

> By 1900 the Boer War had revealed that the horses
> brought out from England were no match for the smaller
> Boer horses, and in that year Sir Walter Gilbey wrote a
> book on small horses in warfare, in which he pointed out
> 'the peculiar suitability of small horses for certain
> campaigning work which demands staying power,
> hardiness and independence of high feeding. (1992: 170)

This sounds like the sort of warfare that was probably
carried out in post-Roman Britain. Native British horses
would have been similar to modern mountain ponies and
other such breeds, commonly coloured dun or roan;
skewbald and piebald ponies were often considered unlucky
in the ancient world so may have been avoided. There may
have been some larger horses bred down from late Roman
mounts in the immediate post-Roman era, but these almost
certainly would have been replaced with hardier British
ponies as time wore on.

Warriors

Early British literary sources make it clear that at least some of the Britons fought from horseback, and they even go as far as to outline the mounted warriors' tactics. *Y Gododdin* states (Jarman, 1988):

> He cast his spears between two armies,
> A magnificent horseman before the Gododdin
>
> With shattered shield he tore through armies,
> His horses swift, racing forward
>
> He threw spears from the grasp of his hand
> From his steaming slender bay horse.

These passages suggest that the Britons rode towards the enemy line, hurling javelins from a distance, as opposed to closing in with a lance; this is supported by late Roman evidence. Holmes draws evidence from *The Anglo-Saxon Chronicle* to support the idea of mounted Britons:

> Under the thigh of Geraint swift chargers,
> Long their legs, wheat their fodder,
> Red, swooping like milk white eagles.
> (1996: 112)

A poem about the death of the British king Cynddylan describes the British mounts as well-trained horses. The ideas of British cavalry tactics shown above are backed up by the better documented use of cavalry in the late Roman army. The light cavalryman played an increasingly important part in the Roman army in the late Empire, indeed the most effective late Roman troops were cavalry. It is also possible that a few heavier cavalry existed in the immediate sub-Roman era, whilst Imperial strategies were still employed, but skirmishing light cavalrymen seem to have been predominant amongst most British mounted contingents. Leslie Alcock believes that the picture created by such sources is 'certainly not one of disciplined cavalry charges' (1987: 334), but also points out that despite the usual use of a javelin as opposed to a lance, a stirrup-less horseman could still charge down a foot soldier with a lance – as evidenced in Greek and Roman accounts. David Nicolle furthers our impression of the Britons fighting from horseback by stating that cavalry dominated in southern Scotland, the Pennines and the West Midlands (all horse-raising areas), and that:

> The warrior aristocracy of Arthurian Britain generally fought as light cavalry with sword and javelin. (1984: 11)

Late Roman cavalry tactics, such as charging in wedges and utilizing close formations, do not lie happily beside the heroic ideals shown in British poetry. The mounted Briton would probably still have charged forward flinging javelins, but may have continued his assault into his enemies' ranks with the sword or hand-held spear; individual feats of arms would almost certainly have impressed such warriors more than a feigned retreat.

Warriors

The ratio of mounted to foot warriors would almost
certainly have varied according to two factors: the
geographical location of the warband, and the period in
which the warband fought. In the early post-Roman, a
continuation of late Roman strategy would have occurred,
meaning that a balanced force of both foot and mounted
troops would have been used. However, the cavalry may have
been more mobile and used as a roving force, while the
infantrymen may have seen more garrison duty. In the
warband period, when armies were small and consisted of a
social elite of well-equipped and well-motivated warriors,
horses may have been widely available for use amongst such
men, through the warlord's generous patronage. Similarly, as
kingdoms began to grow larger, and armies were organized on
a less personal basis, the gift of, and therefore use of, horses
may have declined – leading to largely foot-based armies.

War cries seem to feature in descriptions of several battles
in our period; *Y Gododdin* mentions battle cries four times,
and St Germanus apparently won a battle by his men all
shouting in unison to scare their enemies into flight. It is
assumed that other noise and showmanship would also be
created to make enemies waver – such as banging spears on
to shields, and individual challenges between warriors. Music
may have played a part in battle during this period – three
types of late Roman cavalry instruments are known: the
trumpet, bugle and horn; other instruments may have
included drums, harps and pipes.

Helmets would have been fairly common during the
early part of the Arthurian period; however, there are only

three known later examples, all from Germanic burials. Late Roman helmets came in a variety of designs, but basic construction patterns were similar: helmet bowls were composite in construction, and each bowl section was attached to a central ridged strip running front to back over the helmet. Helmets had cheek and neck guards attached, and occasionally nasal guards were fitted. Chainmail or leather aventails may also have been fitted (as on the later Anglo-Saxon Coppergate helmet, found at York). Spangelhelms were popular amongst Germanic peoples, and warriors in Roman service wore many examples. It is likely that the Britons would have used similar protection, although *Y Gododdin* makes no mention of helmets. The three Germanic helmets known from our period had the seeds of their design laid in late Roman examples. The Benty Grange helmet was excavated in the nineteenth century; it is a spangelhelm, and the excavator believed that it was covered with horn scales. It is decorated with a boar on its crest – a design often mentioned in Germanic literary sources. The second of the three known helmets from this period in Britain – the Pioneer helmet – was excavated in Northamptonshire during 1997, and this helmet also had a boar crest. The third helmet is one of the most well known symbols of British history – the Sutton Hoo helmet. It was excavated from a high status Germanic burial site in Suffolk. Unlike the other two helmets, it has an enclosed face (rather like a Roman parade helmet) and its style is derived from late Roman and Scandinavian *Vendel* designs. If used in combat (and I believe it highly unlikely that it would not have been), the wearer almost certainly would have had to have been fighting a very static battle as the facemask would have greatly impeded vision. The Sutton Hoo helmet was highly decorated, despite its basic design being copied from a mass-produced late Roman item. Study of Anglo-Saxon vocabulary and material culture has identified the use of crests on helmets, cheek-pieces, visors and neck armour.

Cuirasses of both chainmail and leather were used; scale and lamellar armour may have been utilized by the late Romans, but there is little real evidence for their continued use in Britain. Body armour may have become increasingly rare as the Roman Empire collapsed, but the Byzantine manual *Strategikon* called for at least the front two rows of a formation to be armoured. Gildas mentioned that the Romans left the Britons patterns to manufacture arms, and armour, cuirasses and chainmail are mentioned seventeen times in total in *Y Gododdin*. *Y Gododdin* contains references to 'dark-blue armour', and 'armour' – which may imply that 'armour' was leather, compared to 'dark-blue' or 'chainmail' metal armour. Leather armour may have been very common, although a leather jerkin with a pair of gold shoulder clasps was suspended in the boat burial of Mound One, Sutton Hoo. A common assertion is that chainmail was rare, and worn only by those warriors of the highest rank; other ranks wore leather jerkins or no body armour at all. The style of all types of body armour, whether iron or leather, would have been similar during this period; the cuirass may have stopped at the waist or at the knee, and would usually have been short sleeved (although long sleeved examples may have existed). It is even possible that both leather and iron armour were worn at the same time, to heighten their effectiveness. Leather armour would probably have pteruges at both the waist and upper arms for additional protection with a degree of flexibility.

Shields, along with spears, constitute the basic warriors' equipment in the period AD 400–700. It is very likely that many warriors would have gone into battle armed only with these. Härke noted that 26 per cent of Germanic inhumation burials in Britain were accompanied by a shield (Welch, 1992), and shields are mentioned twenty-four times in *Y Gododdin* – and a further twelve times with regard to a shattered or broken shield. They are also well evidenced from Germanic burials with grave goods, and most appear to have been of leather-covered ply wood around 30 inches to 3 feet in diameter and up to a ¼ inch thick. Irish shields, at least, may have been smaller – this being inferred by their smaller bosses. British shields were oval or round, made of hide-covered alder wood, and the boss was used as a weapon. Skirmishers may have used smaller shields, as had been the case in late Roman armies, but a large shield would have been desirable for the warriors in a shield wall. In all probability, geometric late Roman designs were used by the sub-Roman Britons, and were gradually superseded by less Romanized designs. Many accounts suggest the Britons used religious symbols such as the *chi-rho*, but this presumes that all Britons were Christians (which was probably not the case). Medieval Welsh shields are recorded as being yellow, silver, white or blue, and *Y Gododdin* mentions 'icy hued shields'; the *Annales Cambriae* refer to a cross motif, and many other forms of decoration may well have been used. Pictish shield designs, in common with the other rich evidence of their artwork, appear to have been extremely intricate and delicate. Heath records that the Anglo-Saxons used shields of leather-covered lime wood.

Spears were the most common weapons amongst the fighting men of our period; Härke points out that 44 per cent of Germanic inhumations in Britain during this period were accompanied by at least one spear (Welch, 1992). Included in the broad category of 'spears' are both lances and javelins – it is hard to judge the difference between these three weapons by looking at the metal head alone. The British war poem *Y Gododdin* refers to spears thirty-eight times, javelins or thrown spears three times, and a lance on one occasion and David Nicolle notes that 'an extraordinary variety of spearheads have been found' during our period (1984: 15). Spearheads were angular, leaf-shaped or long tapered blades, exceptionally up to 16 inches long and with shafts of up to 7 feet. The most cited British spearhead, from Buston, is 8 inches long and of a heavy construction. References in *Y Gododdin* to 'square pointed spearheads' may parallel the four-sided mail-piercing weapons mentioned in Scandinavian sagas.

Javelins with heads of no more than 6 inches have been found in both Germanic and Irish contexts. There is less evidence for British weapons during this period, as their burial practices (the usual area to look for weapon evidence) appear to have been unaccompanied inhumations – meaning that no grave goods were included. Late Roman *lancea* javelins were carried five to a man, but the warriors of post-Roman Britain may not have been so well equipped. A special type of javelin, very similar to the Roman *pilum*, was the *angon*. Only a few of these weapons have been found in Britain, all in Germanic graves (although this may not mean that only the Germanic people used them). These were prestige weapons with a thin 2-foot metal head and neck, mounted on a 6-foot wooden shaft – the idea being that this would bend in an opponent's shield, rendering the shield useless.

Swords were common in the late Roman period, but after Roman influence had died out, swords appear to have been weapons for those of a high status, and examples become fairly rare during the period AD 500–700. It is possible that their high status later in this period was an attempt to mimic the Imperial splendour of the late Empire (evidenced elsewhere, including the Sutton Hoo helmet and possibly through military belts). The late Roman army used the *spatha* long-sword and the *semi-spatha* short-sword. It is likely that the Britons would have carried on using these weapons at least in the 'sub-Roman' period, although David Nicolle suggests that later on, the Britons may have been armed 'perhaps with small swords of Irish type' (1984: 19). Although not nearly as common as spears, swords are mentioned in *Y Gododdin* fifteen times, and unspecified 'blades' are mentioned a further eighteen times (although these may not necessarily be swords).

Swords are occasionally endowed with mystical qualities in Germanic sagas, and in keeping with this, they are uncommon in Germanic graves in Britain, occurring in high status burials only. Anglo-Saxon swords were about the same length as a *spatha* – around 3 feet. Irish swords were shorter, varying between 14 and 26 inches in length. Single-edged short swords, popularly known as a *seax* after their Saxon users, actually appear to have been used by German and Celt alike. They were mostly between 12 and 20 inches long, and are quite rare finds in graves: they should not be confused with smaller non-military knives, which were common grave goods.

Axes were rare weapons. One reference exists in *Y Gododdin*, and it is known that late Roman light infantry used the axe. Axes are often thought of as being popular amongst Germanic warriors; and although this is true of the Franks on the continent, who threw their *francisca* axes at close range to break an enemy's formation, such axes were uncommon in Britain. Several *francisca* axes are known from graves in Frankish-influenced Kent and on the Isle of Wight, but are less well known elsewhere. Hand-held axes are even rarer than the tapered *francisca,* which was used for throwing.

Bows were used by the late Roman army, and were known to the Germanic peoples in Europe, but appear to have been unfashionable in warfare in Britain. Only six occurrences are known from Germanic graves in Britain, and these all occur in Frankish-influenced areas. David Nicolle, speaking of the Anglo-Saxons, suggests that archers were of 'little social significance' (1984: 16). He also mentions that 'archery played a minor role' in sub-Roman British warfare, although he suggests that there was some archery, mostly the flat bow amongst the later Britons and Welsh – attributing this to the flat bow's usefulness in the close conditions of upland Britain.

Slings were 'a popular weapon among poorer folk' (Nicolle, 1984: 24) in Germanic society. It is likely that many lower class warriors would have carried a sling – it was a simple weapon to make (consisting of a strap of leather and a collection of stones), and would allow the poorer warrior to have an impact in a battle without resorting to close combat against a better armed opponent. Sling staves according to Nicolle were also still in use, at least amongst the Germanic peoples. They had been used by the late Roman army, and therefore possibly also by sub-Roman armies.

An illustration of Romano-Celtic soldiers in a manuscript by Prudentius shows them in late Roman style tunics. Southern and Dixon describe late Roman tunics as being woven in one piece, with bands on the cuffs, and a single, double, or treble *clavus* band riding over the shoulder and down onto the chest. Other geometric patterns were also used, and by the mid fifth century AD, squares were becoming popular for such decoration. The colour of these tunics could vary: late Roman soldiers bought their own tunics, so there was no 'uniform' colour – although red or undyed tunics seemed most popular; decorative designs and the *clavus* were popular in purple, red, or blue. Other possible colours included brown, beige, white, scarlet, and yellow. Blue was notoriously difficult to set into clothes, and dyed cloth was not always used in the ancient world, especially in the poorer elements of society.

Warriors

When Roman influence began to die out, the lower classes wore wool and upper classes wore silk – both apparently in chequered, striped, or spotted styles. Eighth-century Irish laws (which *may* have borne a similarity to British laws), allowed only certain colours to be worn by each strata of their society: subjects could wear only yellow or black, nobles could wear grey, red, or brown, and kings could wear purple or blue; the upper echelons of this 'social colouring' match British sources to some extent. Also, slaves could wear only one colour, subjects two colours, 'learned' classes six colours, and royalty seven colours. Anglo-Saxons are recorded as having worn clothing of scarlet, red, brown, dark green, purple, indigo, deep blue and white at various stages between the seventh and tenth centuries. Several references exist to coloured clothing, including some in *Y Gododdin* – red and white costumes are referred to in this poem. David Nicolle suggests that the Britons would have used the ubiquitous Celtic chequered fabric in less Romanized areas, in a variety of shades of brown and undyed wool.

Standards and banners were 'extremely important' for rallying troops and also for communication. Assuming that the Britons utilized late Roman standards (as did most successor kingdoms at this time), the most common would have been *draco* windsocks, and *vexillum* square flags. Heath states that the Britons probably used golden or red-gold *draco* standards; the usual colour for a *vexillum* was red or purple. Arthur is reputed to have carried an image of the Virgin Mary at one of his battles, although whether this was on a shield or standard, we cannot ascertain.

Arthur: King of the Britons

Above and beyond all of the other warriors featured in this book, the stories of Arthur have hijacked and eclipsed the history and known warriors of an entire period of history. Developed from humble beginnings as a skilled warrior and general in Welsh legend, King Arthur became a hanger from whom the mantle of chivalry could be explained and demonstrated in the high medieval period. The known events of Arthur's historical period has made it difficult to extract a detailed study of his historical authenticity, yet a great deal of time has been spent by scholars ancient and modern in trying to prove his existence. Warfare in Arthur's historical era was dominated by loyal bodyguards of professional, mounted warriors, with weapons and tactics falling between those of the late Roman emperors' armies and the heroic, individualistic combat of the Viking Age. Although not a king in the sense of Malory or Tennyson's writings, a battle leader in the historical Arthur's time would have held many of the same political qualities albeit on a smaller geographical scale – however, the idealism of chivalry would probably have made little impression on such a warrior.

DRACULA
The Transylvanian Vampire

T he legend of Dracula combines two distinct stories:
the tale of a fifteenth-century Wallachian leader, and
the folklore of the vampire. These two strands of
Dracula's legend were popularized as one by Bram Stoker in
1897. In Montague Summers' early twentieth-century study
of the vampire, the author explains what a vampire is by
quoting from Webster's *International Dictionary*. The simplicity
of this short definition belies its accuracy, drawing on the
many folklore traditions from across Europe in which the
vampire is present:

> A blood-sucking ghost or re-animated body of a dead
> person; a soul or re-animated body of a dead person
> believed to come from the grave and wander about by
> night sucking the blood of persons asleep, causing their
> death. (this edition 1996: 1)

The superstition of the vampire as we know it today has its
origins in Slavonic culture; earlier vampires exist in Greek
and Roman lore, and blood-sucking creatures can be found
in the folk tales of many cultures. A ghost of a heretic,

Dracula: The Transylvanian Vampire

criminal or similar ill-doer, the European vampire returns from the grave to suck the blood of sleeping people, who often then become vampires themselves. The only way to destroy a vampire was to drive a stake through its heart.

Most historical records of vampirism note events in central and Eastern Europe – in countries such as Moravia, Bohemia, Romania, Hungary, Serbia and Yugoslavia. Despite the assertion that vampires should be killed with a wooden stake, all manner of weapons and tools were used to rid communities of the undead of historical records. For example, a thirteenth-century Moravian vampire was stunned when pushed from a church spire and then beheaded with a spade. A sixteenth-century Turkish vampire was despatched with a knife, and a seventeenth-century female vampire in Romania drowned in the River Jiu (according to certain folklore, vampires are killed by or cannot cross water or holy water). A more traditional form of death befell a suspected vampire in Transylvania in 1905, when the body of a gypsy which did not suffer rigor mortis after death had a stake pierced through his heart before burial.

For many centuries, vampirism remained an enigmatic and often taboo subject, yet one writer pulled the subject away from its traditional roots and audiences and presented vampirism to a wide audience on a grand scale. That writer, as mentioned above, was Bram Stoker. Since the first publication of *Dracula* in 1897, the novel has never been out of print.

Written as a series of diaries, letters and news items – a style quintessentially typical of the Victorian English crime writers – a tale evolves of an extremely long-lived Transylvanian count,

whose life is prolonged by his vampirism. The story opens
with Jonathan Harker, a London solicitor, who is required to
travel to Count Dracula's Transylvanian castle on the business
of organizing for the Count's purchase of an English estate
called Carfax, arriving in Dracula's domain. He described
Dracula upon meeting him:

> His face was a strong – a very strong – aquiline, with
> high bridge of the thin nose and peculiarly arched
> nostrils; with lofty domed forehead, and hair growing
> scantily around the temples, but profusely elsewhere …
> The mouth, so far as I could see under the heavy
> moustache, was fixed and rather cruel-looking, with
> peculiarly sharp white teeth;
> (Stoker, this edition 1993: 23)

And, while held at the castle for – as the Count told him –
protection from the wild country outside, Harker began to
see more of his host's life:

> As he went down the wall, lizard fashion, I wished I
> had a gun or some lethal weapon, that I might destroy
> him; but I fear that no weapon wrought alone by man's
> hand would have any effect on him.
> (Stoker, this edition 1993: 50)

Harker became mesmerized by the vampiric Count's
advances, and the action then shifted as Dracula was
transported to England in a coffin of Transylvanian soil,

Dracula: The Transylvanian Vampire

landing at Whitby and then moving on to his new estate of Carfax near to Purfleet, Essex. Stoker's Dracula had the power to turn himself into a wolf, which he did aboard ship after killing the crew. At this point in the novel, Harker's fiancée, Mina Murray, takes up the narrative along with her friend Lucy Westenra and Dr John Seward. The knowledgeable Professor Van Helsing, a Dutch expert in vampirism and Seward's mentor, attempted to foil the Count's bloodlust in England, although Lucy fell victim to the Transylvanian Count, condemning her to become a vampire also. Lucy was killed by Van Helsing's party, saving her from immortality as a vampire. Dracula then attempted to turn Mina into one of his undead minions, but, with the aid of Jonathan Harker, Dr Seward, Van Helsing and other stalwarts, she was saved from that gruesome fate and Dracula fled back to Eastern Europe. The vampire-hunting party traced Dracula back to his lair and slew both his gypsy band and himself, ending the life of the Vampire-King; Mina described the Count's final moments:

> As I looked, the eyes saw the sinking sun, and the look of hate in them turned to triumph.
> But, on the instant, came the sweep and flash of Jonathan's great knife [a kukri]. I shrieked as I saw it shear through the throat; whilst at the same moment Mr Morris's bowie knife plunged into the heart.
> It was like a miracle...the whole body crumbled into dust and passed from our sight.
> (Stoker, this edition 1996: 333)

Warriors

Stoker's Dracula possessed the ability to turn into a wolf, and to become incredibly powerful at night-time – a portent of evil. Vulnerable to beheading or having a stake driven through the heart, and sometimes capable of turning into other beasts (such as a bat) or smoke, many diverse strands of eastern European folklore have been drawn together into the vampire legend in the century since Stoker's novel popularized vampirism in a Christian, western sense.

It is shrewdly noted, signifying both the impact of Stoker's skilfully devised novel and of the fascination that mankind holds with the supernatural, that:

> Like *Frankenstein, Dracula* has become a modern myth – the subject of many film versions, imitations and parodies. Tourists to Romania, a country Stoker himself never visited, are now shown 'Dracula's Castle' as tourists to Verona are shown 'Juliet's balcony'.
> (Ousby [ed], 1994: 271)

Former Detective Superintendent John F Plimmer stated in his book *In the Footsteps of the Whitechapel Murders* (1998) that modern police psychological profiling methods consider that any assault that has taken place on a victim's neck to be a sexually motivated attack; the connotations of a vampire's bloodsucking on the neck is therefore obvious, and modern interpretations of vampiric tales have drawn on this notion. The legend of Dracula has, at least in the works of Stoker and movie scriptwriters, flowed steadily along with sexual tension and undercurrents. Perhaps titillating to the repressed

Dracula: The Transylvanian Vampire

Victorian reader, the actions of a creature of the night in seducing and drinking the blood of a pure, innocent virgin is a highly charged sexual image and has been played to the full – sometimes at the expense of other aspects of the vampiric folklore.

The name Dracula derives from Vlad's 'Order of the Dragon'; however, 'dracul' in Romanian also means 'devil'. Stoker's Count Dracula is a composite figure derived from Vlad the Impaler and Countess Bathori; the Countess was arrested in 1610 for murdering girls and bathing in their blood, hoping to maintain her skin in a youthful condition. The Countess had several hundred female victims.

Vampires in Wallachia at the time of Dracula's rule were, to the superstitious people of the medieval period, as real as any army marching through their villages. The practice of driving a stake through the heart of a suicide victim continued as late as 1905; unnatural deaths such as by suicide or from undiagnosed illness were often believed to have been caused by the teeth of a vampire. Other beliefs recorded that anyone remaining unbaptised before death – or even a bastard child – could become a vampire at death. Dracula's renunciation of the Greek Orthodox faith (becoming a Catholic in Hungarian captivity) placed him firmly within the realms of becoming a vampire in a fifteenth or later century Wallachian's mind. It can be argued that his eventual death – beheading followed by the despatch of the head to the Sultan in Constantinople – was not just a sign of obedience to the Ottomans, but a safeguard against Dracula's supernatural return.

Dracula on the Silver Screen

Perhaps the most famous actors ever to play Dracula are Christopher Lee and Boris Karloff. In such movies, Dracula has traditionally been a gaunt, pale and angular figure, garbed in a black cloak (usually with a red velvet lining) and well-tailored dark suit. The ability to metamorphose into a bat, and occasionally into other animals or a smoke cloud, enables Dracula to escape from impossible situations, or obtain access to sleeping women through closed windows high in walls. In such films, Dracula – having often survived and routed a lynch mob from the local village – is hunted down by a small group of plucky adventurers, and killed with a stake through the heart or by heavy curtains being thrown open to reveal his skin to daylight, turning the vampire to dust.

As well as the more 'traditional' versions of Dracula as a vampire, a number of bizarre spin-off movies have occurred. *Zoltan Hound of Dracula* featured a hellish black Doberman dog intent on reviving its master and creating chaos in modern-day America. Several female vampires (usually 'Wife of' or 'Daughter of' Dracula) have appeared to suck the blood from unwary men and occasionally women – usually in a more graphically sexual way than their male vampire equivalents. Dracula and vampirism have not escaped parody on the cinema screen, either. A number of woefully inept, and sadly at times less than amusing, vampires have been played by actors as diverse as Leslie Nielsen and the singer Adam Ant.

Vampirism has also been dragged forward into late twentieth-century settings and beyond with some success (most movies filmed up to around 1980 were set in the nineteenth century), with varying folklore elements still contained within them. Examples of such modernization of myth include *The Lost Boys*, *Blade*, *From Dusk Till Dawn* and *Buffy the Vampire Slayer*.

In History

Bram Stoker certainly chose a good figure from history to hang the mantle of a bloodthirsty vampire upon: the true story of Dracula is bloodier than the legend. The Dracula of Transylvanian and Hollywood legend originates in the reign and actions of a prince of a neighbouring province to Transylvania, Vlad V of Wallachia (1430–1476), known now to history as Vlad the Impaler or Dracula.

Born around 1430 in the town of Sighisoara in Transylvania (now present-day northern Romania), Vlad Dracula entered a turbulent political arena as one of the three sons of Vlad Dracul, Prince of Wallachia. Dracula's father belonged to the Order of the Dragon, formed by the Holy Roman Emperor Sigismund for the purpose of defeating the Turks. Vlad Dracul used the dragon symbol on his coins and went by the name 'Dracul' ('dragon' or 'devil'). Hence the diminutive '-a' on his son's name, Dracula. As the younger Vlad's talent for torture became known, however, the name Dracula came to be interpreted more and more as the sinister 'son of the devil.'

Warriors

At this time, Wallachia was in a constant state of strife, playing a dangerous game of political appeasement between the powerful Turkish Ottoman Empire and Christian Hungary. Vlad Dracul was attempting to keep the balance between both countries, whilst preventing either of them becoming tired of him and replacing his rule with a puppet of their own. This he did successfully until 1442, when he allowed the Turks to pass through his land to raid Transylvania. Janos Hunyadi, Hungary's most successful warlord, defeated the advancing Ottomans and removed Dracul from his throne. Dracul fled to the Ottoman court and secured an alliance with Murad II to reinstate him on the Wallachian throne with

Portrait of Dracula based on a fifteenth- or sixteenth-century German publication. (From Ioan Bogdan's *Vlad Tepes*, 1896)

Turkish help. This he achieved in 1443, but in order to retain Dracul's loyalty, the Sultan took his two sons, Radu and Dracula as hostages (a common means of medieval rulers achieving their desires).

A medieval hostage did not suffer the same fate as their modern-day counterparts, and were usually treated in accordance to their class. It is not known what hospitality Dracul's sons enjoyed, but as the Ottoman Empire's war with Hungary continued, and Dracul's loyalty shifted according to the political situation, the boys must have been very concerned about their welfare. It is sometimes suggested that Radu became a harem favour of the Sultan, but it does not appear that Dracula was treated in a similar fashion.

The Vampire in Britain and America

Vampirism is a mostly eastern and central European folk legend, yet several cases have been reported in Britain and America since the mid nineteenth century. The two most intriguing both occurred in the 1840s, one either side of the Atlantic Ocean.

In 1845, the members of the family of Horace Ray in Jewett City, Connecticut, all fell ill from a 'wasting disease' after his death in 1845. This became very serious, with all of the family dying until, when only one son remained alive, the body of his father was exhumed – and found to be lying in an un-decomposed state, in the same condition in which it had been buried. The corpse was burned, and the remaining Ray made a rapid recovery, convincing some that his father had been a vampire.

In 1848, the Cranswell family claimed to have been stalked by a vampire at their isolated home, Croglin Grange, in Cumberland, England. The vampire apparently made repeated attempts to break into the house to attack the family's young daughter, Anne. Anne's brothers tracked the vampire to its lair in a local churchyard. They burned the coffin with the body inside, and the vampire returned no more.

Warriors

After the defeat of the Hungarians by the Turks at Varna, Dracul took Janos Hunyadi prisoner as he retreated through Wallachia. Hunyadi was eventually released, but was never to forgive Dracul for this humiliation; Dracul presumably took the Hungarian warlord prisoner not to humble him, but to impress the Turkish Sultan – his children, after all, were hostages of the Turks. In 1447, Janos Hunyadi returned to Wallachia, overthrowing and slaying Dracul and his oldest son Mircea. The triumphant Hunyadi placed his own puppet – Vladislav II – on the throne, intending Wallachia to act as a buffer zone between his own Hungarian homeland and the mighty realm of the Ottomans.

In 1448, Dracula was released, whilst the armies of Hungary and the Turkish Empire fought over the area around Kosovo. Dracula returned to Wallachia to ascend the throne, whilst Vladislav II was engaged in the Kosovo campaign. The thrill of ruling over his own people was short lived for Dracula, as his small army was defeated on Vladislav's return. Dracula was sent once more into exile.

Dracula disappeared for the next seven years, emerging once more in 1455; this time, Dracula pledged his loyalty to Janos Hunyadi, who accepted the prince's offer of service. Dracula served with the Hungarian army until the following year, when Hunyadi died, succumbing to disease. At this point, freed from any of Hunyadi's restraint, Dracula again marched into Wallachia, this time killing Vladislav and re-installing himself on the throne. This time, Dracula was determined that his reign would not be so short lived.

His first act as Wallachia's ruler was to call a meeting of all

Drawing based on a contemporary woodcut of Dracula's atrocities. Here, Dracula sits at a dining table with slabs of meat carved from his impaled victims' bodies. (Author's collection)

of the boyars – the noblemen of the country. They were summoned to Dracula's capital at Tirgoviste. Dracula, a cunning ruler who had evidently learnt much from his time with both the Hungarians and the Ottomans, realized that much of the previous scheming and intrigue amongst the Wallachian boyars had made previous rulers – including his father – very weak. Determined to break this power, Dracula waited for the noblemen, who numbered in the hundreds, to arrive at the feasting hall within his castle, and then blocked the exits with his loyal bodyguard. Then, one by one, the boyars were dragged outside and impaled. Dracula replaced the vacuum of nobility with his own followers who had previously proved their loyalty under ample conditions, such as Dracula's two rises to the throne of Wallachia, and in the massacre of the boyars. Dracula placed loyalty above high birth, securing his place on the throne in one swift, if bloody, swoop.

Settled as the ruler of Wallachia, and feeling content after the destruction of the boyar's power, Dracula then set about reviving Wallachia's economy, which at this time was dominated and constricted by Saxon merchants. Dracula closed the Wallachian borders and set about negotiating trade deals with the powerful and greedy Saxon merchants. This may sound, to the casual reader, a rather mundane act from one with such a bloodthirsty reputation, but through this, Dracula demonstrated that he was a shrewd ruler, not only a powerful warlord. That is not to say that the methods supporting Dracula's intelligent economic policies were so mundane; the merchants who did not agree to his one-sided treaties were impaled, and those others who remained were driven from Wallachia in fear. This placed the control of the economy once more into the hands of the native merchants, who would take care in the future not to offend Dracula with their greed.

Dracula's methods appear cruel to the modern reader, yet they were certainly effective in this period of plundering armies and persecuted countryside. In an attempt to solve rising crime levels and spreading disease in Wallachian towns, Dracula gathered together the vagrants and common thieves; they were placed into a large feasting hall, ostensibly to eat a feast (one must wonder if they actually believed this though), which was then locked and burned to the ground. People were impaled for trivial crimes – some reportedly even for fictitious crimes – and Dracula soon earned himself the title of *Tepes*, meaning The Impaler.

Impalement was a particularly gruesome form of execution. The victim was impaled between the legs upon a large, sharpened stake the width of an arm. Dracula reputedly enjoyed mass executions, where several victims were impaled at one time, and their stakes hoisted upright. As they hung suspended above the ground, the weight of their bodies would slowly drag them downwards, causing the sharpened end of the stake to pierce their internal organs. Vlad routinely ordered a banquet table set up in front of his victims, and would enjoy a leisurely supper amid the pitiful sights and sounds of the dying.

Unsurprisingly, crime ceased to exist in Wallachia. To demonstrate this, a gold cup was placed beside a drinking fountain in one of Dracula's towns for the people to use, and it was not stolen; nobody dared to steal it. A merchant travelling through Tirgoviste had a bag of gold stolen; Dracula publicly announced that he wished for the bag to be returned and it was. An interesting addendum to this particular story is that Dracula added a gold coin to the returned bag himself, and asked the merchant to count his returned gold to check that all was present. The merchant was honest, saying that there was one coin too many; given Dracula's previous treatment of greedy merchants, this one was probably very wise to be so honest.

By 1460, Wallachia was a revived country; it was strong enough to resist Ottoman or Hungarian invasion. During every year of his reign, Dracula had paid a tribute to the Sultan to divert war, and had provided Wallachian boys to be trained as Janissaries. However, the Turks became bold, and raids began to occur along the Wallachian border. After several Wallachian castles had been captured by the Turks, Dracula's patience wore thin, and his army marched on campaign in 1461. Avoiding an ambush laid by Turkish forces, Dracula recaptured his lost land and went on to distinguish himself further by capturing the Turkish possession of Giurgiu. At Giurgiu, the Wallachian forces entered the walled town disguised as Turks – on Dracula's orders – took the town by force, and Dracula furthered his name and reputation of 'Tepes' by impaling all of the surviving Turks. Dracula himself described the acts he carried out on his campaign in that year:

Dracula: The Transylvanian Vampire

I have killed men and women, old and young…23,884
Turks and Bulgars without counting those whom we
burned in their homes or whose heads were not cut
by our soldiers…
(quoted in McNally & Florescu, 1992: 48)

The year 1462 saw the Sultan, Mehmet II, raising an army to
invade Wallachia. Dracula's cruel treatment of the Turkish
border forces had tested the Sultan's patience too long; with
the Turkish invasion force rode Dracula's brother, Radu, who
the Sultan intended to place on the throne over Dracula's
bloody corpse. Dracula was aware that, despite his successes in
the so far relatively minor border conflict, he would be hard
pressed to turn back an entire invading army of Turks; he
appealed to the Christian enemies of the Ottoman Empire for
aid. Hungary and several other western realms promised
support, but as the Sultan's army prepared to march into
Wallachia, no help came. He would be facing an invading force
of some 60,000 battle hardened Turks with just 30,000 men.

As the Sultan's army crossed the Danube, their first contact
with the Wallachian army occurred. As the Turks disembarked
from their boats, Dracula's skilled light cavalry dashed to and
fro, attempting to prevent an easy landing or the Turks
establishing a beachhead. This was a shrewd tactic on Dracula's
part, using the advantage of favourable terrain to hold back a
stronger opponent. Eventually, the Sultan sent across his feared
Janissaries – the best soldiers in the entire Ottoman Empire.
After inflicting heavy casualties on the troops emerging from
their boats, the Wallachians were driven away when the

Janissaries managed to hold them back and prepare a landing area for the Turk's most powerful weapons – their artillery. Against such cannons, the Wallachian horsemen knew they stood little chance, so drifted away into the countryside. This was much to the relief of the Turks.

The superior manpower and firepower available to the Turks meant that Dracula would stand little chance in an open, pitched battle. The Wallachian warlord appreciated this himself, and instead opted to follow a scorched earth policy, burning crops and farms as his army retreated, and poisoning wells and other water supplies. This would make it difficult for the Turks to sustain a campaign in an enemy land, as food could only be stolen or foraged (baggage trains did not offer logistical support to the common foot soldiers of medieval armies).

Marching into the land of a warlord with a reputation such as Dracula's must have preyed on the minds of the Turkish troops. The prevention of easily acquired food and booty would also have further unsettled them. Even the weather appeared to be against them – by daytime, the heat made for uncomfortable marching, and by night, Wallachian horsemen harried the Turkish column. Despite the small size of Dracula's force, they excelled at guerrilla tactics, keeping the Turkish guards constantly attentive, and adding to the rising fatigue levels of the marching Turkish invasion force. Accounts of the invasion written by Janissaries recorded the terrible fear that the soldiers in the column felt, and that at nightfall, they dug themselves into deeply entrenched positions fearing the attack of Dracula's horsemen.

Dracula: The Transylvanian Vampire

This fear was to prove well founded. As the Turks trudged onwards through the hot days and dangerous nights, Dracula gathered a force of 10,000 horsemen in the shelter of woodland close to Tirgoviste. At dusk on 17 June 1462 the Sultan's force encamped close by; Dracula was prepared – he had captured prisoners from the column and tortured details of the camps layout and defences from them. As the Turks

Drawing based on a contemporary woodcut of Dracula's malevolence, showing a similar scene to that in the previous image. (Author's collection)

were now dangerously close to his capital, Dracula attempted a grand plan – to capture or kill the Sultan, and rout his forces from Wallachia. Bursting from their concealed stations in the woodland, the Wallachian horsemen charged into the (unsuspecting) Turkish camp. Crashing firstly into the Asian troops of the Turkish army (we must remember that the Ottoman Sultan was served by empire troops in much the same way as the Roman and later British empires were), the Wallachian's routed them. Advancing in good order, and spreading panic throughout the camp as they surged onwards, the Wallachians were led by Dracula, who was apparently dashing like lightning across the battlefield to wherever he was most needed, and all through the night he and his men caused great bloodshed in the Turkish encampment. Sticking to their orders and keeping close to each other – avoiding the lure of looting tents when their country's freedom was at risk – Dracula's horsemen drove through the camp, looking for the personal tent of the Sultan. Luckily for the Turkish leader, the vengeful horsemen identified the wrong tent, and as they battled with well-armed and armoured Turkish Spahi horsemen, the Sultan's Janissary bodyguard formed around his tent. This pause in the attack lost the Wallachian's their element of surprise, and the stubborn, well drilled Janisarries could not be broken by the time that the Sultan's real tent had been identified. Unable to dent the defensive ring of warriors, and aware of the rest of the Turkish camp springing into action, the Wallachians once again melted away into the Wallachian countryside. Despite their massive numerical advantage, the

Turks did not pursue – such was their fear of Dracula's horsemen. Estimates of Turkish casualties vary from a conservative 7000 to an obviously exaggerated 50,000. Whatever the true figure, the attack was a huge blow for the Sultan and a slight to his reputation – the mighty Mehmet II had fled the camp during the confusion of the vicious battle, and refused to return until the following day when he had been assured that it was safe to do so.

Dracula's gamble had not paid off, as the Turkish army resumed its march on his capital city. However, a few miles outside of the Tirgoviste, Dracula had prepared a special welcome for them.

Reputedly extending across 3 kilometres of open land, and filling a width of 1 kilometre, stood the bodies of some 20,000 Turks. They stood as opposed to lay as each victim had been impaled; carrion birds picked at the corpses and parasites made their home in the decaying bodies. Obviously, this was too much for the invading Turks to cope with; ever since they had entered Wallachia they had lived in fear of the bloodthirsty warlord's small yet almost mystically empowered army; they had suffered furious attacks under the cover of night, marched hungry and tired through an unforgiving, savaged land, and were now confronted by the decomposing bodies of fellow countrymen as far as the eye could see. Retreat was ordered immediately, yet even this was harried by Dracula's triumphant horse warriors.

The repulsion of Mehmet II's invading army was undoubtedly the high point of Dracula's military career. Although the main Turkish force retreated out of Wallachia,

Warriors

Radu remained with a small force entrusted to him by the Sultan. Radu, it should be remembered, gave the Sultan the initial excuse to invade Wallachia in an attempt to wrestle the throne from his brother and serve the Ottoman Empire as a puppet king. Although Radu's force was small, the people of Wallachia had tired of war – a fully understandable point of mind given that Wallachia had been a war zone on and off for the previous twenty years – and Dracula's boyars listened to Radu's promise of peace. Whether Radu was believed or not was really immaterial. The Wallachian people, boyars and peasants alike knew that if Radu did not take the crown, the Turks would be back in even stronger numbers. Many deserted Dracula's army, and shortly after, a civil war broke out between Radu and Dracula. Dracula, presumably toiling under the strain of the previous hard campaign followed so swiftly by this, was defeated within a year; he took refuge within a castle high in the Carpathian Mountains.

Radu ruthlessly pursued his brother – elimination would allow Radu to take the crown. Cornered in the castle, Dracula's wife threw herself from the battlements into the river below and death – preferring that to suffering the humility of capture. Dracula escaped his besiegers through a secret tunnel, swiftly entering Hungary and exile. The callous nature of the man showed itself again if the reports that he allowed his wife to commit suicide rather than taking her with him are to be believed.

Radu was duly crowned as the ruler of Wallachia, and fifteenth-century eastern European politics being what they were, Dracula arrived in Hungary to be imprisoned for the

Dracula: The Transylvanian Vampire

following twelve years. By 1475 however, the situation had
changed, and Dracula was freed to serve in the Hungarian
army under Stephen of Moldovia. In 1476, the King of
Hungary decided that Dracula was once more a loyal and
trusted subject, and set about restoring him to the
Wallachian throne (once more as a reliable buffer state
against the Ottomans); an army under Dracula's rule invaded
Wallachia and he was restored once again to power. The
Wallachian people had not forgotten his previous methods
of government, and many boyars felt unsettled by his return;
within months of his restoration to the Wallachian crown,
Dracula had been ambushed by a force of unknown
assassins. Dracula was most likely killed by his own followers
in an act of self-preservation and vengeance; however, the
Slavic account of his death presents a different story:

> Out of sheer joy, Dracula ascended a hill in order to see
> better his men massacring the Turks. Thus, detached
> from his army and his men, some took him for a Turk,
> and one of them struck him with a lance. But Dracula,
> seeing that he was being attacked by his own men,
> immediately killed five of his would-be assassins with
> his own sword; however, he was pierced by many lances
> and thus he died
> (quoted in McNally & Florescu, 1992: 103)

In whatever manner his death did come about, Dracula's
head was sent as a goodwill gesture to the Sultan from the
people of Wallachia; therefore such a poetic, simple

explanation probably does not do the end of Dracula's bloodthirsty tale the justice that it deserves, and he more likely died in a manner befitting the period's politics and Dracula's own eventful life – in a brutal and bloodthirsty skirmish, at the hands of disloyal followers.

In Battle

Wallachia was situated between two great medieval powers – Hungary and the Ottoman Empire – and drew on both for its methods of warfare. The mid and late fifteenth century saw the pinnacle and swan song of the heavily armed, heavily armoured and heavily mounted western European knight; it also saw the emergence of firearms as a potentially battle winning weapon. Despite this, eastern European battlefields were still dominated by light, skirmishing cavalry and bowmen (both on foot and mounted). The knight played his part, as indeed did firearms, but the main strike forces of most eastern European armies were lightly armoured, mounted bowmen. The Wallachians of Dracula were no exception – in fact, light cavalry (hussars and mounted archers) were significant in both Hungarian and Turkish armies of the time too. Special significance must be given to the Ottoman armies of this period when considering the way in which the Wallachians fought, as most accounts give the impression that Wallachian armies were influenced more from the east than from the west.

Dracula: The Transylvanian Vampire

The ruler of Wallachia was served by a small, loyal bodyguard force, of whom Dracula's became the *Sluji* – who replaced the boyars that he so bloodily murdered early in his reign. Such a bodyguard, and the noble boyars of Wallachia would have been armed in a mixture of styles, showing the influence of European Hungary and the more eastern-influenced Ottomans. Indeed, the traditional Slavic account of Dracula's death sees him being mistaken for a Turk by his own men – presumably owing to the Turkish style of his armour and clothing, which was probably very similar to the Spahis described later in this chapter.

The reliance on mounted archery was influenced in no small part by the various Steppe warriors who had passed through Eastern Europe from the Huns to the Mongols. In the intervening years between these two cultures, each famous for its use of mounted bowmen, the Magyars and Avars also left a great impression of the power of lightly armoured, well armed horsemen. The light cavalry predominant in Wallachian armies were well suited to harassing tactics (these horse men were the forerunners of later hussars, and very similar to the famous Cossacks of Russia). It is therefore not surprising to see the way in which Dracula's men harried the Turkish columns when under invasion. Stories very similar to those told by the survivors of Cossack attacks in Napoleon's retreat from Moscow were probably told by Mehmet II's retreating army several centuries earlier. The favoured weapons of Eastern light cavalrymen were composite bows (made from wood yet reinforced with antler or bone to increase the missile's velocity and penetration power), and wicked, curved sabres, which were deadly sharp and wielded with great accuracy. Lances were also popular, a skilled horseman being able to pluck a fish from a stream without dismounting to steady his spear arm. A Hungarian archive of the late fifteenth century, of King Matthias I Corvinus, described the armament of a light horseman as a long lance, a sword, a composite bow, and recorded such a warrior as being mounted on a high pommelled saddle (of Avar origin), dressed in a colourful embroidered costume with plumed hat, and carrying a teardrop-shaped shield. In Turkish armies these light cavalrymen were known as Akinjis, in Hungary as Hussars, and most wore turban or cap, caftan or cape and baggy trousers – their Wallachian equivalent more often wore tall fur hats with feathers mounted pointing upwards at the front.

The Wallachians were skilled horsemen, and trained their horses well. Wallachian horses would be taught to walk in the style of a camel – moving both legs on one side at the same time. Most of the equestrian skills known by the Wallachians were learned from the East – from both the Ottomans and the earlier Steppe peoples from whom the Wallachians and earlier Vlachs were descended.

One of the mainstay weapons of the Wallachian cavalrymen and their mounted enemies was the composite bow. Composite bows fired arrows 2 feet long, and, according to an Arabic archery manual, over 175 yards. Distances that bows could fire accurately have been hotly debated by many experts however – Sir Ralph Payne-Galway believed a composite bow to be capable of firing over 300 yards and capable of piercing ½ inch of wood at 100 yards (Gush, 1982: 11), for example.

The late fifteenth century was a time of change in battlefield tactics and tools. The crossbow was reaching its design pinnacle, becoming a very powerful weapon with immense penetrative power. The most powerful crossbows could no longer be loaded and wound by hand, but needed mechanical devices to assist the bowman. Aside from crossbows and the various other forms of bow used in the late fifteenth century, hand-held, breech-loading guns were also being experimented with. Although sometimes unreliable, with a short range – sometimes as low as 10

East European horse archers in the fifteenth century, typical of the warriors in Dracula's force. (From H S Williams, *The Historian's History of the World*, 1904)

metres – and variable accuracy, such gunpowder-based weapons came into their own in sieges and gradually developed into the early muskets of the next century. The Wallachian infantrymen fought with a mixture of missile weapons, halberds and other pole weapons, wearing whatever armour they could afford or plunder from their defeated enemies. Although by many standards the poorest arm of the Wallachian army, the infantry contingents of Wallachia and neighbouring Moldavia were 'strong', according to Maurice Keen (Keen [ed] 1999: 281).

The armour worn by Hungarian knights and, if chosen in favour over Turkish dress, adopted by the highest social strata of Wallachian boyars would have been western styled plate armour. By the late fifteenth century, the body was completely enshrouded by metal plated armour, with chainmail underneath at vulnerable joints such as behind the knees and at the elbows. Italian-style armour had smooth, rounded plates, whereas German-style armour was decorated with fluting reminiscent of gothic architecture (and hence known as gothic armour). Gothic armour was designed to adapt to human anatomy, and could be close fitting and relatively light in weight. A whole suit of gothic plate armour usually weighed about 25 kilograms, compared to a less protective suit of chainmail which weighed about 15 kilograms.

The shields used for protection by Wallachian and Hungarian warriors were perhaps the most distinctive used in medieval Europe. Described best as either teardrop shaped or winged, these shields had a flat base, and rose to a point at

the rear top corner whilst being lower at the front end –
allowing protection without impeding vision. This was
crucial for a lightly armoured cavalrymen, who relied
sometimes purely on his shield for protection, and his wits
and vision for survival.

East European Horsemen

The most famous Eastern European cavalrymen in history have,
undoubtedly, been the Cossacks, who were acknowledged as
dangerous and cruel opponents from the sixteenth to the twentieth
centuries. Fighting with lances, wickedly curved sabres, powerful bows,
and much later, muskets, they were among the most effective light
cavalry ever to have taken to the battlefield. They darted to-and-fro
across the battlefield, were difficult to pin down in close combat, and
were deadly over short distances with their missile weapons. The
influence for such lightly armed, yet highly formidable cavalrymen
originally came from farther to the East – in successive waves of
Hunnic, Magyar, Avar, and Mongolian invasions.

With the reputation of being born in the saddle, the cultures that
moved west from the Steppe land bordering Europe and Asia were
skilled fighters from horseback. The Huns were partly responsible for
sparking the mass cultural movements of the Goths, Vandals and Alans
that contributed to the fall of the Roman Empire in the fourth and fifth
centuries AD; they were also famed as the skilled mercenary
bodyguards of several post Roman warlords. Later, in the early
medieval period, the Magyars and Avars swept into Europe from the

Warriors

East and fought hard against the Byzantine and Frankish Empires, influencing and increasing the quality and importance of mounted warriors in all the European forces that they met.

Perhaps most famous of all, the Mongols swept west into Russia and Europe, and east into south-east Asia, China and Japan in the thirteenth and fourteenth centuries. Carving out their own empire, the Mongols chose to exact tribute from those who fell under their influence, allowing the original culture to survive; the influence of the Mongols on later armies in those conquered countries was quite explicit – the Russians notably came to rely upon horse archers and fast moving cavalrymen instead of the heavily armoured European-style knights who first rode to disaster against the Mongol hordes.

Mercenaries served in many armies throughout the fifteenth century in Europe and elsewhere. Depending upon whom the Wallachian army served at the time, it would have included Turkish mercenaries or Hungarian mercenaries. Dracula appealed for help from a wider number of Christian European kingdoms in 1462 – although no help was forthcoming despite empty promises. The Ottoman army did not consist entirely of Turkish soldiers, although it did not technically consist of 'mercenaries' but of 'allied' troops instead. It was a great empire, and like Rome before and Victoria's Britain after, drew on many diverse cultures to make up its armies. Dracula himself fought for the Ottomans against the Hungarians at one stage, and many other European warlords, regardless of their religious belief, also took up arms for the Ottoman cause, scared that refusal would lead to invasion and conquest of their own lands.

Janissaries were the elite of Turkish soldiers. Dracula had provided Wallachian boys to be trained as these crack troops, to serve as the Sultan's bodyguard. Janissaries were Christian soldiers who served the Turkish Sultan. Janissaries were among the earliest troops in Europe to be regularly equipped with firearms; even before this became common practice, they were formidable foes and fearsome warriors; composite bows were used very effectively, and the well-armoured Janissaries were tough opponents in a melée. Contemporary illustrations of Janissaries show them wearing blue, red, purple and black clothing, and they had at least some uniformity in their dress. Caftans were worn along with the characteristic Zarcola (a white felt, tall hat), and heads were shaved apart form a pony tail or scalp

Typifying the contrasting styles of Western and Eastern warfare, this engraving highlights the lance-armed heavy cavalry of the West against the lighter, faster bowmen of the East. The army of Dracula encompassed both of these forces. (Author's collection)

lock. Many Janissaries wore moustaches – in contrast to the
rest of the Turkish army who mostly wore beards. For
Dracula's Wallachian horsemen to scare, rout and disorder
the Turkish Janissaries in 1462 can be considered a major
triumph on Dracula's horsemen's part.

The Ottoman cavalry mostly consisted of Spahis; literally
meaning 'soldier', it specifically referred to the heavy cavalry
wing of the Ottoman army. The Sultans employed two types
of Spahi – paid, well organized regular troops (the Household
Cavalry or Spahis of the Porte), and a larger but less well
trained body of feudal cavalrymen. The feudal Spahis were
expected to bring a contingent of followers with them – of
up to eighteen men, known as Jebeli. Spahi weapons, much
like those of other eastern armoured cavalrymen at this time
comprised a light lance (often, it would seem, painted green
and with a colourful pennon), a composite bow and brightly
decorated arrow quiver, and a vicious, jewelled scimitar (a
curved cavalry sword). Other weapons included steel maces
and occasionally javelins. For protection, a shield was strapped
on to the cavalryman's arm (usually such shields were around
30 inches in diameter), and armour consisted of reinforced
chainmail, quilted or leather armour, and occasional plating
(but not so extensively as a contemporary western knight);
helmets were of various forms, but spiked helmets of Persian
influence were worn alongside more traditional peaked
helmets. Horses could also be armoured, notably with
chainmail, leather or lamellar armour.

Artillery was beginning to play an important role on the
battle field in late fifteenth-century Europe. The Ottoman

army generally excelled in its use, and in Mehmet's campaigns against Dracula, artillery was to feature strongly. It was a weapon that Dracula's essentially guerrilla army could not effectively counter on the battlefield, and the Wallachians would fade away into the dense woods when faced with a fierce artillery barrage.

The Ottoman armies were colourful in their clothing, and such style, combined with a rich variety of western dress, would have made the Wallachian armies and their opponents quite a sight to behold. Accounts of the Turks refer to gold, silver, scarlet, violet, dark blue and green cloths, and caftans and baggy trousers were also common. Traditional Wallachian dress included a fur hat with one or two feathers mounted in the front of it, and riding boots were worn to the knee by horsemen. Other popular colours in Eastern Europe included white, a mouse-coloured dun, and yellow; black and purple could be avoided as they were superstitiously perceived to be unlucky colours.

Numbers involved in battles in Dracula's time would have varied. The large force raised by Mehmet II was recorded as numbering 60,000 – it must be remembered that the Sultan was able to draw on warriors from across the expansive Ottoman world. Against this force, Dracula pitted 30,000 men – a combination of footmen and his valued horse warriors; his night-time assault outside Tirgoviste saw him muster 10,000 horsemen; these presumably came from his initial force of 30,000. Hungarian sources suggest that perhaps 10 per cent of a central or eastern European force would have been mounted, yet the mounted arm of a Wallachian army may have been a significantly higher percentage, given the reliance placed on light horsemen. Later Turkish armies involved vast numbers of warriors too – the Spahis of the Porte were divided into six regiments each 500 strong and divided into squadrons of twenty men; the right wing alone of an early sixteenth-century Ottoman army was supposed to consist of 3500 men. George Gush tells us that, in terms of cavalry only (not including any infantry):

> Under Suleiman the Magnificent [1520–66] the total of the Household cavalry was increased to about 12,000, and according to some sources they were accompanied by armed and mounted slaves who could bring the whole number as high as 30,000.
> (1982: 77)

The Ottoman rulers could also call on 30,000 or 40,000 lightly armed Akinji cavalrymen, and, under the leadership of Suleiman the Magnificent, around 12,000 Janissaries and countless hordes of other infantrymen.

Small skirmishes were also common – these occurred around the edges of invading columns, whose outposts, vanguards, rearguards and flanking troops would have been under constant threat and harassment by unfriendly local and light cavalry. Another form of skirmish that seems to have been prevalent was that between rival nobles, treacherously attempting to remove those who presented the greatest political threat to their own power. Such small skirmishes may have taken place between as few as fifty or so

Dracula: The Transylvanian Vampire

combatants, but could determine the fate of an entire
political dynasty – as shown so poignantly in the historical
version to Dracula's life.

The civil wars which raged throughout Eastern Europe in
the late fifteenth century were played out by these smaller
forces. The constant reference to ambushes and small-scale
sieges in Dracula's military career suggests as such, and it is
likely that only a few hundred men (at most) would usually
have taken part in warfare at this time. This situation does
not appear far removed from the earlier periods when
warriors such as Arthur, Cuchulain and Beowulf would have
taken the warlord mantle of Dracula on their shoulders; if
anything, Dracula's time was more brutal.

His Turkish adversaries have left us some very vivid
accounts of life on campaign against Dracula. The launch
of the 1462 campaign into Wallachia was recorded by one
eye witness:

> [Opposite Dracula's army] we dug ourselves in trenches
> setting the cannons around us. We dug ourselves into
> the trenches so that the horsemen could not injure
> us... And when the whole of the infantry crossed over,
> we prepared and set out gradually against the army of
> Dracula, together with the artillery and other
> impedimenta we had taken with us. Having stopped,
> we set up the cannon, but until we could succeed in
> doing this, 300 soldiers were killed... After that, seeing
> that our side was weakening greatly, having transported
> 120 guns, we defended ourselves with them and fired

often, so that we repelled the army of the prince from
that place and we strengthened ourselves... And
Dracula seeing he could not prevent the crossing,
withdrew from us. Then, after the Emperor had crossed
the Danube following us with a whole army, he gave us
30,000 gold coins to be divided among us
(Quoted in McNally & Florescu, 1992: 50)

Such battles must have been noisy, chaotic affairs. It must be
remembered that gunpowder was still in its military infancy,
and it must have been a frightening experience for many of
the ordinary soldiers on both sides to be fired upon, or even
to be near to firing cannons.

Any densely formed eastern European force, no matter if
it consisted of heavy cavalry or heavy infantry, would have
been screened by a force of light cavalry. Their role was
partly to break up and impede any attacking force before its
full strength could hit home, partly to disguise the actual
number of troops in the formation, and partly to prevent
enemy skirmishers approaching to within missile-firing
range. These light cavalrymen would also act as the eyes of
a force, reconnoitring the landscape and the enemy, and
bringing back vital information to the main body of an
army.

Another tactic, common amongst virtually all mountain-
based or rough terrain-based armies, was to use the available
countryside to its best advantage. In the battle of Posada in
1330, the Hungarian army of Charles I was lured into a
defile in the Carpathian Mountains by a Wallachian force,

Dracula: The Transylvanian Vampire

A Hungarian shield of the winged style common in Wallachia, showing front and back. (Author's collection)

Three views of a Turkish helmet from the fifteenth century, with a mail aventail; Wallachian nobles often wore armour in the Turkish style. (Author's collection)

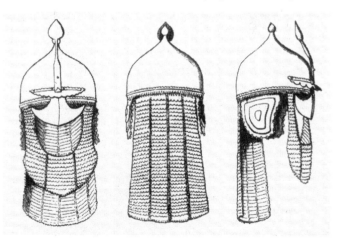

and then defeated in ambush by a Wallachian force armed with no more than composite bows and hurled rocks from above. The Hungarian force included contingents of well armoured knights and foot men, and this battle can be compared to that in which the earlier Frankish paladin Roland died (see Chapter Eight).

Strategy, at least on Dracula's part, but also probably on that of any warlord in this area, included many nasty surprises – both psychological and natural. The psychological attacks made by Dracula's men were outlined earlier in this chapter – the field of corpses and the night attacks and constant harassment on the march. Perhaps contemporary chroniclers exaggerated the events beyond their truth, but even so, this reflects the effect that such events had on those involved. The sun's heat, beating down on the resilient Turkish army which marched into Wallachia in 1462 took its toll, with the soldiers complaining that they could find no drinkable water in the springs; it has been recorded that the African and Asian elements of the multinational Ottoman army, being more used to adapting to such heat, used their shields as giant roasting tins to cook meat upon.

Dracula being described as a warrior may have raised the eyebrows of many readers. This simple statement demonstrates how potent the storytelling powers of modern cinema and literature are. The earliest legends created about Vlad Tepes concentrated on exaggerating his cruelty; the Victorian author Bram Stoker combined this with the wonderful Eastern European

Dracula: The Transylvanian Vampire

folklore of the vampire to create a popular and long-lived image of 'Dracula' the vampire, which has since prospered through many decades in the cinema. As a historical character, Vlad Tepes certainly existed, and a fairly coherent account of his deeds has been made. Like the historical Arthur, Vlad's armies fought in a period of transition between the medieval world of swords and lances and the renaissance world of gunpowder and fortresses. Dracula as a vampire has now become too strong an image for the historical Vlad to ever rise above, yet the Wallachian warlord must be considered as equally bloodthirsty as his legendary namesake.

ACHILLES
Hero of *The Iliad*

Achilles is perhaps the most powerful of all mortal warriors in Greek mythology; however, in addition to his deeds overseen by Zeus and the other Gods, Achilles played a pivotal role in the classical tale of early Mediterranean warfare – *The Iliad*. The epic wars between Greece and Troy were committed to paper by the Ionian poet Homer, an unidentified writer who probably lived in the eighth century BC; other later Greek authors have added many twists to the overall tale, or reinterpreted parts of it. The wars of which he spoke probably dated to the thirteenth or twelfth centuries BC, and, as mentioned above, the focal character of Homer's tale is the mighty warrior Achilles, leader of the powerful warband of the Myrmidons.

The Iliad consists of twenty-four books. The legendary war that Homer narrated was waged for ten years between the men of Greece and their enemies in Troy; however, *The Iliad* really only considers the final year of the siege of Troy. The seeds of the war were sown when Paris, the Trojan king, carried away Helen, the wife of Menelaus, king of Sparta. By all accounts, Helen was an extremely beautiful woman:

Achilles: Hero of *The Iliad*

'Oh, thou art fairer than the evening air,
Clad in the beauty of a thousand stars.'
(Marlowe, quoted in Bulfinch, 1915: 261)

Menelaus induced his Greek allies to accompany him in a
great expedition to lay siege to the city to reclaim his wife.
Achilles, and many other important Greek kings, agreed to
accompany Menelaus; Achilles only arrived through the
eloquent persuasions of Odysseus.

Achilles was acknowledged as a vital component to the
raiding party; he was a formidable warrior. His mother had
dipped him into the mystical River Styx, rendering him
invulnerable in all parts except that by which she gripped
him – his heel. He had been entrusted into the care of a
wise tutor, the centaur Chiron, who had taught many of the
earlier great heroes of Greece.

> From this instructor Achilles learned the arts of war,
> wrestling, poetry, music and song – all, in short, that an
> accomplished Greek warrior was expected to know.
> (Guerber, 1907: 279)

Thus prepared, with the greatest warrior as part of the
invading army, the Greek fleet assembled at Aulis, and a
Greek seer named Kalchas interpreted a portent seen by the
assembled Greeks. A serpent climbed into a tree that held a
nest with eight young birds in it; the serpent ate the birds
and then caught and ate the mother; it was then turned to
stone by the god Zeus. Kalchas explained to the warriors

that this meant the siege of Troy would last for nine years, and only come to an end in the following, tenth, year.

The fleet set out, delayed several times, including (in post-Homeric tales) a wrong direction being taken and the fleet landing at Mysia. The inhabitants mustered under their king Telephos, a son of Herakles, who was wounded in battle by Achilles, despite his own prowess and valour. The Greek fleet departed, having no quarrel with the Mysians, yet the wound inflicted by Achilles to Telephos would not heal, and the Mysian king pursued Achilles, forcing him to heal the wound by applying scrapings from his spear to the wound (this was instructed by Apollo – who declared that he who wounded should also heal, meaning Achilles' spear).

At length, the Greek fleet arrived before the walls of Troy, and the ships were drawn up on the beach to provide a base camp. The Greeks settled down for a long, besieging campaign. Small skirmishes formed the beginning of the war, and in one such skirmish, Protesilaos, king of Thessaly was slain by a Trojan leader (sometimes identified as Hector, but not so by Homer). It had been fated that the first Greek to leap ashore – this being Protesilaos – would sacrifice himself for his comrades. In the same skirmish, Achilles strangled Kyknos to death. However, Kyknos was an invincible son of the god Poseidon, and instead of dying he turned into a swan and escaped.

Inside the walls of Troy, Paris was in overall command. (It had been foretold to his father that Paris would be the ruin of the city; acting against this, his father, King Priam had put to death another, illegitimate child born on the same day.)

Achilles: Hero of *The Iliad*

Another of the important leaders on the Trojan side was Antenor, who disapproved of the kidnap of Helen and urged Paris to give her back. A respected elder, his words fell onto Paris's deaf ears, yet the Greeks appreciated his efforts, and, when Troy finally fell, spared Antenor and those of his family who had not died in the war.

The foremost protector and champion of the Trojan army, the Trojan warrior who would stand most chance of slaying the mighty Greek warrior Achilles, was Hector. Never the diplomat, Hector was nevertheless:

> ...a chivalrous and most valiant warrior, a terror to the Greeks in combat, inferior only to Achilles, and an affectionate husband.
> (Rose, 1958: 234)

The other sons of Priam played their part in battle for the Trojans too; they mostly appeared briefly in battle before being killed or captured by the often superior heroes of Greece. One of Priam's youngest sons, Troilos, was slain in battle by Achilles.

The Greek army that Menelaus mustered brought with it many great heroes. In addition to Achilles, who was 'the strongest, swiftest, most valiant and most handsome of the whole army' (Rose, 1958: 239), one of the most famous Greek warriors present at the siege of Troy was Nestor. Nestor was the king of Pylos (which has actually been shown through excavation to have been an important site in the Mycenaean age) and at sixty years old, he was one of the elder warriors in the Greek army. Age was accompanied in Nestor by wisdom, and he is shown throughout *The Iliad* as giving wise counsel and long-winded stories of old, rather than for exerting much military prowess on the battlefield with his ageing body. Nestor tries to act as a peacemaker, but when this fails, he largely fades out of the tale. He is also present in Homer's other great work, *The Odyssey*.

Odysseus features prominently in both *The Iliad* and *The Odyssey*. He was the king of Ithake, the husband of Penelope and the father of Telemachos. Odysseus was renowned for his sharp intelligence and quick wit; indeed it was he who initially persuaded Achilles to join the Greek army. Although formidable in battle, Odysseus was not one of the greatest Greek champions but was always prepared to give his best – when lots were drawn to decide who should fight Hector, most Greeks warriors hoped that the deed would fall upon Diomedes, Agamemnon or Aias, rather than Odysseus, despite the fact that he had volunteered for the role. Odysseus also entered Troy as a spy.

Diomedes was another Greek hero, and he often acted in conjunction with Odysseus in *The Iliad*. Prominent for his bravery and for his frank advice, he was favoured enough by the goddess Athena to wound both the god Ares and the goddess Aphrodite in battle when they appeared on the Trojan side. Diomedes survived the war, and travelled back to his home of Argos.

Agamemnon, who was the son of Atreus and brother of the king Menelaus, was a man of great political standing rather than a great warrior, yet he stood alongside the other Greek heroes on the plain beneath Troy. His brother Menelaus, who initiated the expedition in order to recover his wife Helen, was an efficient yet uninspired warrior; H J Rose noted that, 'Achilles, Agamemnon, the two Aiantes, Diomedes, and, in the other camp, Hector, outclass him.' (1958: 236)

Thus arrayed, the two armies, led by their various champions, settled down to a long siege frequently punctuated by skirmishes between the opposing heroes, supported by their followers.

> Hostilities had now begun, and the war between the conflicting hosts was waged with equal courage and skill. During nine long years of uninterrupted strife, the Greeks' efforts to enter Troy, or Ilium, as it was also called, were vain, as were also the Trojan's attempts to force the foe to leave their shores.
> (Guerber, 1907: 282)

During the first nine years, a few soulless attempts at diplomacy and peace failed, and the Greeks continued to raid the minor supporting cities around Troy. Troy itself, with its strong garrison and thick walls, protected by the Trojan warriors and their many allies, was considered impregnable to the Greek besiegers. Instead, the campaign was a war of attrition, with the Greeks trying to burn or steal the Trojan resources – from food to chariot horses – and to block trade in and out of the city.

The tenth year – that covered in detail by *The Iliad* – saw a plague falling upon the Greek camp, brought about by the

Warriors

Trojan priest of Apollo Chryses, whose daughter was held
captive by Agamemnon. The Priest's daughter was returned,
in order to bring a halt to the plague, and Agamemnon then
turned his lust to one of Achilles' favourite slave girls.
Achilles was furious and withdrew his crucial support for
the Greek cause, and left the Greek army in disgust.

Menelaus and Paris met in a duel, and Menelaus gained
the upper hand – perhaps after working himself into a fury
against the man who stole his wife. With Paris faltering
badly, his patron goddess, Aphrodite, whisked him away from
the duel, safely back into Troy. Neither the Greeks nor the
Trojans were impressed by Paris' acquittal of himself, and he
was branded a coward by Greek and Trojan alike. Helen also
expressed her disapproval of Paris very strongly.

Even so, without Achilles' support, the Greek battle force
began to falter. Despite a brave attempt to resist him, Hector
drove the Greeks back to their ships, attacking the Greek
base camp and setting fire to one of the beached Greek
ships. In an effort to repel this Trojan sally, Patrokles – one of
Achilles' favourite warriors – donned Achilles' armour and
launched a counter attack on the Trojan force:

> 'Send me at least into the war,
> And let me lead thy Myrmidons, that thus
> The Greeks may have some gleam of hope. And give
> The armour from thy shoulders. I will wear
> Thy mail, and then the Trojans, at the sight,
> May think I am Achilles, and may pause
> From fighting, and the warlike sons of Greece,

Achilles: Hero of *The Iliad*

Tired as they are, may breathe once more, and gain
A respite form the conflict.'
(trans. Bryant, quoted in Guerber, 1907: 288–289)

The Trojans, seeing Achilles' armour and fearing that the
great warrior had returned, routed in disorder back towards
the walls of the city. However, the deceit of Patrokles was
fatally revealed when he fell in battle, the god Apollo
lending the Trojans and Hector a helping hand in his defeat.

The death of Patrokles enraged Achilles; they had been
great friends and Achilles now went partially mad –
appearing unarmed and unarmoured on the battlefield
booming out a defiant war cry. The Trojans immediately
retreated back into the city once beholding the fearsome site
of Achilles enraged. The death of Patrokles brought Achilles
back to the Greek army, eager to make his friend's killers pay
for their deed. The next day, Achilles' warband gained a
major victory over the Trojans, utterly routing the main
contingent and Achilles slaying the Trojan hero Hector in
single combat:

> Achilles went forth to battle, and at last seeing Hector,
> whom alone he wished to meet, he rushed upon him
> with a hoarse cry of rage. The Trojan hero, at the mere
> sight of the deadly hatred which shone in Achilles' eyes,
> turned to flee. Achilles pursued him, and taunted him
> with his cowardice, until Hector turned and fought
> with all the courage and recklessness of despair.
> (Guerber, 1907: 292)

Achilles then dragged the body of Hector around the battlefield on the back of his chariot. Funeral games were held that night for Patrokles, and Priam, Hector's father, came secretly to Achilles to ransom back the body of his son.

With Hector's death and Patrokles' funeral, the books of *The Iliad* close. The siege continued for a time after this, Achilles being killed after routing the Trojan's allies the Amazons and Ethiopians. Finally, as the great heroes of each side gradually fell in battle, with the walls of Troy never looking likely to be taken, the Greeks resorted to a ruse. Epeios, a skilled craftsman, constructed an enormous wooden model of a horse with the help of the goddess Athena. A band of skilled, hand picked warriors was placed inside and the rest of the Greek army sailed away. The horse, believed to be a gift to the goddess Athena, was hauled into the city whereupon the warriors inside spilled out and slew the Trojan garrison. Thus Troy fell to Greek power, and Menelaus had enacted his revenge upon Paris.

The other great work of Homer, *The Odyssey*, follows on from where *The Iliad* ends, and follows the adventures of Odysseus. A few of the surviving characters from *The Iliad* are featured in *The Odyssey*, which to modern readers should very much be viewed as a sequel to *The Iliad*. There has been speculation amongst modern scholars as to whether these two works, both attributed to Homer, were actually written by the same author. A comparison of word usage suggests that they were probably not, but it is unlikely that scholars will ever be able to conclusively prove or disprove this view.

The Death of Achilles

Although the death of Hector brings *The Iliad* to a close, the story of the siege did not end there. The Trojans were reinforced by the arrival of Penthesilea, queen of the Amazons, who offered the aid of her elite band of warrior women. Achilles, setting aside any qualms of fighting women, promptly routed the Amazons and killed Penthesilea in their very first encounter.

Achilles did not feel so angered towards all of the women on the side of Troy, however. In one of the early skirmishes against the Trojans, Achilles had caught sight of the daughter of Priam, named Polyxena. After the death of Hector, Achilles tried in vain to bring peace between the opposing sides, so that he might obtain Polyxena's hand in marriage. Achilles' attempts at diplomacy failed, yet he eventually persuaded Priam to agree to the marriage once the war had ended.

The betrothal ceremony took place just outside the city gates, and when completed, Achilles made to depart back to his own army's lines. Paris, however, showed treachery by approaching Achilles from behind and firing a poisoned arrow into the only vulnerable part of Achilles' body – his heel.

> Thus great Achilles, who had shown his zeal
> In healing wounds, died of a wounded heel.
> (OW Holmes, quoted in Guerber, 1907: 294)

Ownership of Achilles' armour, forged by Vulcan, was the subject of competition between Ajax and Odysseus; when Odysseus finally prevailed, Ajax went insane and committed suicide. Polyxena joined Ajax in suicide, deeply grieved by her betrothed's death, killing herself on the mighty tomb erected in Achilles' memory.

In History

The wars between the Greeks and Trojans have not always been considered to be historical fact. Not until excavations in Turkey in the nineteenth century was Troy assumed to be anything more than a mythical city. The wars of which *The Iliad* speaks probably date to the thirteenth or twelfth centuries BC, but much of what we know is guesswork based on a number of excavations.

Troy was said to overlook the Dardanelles, sitting in the extreme north-west corner of Asia Minor. A nineteenth-century German archaeologist, Heinrich Schliemann, set out to discover the whereabouts of the historical city of Troy, convinced that there was some truth in Homer's story. Schliemann was certainly unusual amongst his countrymen in this:

> German scholars favoured a view which made it unlikely that the Iliad's stories of the Trojan Wars were based on reality, but rather involved miscellaneous separate mythological accounts of heroes.
> (Greene, 1983: 38)

Achilles: Hero of *The Iliad*

Schliemann combined the texts of Homer and other writers on the Trojan War with his own fieldwork analysis, and suggested that the site of Hissarlik in Turkey was the real site of Troy. The site held evidence of a long succession of occupation layers, which had been built up on top of older levels for a great many years; Schliemann thought that the evidence of one of the levels excavated – one containing a great amount of burnt material – was the Troy of legend, the burning representing the final destruction of the city by the victorious Greeks. If Hissarlik was indeed Troy, then the archaeological record suggests that Troy was founded on three economic aspects – wool, shellfish and horses. It was probably a rich society, including many wealthy classes of people, and, one would presume, protected by a representatively well equipped army. Since Schliemann's time, research has continued on the site, and like so many other archaeological sites, it has been very hard to prove or disprove his theory for certain. The fate of the legendary Troy must have been shared by many other emerging cities at this time, for as will be seen below, raiding was a prominent feature of civilization at this time – therefore we are left to ask ourselves whether Hissarlik is Troy or just another unfortunate site of violent raiding.

Despite the gaps in our knowledge, it is possible to recreate a credible written history of the period leading up to and the years around the Trojan War. Between 2000 BC and 1900 BC, the cultures that were to go on to dominate the Greek peninsula arrived in the area; they were to become known as the Mycenaeans. At around the same

time, a culture based on earlier Egyptian models existed on
the southern Greek island of Crete. This culture has survived
in the archaeological record from its splendid palaces; in
Anatolia, the remnants of the Old Assyrian culture were
developing into the Hittite Empire. The palace culture of
Crete – the Minoan – seems to have been the dominant
force in the Aegean Sea, and a unique record of life within
the Minoan world has survived through a number of
excavated clay tablets, which tell us much of daily and
governmental life in Crete.

Disaster was to strike for the Minoans though. Around
1500 BC, some kind of cataclysmic tragedy occurred
which destroyed the palace culture in a short space of time.
Whether this was a natural disaster, such as famine or
plague, or whether the decline of the Minoans was directly
related to the increasing number of Mycenaean settlements
along the coastline, we do not know from the evidence
currently available.

The Mycenaeans, as they expanded through the Aegean
Sea area, seem to have raided their rivals – including the
Minoans and the Hittites. This would almost certainly have
included plundering the rich towns along the coastline – for
example, Minoan palaces did not have purpose-built
defences, and would have made easy targets. The site that has
been identified as Troy – whether this is correct or not –
suffered such a raid or siege, but is probably only one in
many such targets that was attacked.

Minoan and Mycenaean history is classically studied as
one era, but even so, it can be divided into three main

periods – the Minoan Palace Culture (1600–1250 BC), the era of change and assimilation between the two cultures (1300–1200 BC), and the final period, known as the Mycenaean Culture after 1200 BC. It is in this last period that the Trojan War probably occurred, although the earlier periods must also be considered. Perhaps coincidentally, but perhaps more significantly, around the middle of the thirteenth century BC, the archaeological record suggests

Interpretation of the arms and armour shown on the Warrior Vase (c 1200 BC). Drawn by Symmie Tyson. (Author's collection)

a great deal of unrest in the Mycenaean homelands. Perhaps this was the cause of the Mycenaean king to adventure overseas, to either take his subjects' minds away from their problems, or to escape from the strife in his kingdom.

We gain a telling insight into late nineteenth- and early twentieth-century imperial British approaches to history in that the Britons claimed links to the heroes of Homeric epic. One of the legendary founders of Briton, Brutus, was the descendant of a fleeing exile from the defeated Trojan army conquered by Achilles and the Greeks. Ebbutt went further than this in 1910, offering the suggestion that the Greeks were perhaps actually warriors from the Gallic lands of what is now France (and thus, by Celtic association, again to the Britons). Speaking of the Celts in the British Isles, he noted that:

> ...their weapons, their war-chariots, their mode of life and their treatment of women, are all so closely similar to that of the Greeks of Homer that a theory has been advanced and ably defended, that the Homeric Greeks were really invading Celts – Gaelic or Gaulish tribes from the north of Europe. If it indeed be so, we owe to the Celts a debt of imperishable culture and civilization.
> (1994:xiii)

Later cultural and archaeological studies have proved this pro-British flag waving to be inherently unlikely, to speak of Ebbutt's theory in the kindest possible way. John Warry, writing in the late twentieth century (1980: 12–13), made a far more worthwhile comment in reflecting that, as the Greeks and Trojans showed no problems conversing with each other – to offer truces and to exchange battlefield boasts and threats – they were probably both of Greek extraction, as Homer had no word applicable to all Greek-speaking peoples anyway.

Excavations at Hissarlik

Since Heinrich Schliemann's nineteenth-century excavations, archaeological investigations at Hissarlik – the site that he and many other researchers believe was Troy – have uncovered many hitherto unknown or unsuspected facts about the city.

Perhaps most importantly, the city was not only restricted to the hill upon which the earliest excavations focused, but spread into the surrounding land also. At this time, in the late thirteenth century BC, the walled site on the hill was the fortified citadel at the centre of a wider conurbation (Ranitzsch, 1999).

Excavated evidence of material culture at Hissarlik suggests that the city was a cosmopolitan place to live. Pottery from as far as the Baltic and Afghanistan has been found, alongside local wares and imports from many sites both near and far (Ranitzsch, 1999). This is perhaps to be expected from a site settled by a culture intrinsically linked to trade by both land and sea, as the Mycenaean, Hittite and Minoan cultures were.

Despite the high standard and wide chronological spread of artefacts excavated at Hissarlik, as yet nothing has been found to conclusively prove that the site was that of Troy. Evidence of possible civil disruption or warfare in various phases of the city's history is indicated by burnt layers and destruction of buildings, but none of these are dated to the era in which we would expect the Trojan Wars to have taken place.

Much of the excavation work at Hissarlik, from Schliemann's time onwards, has been carried out by German archaeologists, including the most recent project, which since 1988 has been led by Professor Manfred Korfmann.

In Battle

Unlike the mythological battles of say, Malory or Tennyson's King Arthur or the sometimes plate-armoured Roland of medieval French chivalry, it seems that Homer had a good idea of how battle actually took place in the era of Achilles. Although many later interpretations and illustrations choose to show the warriors of the Trojan Wars in Greek hoplite armour, Homer correctly places his warriors in chariots or behind very large tower-shaped shields. The kind of warfare that Homer describes his heroes engaged in is supported by the pictorial and archaeological evidence available to us from the true historical period, and as such, Homer's work is versatile enough to be examined not only as legend, but also, with careful consideration, as a potential source for battle studies.

Achilles: Hero of *The Iliad*

Homer created vivid and brutal images of warriors in battle. The typical way artists have illustrated the events described by Homer is to clad the warriors in classical Greek armour – a bronze, almost bell-shaped breastplate, greaves on the legs, a huge shield to protect the warrior from both missiles and weapons, and a helmet usually of the Corinthian style. Cladding Achilles or his contemporaries in such armour is as inaccurate as William the Conqueror in the uniform of an American Civil War general – the Classical Greek period was around 800 years after the events of *The Iliad* appear to have taken place in real life.

Army sizes in the Trojan Wars were probably far smaller than those of many of the earliest recorded battles or the Classical Greek period several hundred years later. The numbers of warriors involved in these other battles (for which we have slightly reliable sources to interpret from) could vary greatly themselves. For example, the Battle of Kadesh in 1294 BC was fought between around 20,000 infantrymen and chariots on the Egyptian side, and 8500 infantry supporting 3500 chariots on the Hittite army, whereas at the battle of Leuctra in 371 BC, a force of 6000 Thebans met an army of 11,000 Spartans. Instead, the armies of Achilles, Hector and the other great heroes would almost certainly have had more in common with the early medieval European armies of Arthur and Macbeth – both were similar 'Heroic Ages' fought by great warlords and their professional companions numbering in the hundreds at the very most, occasionally supported by the greater populace at arms.

Warriors

Chariots were used by the nobility in the Trojan Wars; darting between armies and fighting dashing duels, the heroes fought their own showpiece skirmishes as the majority of warriors watched on. A chariot of this period was drawn by two horses (although Homer also makes reference to Hector's exceptional four-horsed chariot) and carried two men inside – the charioteer, who was responsible for controlling the chariot and horses, and the warrior, the noble who was well armoured and equipped to do battle. In modern terms, the charioteer was a chauffeur to the noble. The chariot was used to ferry the warrior around the battlefield in his heavy armour, and, upon meeting an enemy, the warrior would dismount to fight on foot while his charioteer waited a safe distance away. If victorious, or perhaps if shrewd and fleeing, the warrior would return to his chariot and be driven to another area of the battlefield as required. Sometimes the charioteer would not withdraw to a safe distance – Homer cites the chariot driver of Hector being killed by an arrow intended for Hector himself. At other times, the warrior would fight from the chariot car itself – presumably if tactics suggested that a running fight was preferable to dismounting; Patrokles hauled an opponent out of his chariot by impaling him on a spear; the same Greek hero also killed a charioteer by the deft throw of a stone.

A chariot needed relatively smooth ground to operate on; crashing over broken ground the yoke or axle were liable to break – Homer recorded this as happening to Trojan chariots as they attempted to cross the defensive ditch on the edge of the Greek camp. In an attempt to make chariots more rugged machines, it is possible that a horizontal strut was placed from the rim of the car to the very tip of the yoke, as suggested on fourteenth-century BC Cretan tablets. Only the richest warriors were able to afford the upkeep of a chariot, the horses and a charioteer, although it is possible that several warriors would share the investment in a chariot between themselves.

The usual material used for weapons was bronze; armour may have been leather or bronze, although Homer makes explicit reference to golden armour, which the heroes of his literature despise. Iron was reserved for arrow heads; at this time, iron appears to have been considered a substitute for bronze as opposed to an improved material.

We have very few illustrative depictions of warriors from the era of the Trojan War. A few vases and pottery fragments contain images of battle or armed warriors – the famous Warrior Vase (*c*1200 BC) depicts soldiers in leather armour with crescent shaped shields and helmets constructed of scales of boar tusk and horns on them; they are armed with spears. An inlaid Mycenaean dagger shows lion hunters armed with bows, spears and huge figure-of-eight shaped shields. They wear no armour but, we must remember, are hunting and not dressed for battle.

The most common weapon in *The Iliad*, as with so many periods of ancient warfare, is the spear.

> Him as he came on I smote with a bronze-shod spear,
> and he fell in the dust and I leaped into the car, and
> stood among the foremost fighter,
> (*The Iliad*, this edition 1995: 158)

And now fight we with straight-set resolve and let
there be no sparing of spears, that we may know
whether Achilles is to slay us
(*The Iliad*, this edition 1995: 308)

Made of ash wood, the Homeric spear was designed for
thrusting at an enemy or for throwing at close range. Indeed,
Achilles slew Hector with a thrust of his spear. Hector's own
spear was recorded as being 11 cubits long, which is about
18 feet in modern terms. Such a weapon would usually be
classified as a pike, and the spears intended for throwing
would have been much shorter – perhaps 6 feet long; the
spears shown on the Warrior Vase of *c*1200 BC are about 6
or 8 feet long. The metal heads of spears during this period
seem to have been unusually long – excavated examples
from Rhodes were up to 2 feet long, and could only have
been from long thrusting spears such as that attributed to
Hector. It is even possible that such long weapons could
have been used in both hands from the car of a chariot.

Swords were double edged and quite large. They were
predominately cutting weapons, heavily weighted from
bronze, and sheathed in a scabbard when not in use. The
sword would have been a secondary weapon for use when
the warrior's spear had broken; the length advantage of using
an 18- or even 8-foot long spear over a short sword would
have been too significant to overlook for a warrior on the
battlefield outside the walls of Troy.

The evidence that we have available suggests that shields
were huge. The most common type of Mycenaean shield

was the figure-of-eight shaped shield, shown on wall paintings, pottery and described by Homer himself. The frame consisted of two bow shaped pieces of wood fastened to form a cross shape. The body of the shield was constructed from layers of toughened bull hide, glued and stitched to a wicker core; the shield of Ajax was constructed of seven layers of hide. The bull's hide pattern seems to have been left on the cover of the shield, giving a black-and-white mottled effect. The shield, being so large and cumbersome, was suspended from a leather strap around the warrior's neck, and protected the whole length of the body so that any other form of armour was less crucial for survival – this made such large shields very useful to the lower class spearmen who could not afford the same body armour as the chariot-driven nobles. Ajax's shield was described as being like a tower, but it is more likely that the chariot borne nobles used smaller shields – perhaps like the crescent shaped ones of the Warrior Vase, or perhaps round shields – inferred by the mention of nobles wearing bronze or fabric greaves. Aside from the natural pattern of the bull hide, there does not appear to have been any form of blazon used on shields at this time.

As just mentioned, the nobles could afford fine armour, and may not have resorted to using the huge figure-of-eight shaped shields of the infantrymen – especially in the confines of their chariot cars. Armour was precious, and the body of a slain hero would be plundered for his armour. Later warriors wore leather or bronze breast plates or bell shaped cuirasses (in fact, such protection forms were early typologies of the later Classical Hoplite armour), but an intriguing suit of armour, dating to around 1400 BC, known as the Dendra Panoply, may also have survived into the Homeric period. The Dendra Panoply comprised a series of segmented metal strips, held together by leather straps; it had articulated shoulder and skirt pieces, and gave such complete protection to the upper part of the body that a shield would be unnecessary. In other words, the Dendra Panoply would have been ideally suited to a warrior in a chariot, allowing his shieldless arms more balance and dexterity. Arm guards and greaves have also been found dating to this period, but it is not certain that they were part of a Dendra suit; nor indeed are we certain if the Dendra armour was unique, or of a common pattern. Summing up these points about armour, John Warry stated that:

> Homeric arms and armour, it must be remarked, are the subject of much controversy. In the present context, we must limit ourselves to generalizations; but even so it is difficult to avoid statements which are open to challenge.
> (1980: 14)

Indeed, this state of affairs remains valid beyond the issue of armour and into many aspects of life, culture, warfare and society in the period around that in which *The Iliad* is set.

Helmets, when worn, could have been of several materials. Bronze helmets are referred to – especially on the heads of prominent heroes. The less privileged may have worn leather helmets, and the Warrior Vase shows a helmet constructed of boar tusk – including horns mounted on the front. Homer's accounts sometimes record swords shattering on helmets, so they must have had some resilience against blows. Bronze helmets at least could be plumed with horse hair:

> Now Meges smote with sharpened spear at the topmost crest of his helmet of bronze with horse-hair plume, and brake off his plume of horse-hair, and it all fell earthward in the dust, shining with its new scarlet dye. (*The Iliad*, this edition 1995: 215)

The Myrmidons

Achilles' Myrmidon warriors have attracted much attention from scholars of the Trojan War. Regarded as an elite among the assembled Greek army, they have been remembered for their ferocity on the battlefield, yet they were also famed for other valued mannerisms, noted by a legendary King of Athens as:

> ...a diligent and industrious race, eager to gain, and tenacious of their gains. Among them you may recruit your forces. They will follow you to the war, young in years and old in heart.
> (Bulfinch, 1915: 120–121)

Warriors

Such plumes would give a similar morale-shattering effect to the Bearskin shako of the nineteenth century – making the wearer seem physically larger and endowed with animal-like powers. Achilles drags his opponent and defeated victim Hector around the battlefield by the plume of his helmet, and perhaps this should be seen as symbolic of Hector's martial humiliation and loss of power.

Whilst the champions and nobility of the Greek and Trojan armies dashed around in chariots, the majority of warriors on both sides fought with spears and large shields as described above. Generally, the spearmen fought against each other or watched on as their champions duelled; it could potentially take a large number of ill-armed spearmen to overcome a well armoured, chariot-agile champion, and perhaps the general feeling was that it was better to allow the champions to duel amongst themselves. Spearmen appear to have fought in fairly dense bodies, probably using their large shields for mutual protection; some commentators have likened these formations to the later phalanxes and phalanges of the Classical Greeks and Macedonians respectively. According to John Warry, battle between the massed warriors of opposing forces would have appeared as thus:

> Both sides were marshalled by their leaders in good order, but after battle was joined the scene was confused and sanguinary. The enemy ranks were more easily broken when one of their leaders was killed. This might lead to a full-scale rout, when chariots were useful in pursuit.
> (1980: 16)

Achilles: Hero of *The Iliad*

Aside from the chariotry and spearmen, the other type of
warrior to be found on a Mycenaean battlefield was the
skirmisher. Armed with a bow, a sling, javelins, or even just
stones picked up from the dusty plain of Troy, such warriors
would swarm around the battle, lending their support from
the periphery. Chariot horses could be targeted and slain, or
accurate shots could incapacitate a driver or champion:

> Alexandros…had smitten with an arrow upon the top
> of the crest where the foremost hairs of horses grow
> upon the skull; and there is the most deadly spot. So
> the horse leapt up in anguish and the arrow sank into
> his brain, and he brought confusion upon the steeds as
> he writhed upon the dart.
> (*The Iliad*, this edition 1995: 102)

The highest class of warrior felt no shame in using missile
weapons if necessary in battle; Paris used a bow against
Achilles, his fellow Trojan Pandarus was also noted as a
bowman, and Patrokles killed a chariot driver with a hurled
stone. The best Greek archer was Teucer, who is recorded in
The Iliad as having shot nine enemies during the course of
the books. Trojan archers, and possibly their Greek enemies,
used shields for protection on the battlefield.

Around 1300 BC, it appears that battle moved more
towards the dashing chariotry and personal duels and away
from formed bodies of spearmen attacking each other.
Champions would only fight other champions, if the sources
are to be taken at face value. Indeed, there would be little

point in an unarmoured spearman attempting to slay a well armoured, skilled fighter driving around in a chariot – such warriors were the Bronze Age equivalent of a modern battle tank. This exclusion of lower class spearmen in duels suggests that the standard of armour available had improved to the standard of bronze armour outlined above. The champions of each army would dismount from their chariots, approach each other and hurl one or two javelins at his paired off enemy; if neither warrior did significant damage with these weapons, they would close in with sword or long spear, and fight using brute force and martial skill in the absence of sophisticated weaponry or ploys. Large stones were occasionally hurled at opponents, perhaps to unbalance or concuss them. War cries and insults were also hurled at regular intervals, according to Homer's account. The duel between Hector and Ajax was typical of such skirmishes:

> Ajax shouted defiance, to which Hector replied, and hurled his lance at the huge warrior. It was well aimed and struck Ajax, where the belts that bore his sword and shield crossed each other on the breast. The double guard prevented its penetrating and it fell harmless. Then Ajax, seizing a huge stone, one of those that serve to prop the ships, hurled it at Hector. It struck him in the neck and stretched him on the plain. His followers instantly seized him and bore him off, stunned and wounded.
> (Bulfinch, 1915: 268)

Achilles: Hero of *The Iliad*

Three styles of clothing appear to have dominated the whole of the period during which the Trojan Wars may have been fought. These were fringed kilts, short sleeved tunics, and scanty loincloths. Most clothing would have been a natural, off white linen, or perhaps bleached white. Red, green and purple clothing and ornate embroidery were also recorded, however, and may have only been worn by those of the upper classes who could afford dyed and embroidered clothing.

As well as the armies of Greece and the Trojans, many other confederated armies were present. Trojan allies included the Ethiopians, the Lukka or Sea Peoples, the Thrakes and Kikrones – fierce mountain tribesmen – and the infamous Amazons – warrior women commanded by Penthesilea, the daughter of the god Ares.

Achilles' personal warband were the Myrmidons. 'They were noted for their fierceness, diligence and devotion to their leader, hence their name is applied to a servant who carries out his orders remorselessly.' (*Brewer's Concise Dictionary of Phrase & Fable*, 1992, 701) 'Myrmidon' comes from the Greek word *myrmix*, and literally translates as 'ant people', defining their industrious hard work for their master, and also dehumanizing these worthy warriors psychologically in the minds of their enemies on the battlefield. Renowned for their wild charge into battle, some commentators have suggested an early Celtic provenance for the Myrmidons, yet the Thracians – settled just to the north of the later, Classical Greeks – are far more likely to have been the descendants of the Myrmidons. Given the multi-cultural make-up of the forces involved in the Trojan War, it is even possible that Achilles' men came from further afield, from Africa or Scandinavia, although we have no evidence which is able to confirm or disprove this notion.

Strategically, the siege of Troy was probably not a siege as we would think of it in modern terms; the Trojans were able to gather food from outside the city, and their allies seem to have arrived and departed without restriction from the besieging Greeks. The Trojans were also sufficiently free to organize a sally to attack the Greek camp, which flowed over the defensive Greek ditch and into their beached ships. There is no evidence of Greek or Trojan knowledge of siege craft; the Trojan Horse ploy came about through the Greek's inability to break into the city of Troy through or over the walls. This lies unhappily in contrast to the armies of the Old Testament, who appear to have excelled at siege warfare, capably and successfully attacking fortifications. Spies, on the other hand, seem to have been used by both sides in the siege of Troy; their task was to gather information and return with news of the other side's morale and intentions. A captured Trojan spy led to the defeat of Troy's Thracian allies, as they lay in wait to attack the weary Greeks.

If Hissarlik has been correctly identified as Troy, it had a wealthy economy, and was well supplied with horses. This would suggest that the army of Troy would have been relatively small, but well equipped, and essentially an army of aristocrats. This connects well with Homer's depiction of the Trojans, their heroes mostly coming from the family of King Priam; perhaps the nineteenth-century enthusiast

Achilles: Hero of *The Iliad*

Schliemann was correct in his identification, despite our present uncertainty?

Achilles is really a myth within a myth. Aside from Homer's study of Achilles in the Trojan Wars, the warrior is also featured in other Greek legends. For many centuries, the world of which Homer wrote was considered to be as historically unlikely as that inhabited by the Classical Greek gods, superhuman heroes and mythological creatures. However, nineteenth- and twentieth-century archaeologists have uncovered enough evidence to suggest that the war may actually have happened – and if the siege of Troy did not itself occur, other, similar sieges certainly did. Homer's analysis of warfare in Achilles' world is also supported by contemporary material evidence uncovered through excavation. Achilles stands out among the other great warriors in Homer's tales – he is the Greek hero to whom all others aspire in terms of ability and strength. His name has been remembered to the modern reader for just the same reasons, for an Achilles among men has the same attributes in the twenty-first century, although these skills may now be either physical or mental.

BEOWULF
Warrior King of the Geats

We know Beowulf through a poem of the same name, composed at some time between the mid-seventh and late tenth centuries AD. The poem as we have it was written in England, but describes events in Scandinavia (part of the original homelands of the Anglo-Saxons). Our knowledge of the poem comes from the one surviving copy of it, currently housed in the British Museum; *Beowulf* is the oldest epic in English, indeed in the whole group of Teutonic languages.

As a piece of literature, scholars have studied *Beowulf* for generations, to examine the language and style of the piece. The original tale, however, would have been spoken from memory by a bard or poet – probably in a warlord's hall very similar to that described in the poem. The poem no doubt originated in the Saxons' homeland before they came to Britain, and was later updated to include Christian references.

Beowulf begins by explaining a basic (and fictitious) history of the Danes, noting their great founder Scyld Scefing. This great king came to Denmark in a mysterious manner, yet his power grew with his age, and his fame spread among the Germanic tribes. When Scyld died, his throne was secure for his family, and his body was returned to the sea – from whence he had first come.

Scyld's great grandson was Hrothgar. Hrothgar was a great warrior and conqueror, who won glory in battle and whose fame was such that nobles in their own right flocked to become members of his personal warband. In a show of his own power, Hrothgar ordered the building of a great feasting hall, which would serve as a council chamber, meeting hall, and symbol of his political power. The hall was built speedily, majestically adorned, and, at the first feast held there, Hrothgar announced that this hall – with its antler-like gables – would be henceforth known as Heorot ('The Hart'). Pride rose within Hrothgar's heart, and in the hearts of the men of his warband, when the grandiosity of the hall was seen by all.

Day by day, the feasting continued, and became so great in noise as to raise an unspoken enemy from his fearsome fenland grotto. Grendel 'the loathsome fen-monster', dwelt in the marshy fens near to Heorot, living on the corpses of travellers that he captured; enormous in both stature and strength, he was a formidable foe, covered in a green, scaly skin into which no sword could bite. Likened to goblins, giants, demons and sea monsters, Grendel was a descendant of Cain, and lived a suitably outcast life. But now, the joyous revelry inside Heorot roused him, and he determined to put an end to such happiness.

In the still of night, when Heorot's revellers had dropped into mead-induced slumber, Grendel struck. Bursting into the hall, Grendel slew and dragged away thirty proud thanes from Hrothgar's bodyguard, leaving behind a trail of destruction as the remaining warriors looked on helpless. Hrothgar's grief was as profound as his previous joy had been; his morale became lower as Grendel returned on successive nights, to claim yet more men from Hrothgar's hall. Too old to face the monster himself, Hrothgar sent his mightiest champions against Grendel; all met the same fate in the hall at night; all that remained of them was a blood trail leading deep into the desolate fenland.

Finally, not one of Hrothgar's remaining champions would face Grendel, and Heorot fell into silent disuse after nightfall. This affliction continued for twelve years, yet every night Grendel returned in the hope of finding a fresh meal in the form of Hrothgar's bodyguard. Word spread across the land and beyond the borders of Denmark; many boasted of their prowess, yet not one warrior came forward to successfully champion Hrothgar's cause. Eventually, even the bravest warriors from abroad refused to come, and Hrothgar and his Danes settled into a life of night-time bondage.

As the sad saga of Heorot continued, so grew a boy into a warrior in the realm of the Geats. The Geats were ruled by King Hygelac, a strong and powerful ruler who conquered many of his neighbours. His only sister was the daughter of the dead king Hrethel, and the boy in question was her one son – Beowulf – who from the age of seven was brought up in Hygelac's court. Although of great stature, Beowulf greatly disappointed his grandfather, King Hrethel, by his peaceable and sloth-like nature; as a youth, he was despised by his peers and elders for his sluggishness and unwarlike character.

Beowulf: Warrior King of the Geats

Yet wise men saw something within Beowulf – perhaps the strength of his grip, his anger when aroused or the force of character in his great blue eyes. Beowulf also distinguished himself when challenged to a swimming competition by a famous Geatish champion – Breca – which Beowulf proceeded to win. Beowulf's hand grip was said to hold the strength of thirty men, for which the hero was already famed when news travelled to the land of the Geats of Grendel's reign of terror.

Obtaining the permission and blessing of his uncle, King Hygelac, Beowulf chose fourteen loyal and courageous companions to accompany him to the realm of Denmark. Bidding their families and kinsfolk goodbye, the fifteen Geats set out to make their own fame and fortune against Grendel.

The Warden of the Danish coast observed from the white cliffs a foreign war vessel running ashore; the vessel's banners were unknown to the Warden, and the strangers aboard were equipped with war gear. As they landed, they appeared to be preparing themselves for a march inland. Though the Warden was alone and knew there to be fifteen strangers, he rode down to challenge them, and demanded:

> 'Warriors! Who are you, in your coats of mail,
> who have steered your tall ship over the sea-lanes
> to these shores? I've been a coastguard here
> for many years, kept watch by the sea,
> so that no enemy band should encroach
> upon this Danish land and do us injury'
> (Barber, 1999: 189–90)

Warriors

Unsure as to their motive, he beheld the boar-helmeted Beowulf – undoubtedly the leader of the group due to his stature and lordly air. Beowulf addressed the Warden in return:

> 'We are warriors of the Geats, members of the King
> Hygelac's bodyguard. My father, well known among
> men of wisdom, was named Ecgtheow, a wise
> counsellor who died full of years and famous for his
> wisdom, leaving a memory dear to all good men.'
> (Ebbutt, 1910: 7–8)

The Warden judged from Beowulf's speech that the seamen's disposition was not unfriendly to the Danish king, and chose to lead the small band to King Hrothgar himself. Bidding his men to guard Beowulf's ship, the Warden started on the trail up the cliffs towards the hall of Heorot, the Geats followed him, resplendent in their shining armour, boar-crested helmets, shields, spears and gleaming swords in hand. Eventually, Heorot entered into view, splendid in the daylight – yet little could the Geatish band expect of the fear to await them at night, beyond the tales that had travelled afar about Grendel.

Shining brightly white in the sunshine, Heorot seemed glorious as the Geats approached. The Warden turned to the men who had followed his horse on foot from the coast, bidding their way forward to the hall, whilst he himself returned to his coastal vigil. The band of Geats strode towards the Danish royal hall, setting their broad shields down beside the door to show they meant no evil intent. As they entered the hall and were greeted, Beowulf addressed the throng:

> 'We are Hygelac's chosen friends and companions, and I am Beowulf. To King Hrothgar, thy master, will I tell mine errand,'
> (Ebbutt, 1910: 9)

Impressed by his speech, Hrothgar's house men ushered Beowulf along the hall, to the high seat where Hrothgar sat amidst his bodyguard of handpicked champions. Beowulf bowed respectfully and announced himself as Beowulf, who had travelled from overseas to be of service to the Danish king. The aged King exclaimed that he knew Beowulf as a boy – the son of Ecgtheow, who wed the daughter of the Geat king Hrethel. Hrothgar announced:

> 'His fame has come hither before him; seafarers have told me that he has the might of thirty men in his hand-grip. Great joy it is to know of his coming, for he may save us from the terror of Grendel.'
> (Ebbutt, 1910: 10)

A striking figure was Beowulf, in his shining armour, clasping his mighty sword. Perhaps, the assembled Danes felt, King Hrothgar's words were true – yet many of their own great champions had perished by Grendel's hand. Beowulf explained to the mass of people that he had heard of the horrors caused by Grendel, and intended to rid Heorot, the hall of Hrothgar, of this menace. Not only this, but he intended to confront Grendel after laying down his sword and his linden shield – fighting the fen monster with his bear hands alone. This, Beowulf explained, was because Grendel himself scorned the use of weapons, and Beowulf's pride and honour made it difficult for him to enter such a fight at an advantage.

King Hrothgar had listened intently throughout Beowulf's speech, and spoke again:

> 'thou hast remembered the ancient alliance between Ecgtheow, thy father, and myself, when I shielded him, a fugitive, from the wrath of the Wulfings, paid them the due wergild for his crime, and took his oath of loyalty to myself... [yet] many a hero has boasted of the great valour he would display in strife with the monster, and has awaited his coming in this hall; in the morning there has been no trace of each hero but the dark blood stains on benches and tables.'
> (Ebbutt, 1910: 11)

Room was made on these same benches for Beowulf and his men, and much feasting took place. Beowulf, as befitted his honour, sat opposite the king. Great carved horns of ale were brought to the Geats, along with a large amount of food; as they sat, bards sang of the heroic feats of the ancestors of the Danes. As the evening drew to a gluttonous close, Hrothgar and his people left the hall of Heorot, to sleep somewhere further away and more secure. Beowulf and his men prepared themselves for the perils of the night ahead. The fourteen Geats made ready for sleep; Beowulf's men lay down to catch what sleep they could fully armoured and with spears and swords by their sides. Beowulf himself took off his armour and gave his sword to one of his men to bear away. True to his earlier boast, he did indeed intend to tackle Grendel unarmed – he intended to wrestle with the beast and overcome him in that way. They slept – perhaps restlessly – yet certainly brave, as they knew they would be called upon to risk their lives in a native land against an inhuman foe.

In the dead of the night, Grendel came. From the fen vastness, along the marshy tracts, through the dense mists and swamp fogs, the hideous monster made his way to the house that he hated so bitterly. Grendel crashed through the door of Heorot, the hall's locks and bolts not barring his progress. From his eyes shone an uncanny green light, which showed him the troop of Geats lying asleep. Quickly seizing one of the slumbering Geats, Grendel tore the warrior limb from limb before any in the hall could react. He drank the blood and devoured the flesh, and was surprised as he felt a tremendous grasp take hold of his arm – a grasp far stronger than any he had felt before. Beowulf had sprung from his bench, and began to wrestle the fen monster in the gloomy, darkened hall. The Geats felt for their weapons, but feared to strike blows on the grappling pair before them, who rolled across the hall, breaking benches and tables underfoot. Occasionally, they caught a gleam of Grendel's eyes, and struck the occasional blow when the monster was exposed – yet their weapons glanced harmlessly from the scaled skin of Grendel. Outnumbered and worsted in the wrestling contest, Grendel tried to break for the hall's doorway, but Beowulf held on fast, with a grip that no man or creature would have been able to loosen. Finally, Grendel wrenched himself free with one great effort, and staggered to the door, for his arm had stayed in the grip of Beowulf, torn from the green scaly body of the fen beast. Screaming, Grendel fled from the door, leaving his limb in the victor's grasp.

Beowulf sank to the ground, panting and gasping for breath, struggling to believe his victory as his men gathered around, bringing lighted torches. In the white light of the flame, the Geats looked at the green arm of Grendel. It looked threatening even when detached from the powerful body of their foe. Happy that Grendel would die from such a serious wound, the Geats shouted for joy and for their leader's victory, and fastened the fearsome trophy to the roof of Heorot.

In the morning, many warriors came to Heorot, unsure as to the sights that would greet them. Few expected to see the Geats alive, and fewer still expected to see the grisly arm of the defeated Grendel hanging in the hall. Joyously, some followed the blood trail left by Grendel, deep into the fens (which were safe by daylight). The trail led to the edge of a dark lake, and all felt satisfied that this was the final resting place of the fiend.

Hrothgar addressed the throng:

Beowulf: Warrior King of the Geats

'Thanks be to the All-father for this happy sight! Much
sorrow have I endured at the hands of Grendel, many
warriors have I lost, many uncounted years of misery
have I lived, but now my woe has an end!… Often
have I rewarded less heroic deeds with great gifts, and
to thee I can deny nothing.'
(Ebbutt, 1910: 18)

Beowulf answered that he had indeed performed his boast,
yet did not fully succeed, as Grendel had escaped. Yet this did
not prevent the feasting that occurred from being even
grander than before; the bards sang of deeds of old – the
Fight in Finnsburg, the deeds of Hnaef and Finn, and of
Queen Hildeburh. Hrothgar showed his lavish generosity
and great debt of gratitude to the Geats through his gifts.
Beowulf received a gold-embroidered banner, a magnificent
sword, a helmet and hauberk, a golden goblet, and eight
fleet-footed horses. His men were equally well rewarded, as
befitted their rank, and the entire Geatish band was escorted
to another lodging, whilst the carnage of Beowulf and
Grendel's mighty struggle was cleaned up.

In the darkness of the following night, a powerful avenger
came to the hall – with the very same silence and stealth as
Grendel had. Grendel had indeed gone to die, to his home,
and now his mother arrived to avenge her son. An horrific
panic spread as the sleepers in the hall saw her enter, and
brave warriors fled in all directions, vainly attempting to
attack her and escape from her all at once. No weapons
harmed her scaled skin, and the she-monster seized King

Hrothgar's most valid thane and advisor, Aschere. Leaving the
hall in a state of disarray and lamentation, in place of the
rejoicing of only a few hours previously, Grendel's mother
left, boring away her trophy of the King's thane.

Hrothgar summoned Beowulf, intent on his new
champion reaping revenge on the mother of his vanished foe,
in return for the loss of Hrothgar's wisest counsellor and
dearest friend. Hrothgar asked Beowulf to find Aschere's
body, and slay Grendel's kinswoman. Hrothgar's men searched
high and low through the marshland, and eventually found
the lair of Grendel's mother; Hrothgar mounted his horse,
and joined by a mixture of his own men and the Geats, rode
towards the dread, monster-filled lake that had been
identified as the lair of Grendel's mother. When they arrived,
the head of Aschere was found lying on the lake's shore.

> The water boiled with blood, with hot gore;
> the warriors gaped at it. At times the horn sang
> an eager battle-song. The brave men all sat down;
> then they saw many serpents in the water,
> strange sea-dragons swimming in the lake,
> and also water-demons, lying on cliff-ledges,
> monsters and serpents of the same kind
> as often, in the morning, molest ships
> on the sail road.
> (Barber, 1999: 216–7)

Beowulf watched these creatures from the shoreline, and
drew his bow and suddenly shot one through the heart. The

other creatures fled, whilst the Danes dragged the floating corpse of Beowulf's victim onto dry land, where they surveyed it with wonder. Meanwhile, Beowulf made ready to enter the lake to reap revenge for Aschere's death.

> He trusted to his well-woven mail, the corslet fitting closely to his body and protecting the breast, the shining helm guarding his head, bright with the boar-image on the crest, and the mighty sword Hrunting... an ancient heritage: steel was the blade itself, tempered with poisoned twigs, hardened with battle-blood: never in a fight it failed, Any who wielded it, when he would wage a strife In the die battlefield, folk-moot of enemies.
> (Ebbutt, 1910: 23–4)

Thus prepared, Beowulf dived down into the lake, and swam for an entire day, fighting sea creatures all the way down to the lake's dark bottom. As he reached the floor, Beowulf was seized by a long scaly arm, of gigantic strength. The sharp, fierce, ripping claws of Grendel's monstrous mother strove to claw through his chainmail, but her attempts were in vain. A superhuman contest developed between Grendel's mother and her son's slayer; the sea-woman flung Beowulf on his back and stabbed at him with a broad bladed knife – again the hero's chainmail saved him. Exerting his own mighty force, Beowulf threw her to the floor and sprang to his feet. Hrunting flashed threw the water, yet Grendel's mother's scaly skin turned the mighty blade aside. Angrily, Beowulf cast his trusty sword away, useless as it was in this contest – once again he resorted to fighting a fen monster with his bare hands alone. The son was evidently not as strong as his mother, and Beowulf's hand grip faired no better – he needed another weapon. Gazing around the creature's lair, he saw, amongst the trophies that had been carried away from Danish halls in the past, a gleaming, invincible sword:

> wrought by the giants, massive and double-edged,
> the joy of many warriors; that sword was matchless,
> well-tempered and adorned, forged in a finer age,
> (Barber, 1999: 219)

Beowulf snatched the huge sword, bigger than any man could wield. Swinging it at Grendel's mother, a fierce blow crushed down onto the neck of the monster, breaking her bones and forcing the lifeless body to the lake's floor. Exhausted yet casting his eyes around the lair, Beowulf saw the body of Grendel lying on a bed in the hall. Beheading his former foe, Grendel's poisonous blood melted his new weapon's blade. Carrying the head of Grendel and the hilt of the mighty sword with him, Beowulf swam to the surface.

All this time, above the surface, the Danes and Geats waited eagerly; by nightfall, the Danes had left, believing that Beowulf would never return – but the Geatish band remained, as a worthy warrior's companions should, waiting for his return. How gladly they greeted him when Beowulf broke the surface. Proudly they followed their leader back to

Beowulf: Warrior King of the Geats

Heorot, the startled throng parting before them, as Beowulf
threw Grendel's head down at the feet of King Hrothgar.
Proclaiming that god had guarded him against unnatural
foes, Beowulf explained that the head of Grendel was
brought for the King's pleasure – and indeed, Hrothgar was
now more pleased than ever as he gazed at the head of his
enemy and for the return of his friend and champion. Now,
Beowulf felt he had fully achieved his earlier boast, bringing
evidence of Grendel's death to his patron.

With thanks and fresh gifts, Hrothgar again rewarded the
Geats, and spoke of a new alliance between the Danes and
the Geats of King Hygelac – pledging a thousand thanes to
the Geats in time of strife. Their job accomplished the little
band of Geats returned to their vessel that the coastal
warden had diligently guarded. Loading on their many gifts
from the Danes, they set sail for Geatland in their dragon-
prowed vessel.

Eventually the cliffs of their homeland came into view,
and soon they were landed. Upon their return, and the
telling of their deeds, another splendid feast took place.
Beowulf was called upon to describe the terrors and
adversity which he had faced, and the boundless gratitude
and generosity bestowed upon him by King Hrothgar. As
Beowulf showed the treasures given to both his men and he,
he distributed them amongst the Geatish kinsmen and
women. Queen Hygd received a jewelled necklace and King
Hygelac was given Beowulf's best new steed. For his bravery,
martial skill and own generosity, Beowulf became the King's
Champion, and settled back amongst his own people.

Warriors

Half a century later, great changes had occurred in the lands of the Geats and Danes. Hrothgar was dead, succeeded by his son Hrethic, and Hygelac had been slain in a campaign against the rival Hetware people. In this fatal expedition, Beowulf had done all he could as the King's Champion – when his king was slain, he fought his way through the enemy and swam back to Geatland.

Queen Hygd offered the crown to Beowulf, but he refused, instead acting as the king's young son's protector until he came of age; when this son died in battle, Beowulf was again offered the kingship, and, as no Geatish royal male remained, he accepted the crown. Beowulf ruled as a perfect king – a powerful war leader and a just man. However, in the fiftieth year of his reign, a monstrous, fire-breathing dragon came to ravage his kingdom. A thief had broken into the dragon's cavern and stolen from the beast's treasure hoard. The wrathful dragon reaped revenge on the countryside, intent on making the thief's kinsfolk pay for his crime.

Beowulf had to act, despite being an old man. He decided to attack the dragon, to save his land from complete devastation. Still wily, he ordered a huge shield to be made, completely of iron, to protect him from the dragon's fire breath – a usual linden wood shield would be consumed in flame. Beowulf set off to confront the great beast with eleven hand-picked warriors – the best of his bodyguard. They marched on the lonely spot where the dragon's barrow was situated.

Beowulf: Warrior King of the Geats

Payment for Loyalty in the Heroic Age

One of the most significant themes running through Beowulf is that of
service to one's warlord, and the benefits of loyal service. In addition to
the weapons, armour, and ancient heirlooms passed to loyal warriors
on a regular basis throughout the poem, Beowulf himself is explicit in
his reference as to the gift of land, and the benefits that loyal warriors
such as he brought to their warlords:

> 'The treasures that Hygelac lavished on me
> I paid for when I fought, as fortune allowed me,
> with my glittering sword. He gave me land
> and the security land brings, so he had no call
> to go looking for some lesser champion,
> some mercenary from among the Gifthas
> or the Spear-Danes or the men of Sweden.'
> (Heaney, 1999: 79)

Beowulf raised his voice and shouted out a defiant
challenge. The dragon sprang out of his lair, fiery breath
before him. The sight of the dragon's blue and green scales,
his flaming nostrils and his eyes frightened Beowulf's men;
not as brave as he, they fled.

Beowulf's bright sword flashed as it cut into the beast, and
the Geatish king sheltered behind his iron shield as the

creature breathed flames back at him. The shield glowed red and Beowulf burned badly behind, yet without its protection he would have died. As the battle waged on, one of the king's cowardly bodyguards roused himself to return and aid his king:

> '…we have betrayed and deserted him, and left him alone against a terrible foe. Now the day has come when our lord should see our valour, and we flee from his side!… He and I will die together, or side by side we will conquer.'
> (Ebbutt, 1910: 36–7)

So Wiglaf returned to Beowulf's side, plunging into the fiery cloud around the combatants. The arrival of a second Geat enraged the dragon more, and the battle became yet more violent. The two Geats fought on manfully, and Beowulf struck the dragon such a blow that his ancient sword shattered. The dragon seized Beowulf by the neck with his poisonous fangs, as Wiglaf dashed forward from behind the iron shield and slashed into the dragon's body with a fatal blow. The fire began to fade, and Beowulf, with his strength waning from the neck wound inflicted by the creature, drew his knife and cut the reptile's neck. Releasing the Geatish king, the dragon slumped down dead.

Beowulf, collapsed with pain, spoke to Wiglaf:

> 'Now I bequeath to thee, my son, the armour which I inherited. Fifty years have I ruled this people in peace, so that none of my neighbours durst attack us.'
> (Ebbutt, 1910: 38)

Beowulf: Warrior King of the Geats

Wiglaf entered the barrow, and discovered the dragon's hoarded treasures. Filling his arms with as much as he could carry, he took the prizes to Beowulf's prone, dying body. He flung the treasures down for his lord to see – magic armour, dwarf-wrought swords, gems, jewellery, goblets and a golden standard – so that the Geatish king could see what he had won for his people in battle. Happy having seen this, Beowulf then died.

Since the battle had ended, a number of Geats – including the shamed bodyguard – advanced to the battle site. Wiglaf, cradling the body of Beowulf, addressed them:

> 'Better is death to every man than a life of shame!'
> (Ebbutt, 1910: 40)

The Geats stood abashed and silent, as Wiglaf foresaw what lay ahead of them – enemy raids on a weak nation. Indeed, this future was in store for the Geats, yet Beowulf deserved and was given a hero's burial – a mighty funeral pyre, upon which the dragon's treasures were placed with the king's body, and overlaid by a cairn when the flames dwindled.

> So all the Geat chiefs
> Beowulf's bodyguard,
> Wept for their leader's fall:
> sang in their loud laments
> That he of earthly kings
> mildest to all men was,

Warriors

Gentlest, most gracious,
most keen to win glory.
(Ebbutt, 1910: 41)

In History

Beowulf is one, perhaps the only, warrior in this book
whom we are fairly certain did not exist historically.
However, as Seamus Heaney explains, the poem
describes events which 'are set in Scandinavia, in a "once
upon a time" that is partly historical'. Some authors have
argued the case for *Beowulf* being set in England, shortly
after the Anglo-Saxon dominance of the lowlands began in
the seventh century AD. This Anglo-centric viewpoint rather
ignores the fact that the early Anglo-Saxons and their
Scandinavian contemporaries were intrinsically linked in
their mythology and, for the most part, non-Romanized
culture; it would seem most likely that the Geats were based
in Gotland, in southern Sweden. The poem probably
originated in the Saxons' homeland long before they came
to Britain, and was later updated and recorded in a written
form in England to include Christian references. Some
writers have gone so far as to suggest that *Beowulf* could be
set in any time from the European Bronze Age to the
Frankish empire of Charlemagne, but I feel that we should
consider the history of Beowulf's time in the context of the
time when our version of the poem existed, between the
seventh and tenth centuries AD.

Highdown Anglo-Saxon Cemetery

Highdown Hill is located between Worthing and Littlehampton on the Sussex coast of England, and sitting astride the hill is a very typical early Anglo-Saxon cemetery. Excavated mostly in the late nineteenth century, around 150 burials have been found, both inhumations and cremations, dating to the fifth and seventh centuries AD.

A typical male grave in the Sussex cemetery contained a bronze or iron buckle to secure a belt around the waist, and an all-purpose short knife (not a military weapon). Swords were rare, but from the number of spearheads found in the graves, it would seem that many men were buried with spears. Many spearmen were also buried with a shield, surviving in the form of an iron shield boss.

Two swords were excavated, reinforcing the theory that such weapons were owned by only the richest aristocrats. Each of the Highdown swords had a broad blade between 28 inches and 31 inches long, and was edged on both sides. Both swords were pattern welded. Traces of wood preserved on the blades showed that the swords were carried in wooden and leather scabbards. The handles were also wooden, and the decorative fittings of one scabbard's mounts were excavated.

All of the spearheads recovered were typical of their typology with one exception. A single example of the throwing spear – or *angon* – was excavated at Highdown. The barbs on the head of this weapon had broken off, either in an opponent's body or shield, and the metal head and shaft were 30 inches long. Notably associated with the Franks, this rare angon may suggest the cultural heritage of those buried at

Warriors

Highdown – although pottery found at the site is closely matched to that of Niedersachsen in Lower Saxony in Germany.

No helmets or body armour were found at Highdown (these being extremely rare in Anglo-Saxon burials), and shields appear to have been about 2 feet in diameter. The protruding metal boss, often carrying a knob on its tip, could have served as a secondary weapon if necessary.

Overall, the cemetery evidence presented from Highdown builds a picture of a typical Anglo-Saxon warrior at the time of Beowulf – going to war with spear and a shield only, looking jealously on at his chieftain, who was able to wield a sharp, double-edged slashing sword in battle, and, if rich enough, could afford the protection of a helmet or metal body armour.

Our knowledge of Scandinavian and early English history during the early medieval period comes mostly from archaeology and genealogy. Beowulf's period is pre-Viking, before the warriors of northern Europe dramatically announced themselves on the rest of the continent. Being outside of the main sphere of Roman – and therefore written – history, the early English and Scandinavians remain a relatively mysterious culture. As has been described in the chapter on King Arthur, the earliest English settlement of the British Isles is no less confusing. It would appear that the Britons invited Saxon mercenaries into Britain shortly after the Romans withdrew, in order to help defeat Pictish, Irish, and probably even other Germanic raiders and invaders. The

Beowulf: Warrior King of the Geats

Saxons arriving in England brought their own culture with them, and after establishing themselves along the eastern seaboards, continued their links to their homeland. Effectively, this turned Britain's global outlook from north-south to west-east, with Scandinavia and northern Germany to the south, and the Celtic regions of Wales and Ireland to the north.

Early medieval Scandinavia is often overlooked by historians, who tend to view it as a cultural backwater, untouched by the Roman empire, and untouched by Christianity for far longer than the rest of mainland north-western Europe. However, Scandinavia was culturally important – the descendants of Scandinavian travellers founded the early English kingdoms, the later Norman kingdom in France, discovered North America, and made their presence felt through trade and warfare across the Mediterranean. These substantial contributions to medieval history should really not have been overlooked for so long in the study of the development of medieval Europe.

The history of early medieval Anglo-Saxon England and of Scandinavia is a history of small kingdoms evolving into larger ones, and eventually uniting under powerful kings into nations. The border wars alluded to in *Beowulf* are indicative of such cultures, and equally show the dangers of, and the potential prizes of, such campaigns. The motley collection of Saxons, Jutes, Angles, Frisians and others who arrived in Britain towards the end of the Roman empire did not fully confederate into one nation, a united kingdom, until almost the eleventh century. Instead, small kingdoms were carved out, numbering from five at some times to eleven at others, and, as the country eventually began to unify, a Bretwalda (meaning 'wide ruler') was elected to an honorary role which gradually evolved into kingship. A similar situation occurred in the Scandinavian countries, where individual kings came to dominate their neighbours.

The period in which *Beowulf* is set saw a fundamental change in everyday life for the Anglo-Saxons in England. Christianity arrived to replace the pagan gods previously worshipped, and *Beowulf* contains interpolations with overtly Christian ethics and morals, which sit somewhat uneasily beside the generally heroic pagan themes from which the poem is constructed. Christianity worked hard from it's earliest incarnations to impose itself over pagan festivals and customs – hence the number of Christian events which fall on previously pagan celebrations, the number of churches which were founded on older, pagan sites, and the number of extremely ancient folk tales that have had Christian sentiments and ethics woven into their storylines through the centuries. Christianity did not become as popular in Scandinavia as quickly as it had done in England; St Augustine converted the first English kingdoms to Christianity in the last four years of the sixth century AD, and others followed in the seventh century, whereas the contemporary Scandinavian rulers were entering their most ostentatious era of lavish boat burials in the seventh and eighth centuries. Some Scandinavian warlords maintained their pagan beliefs well into the medieval period, and were the subjects of the most bloody and brutal crusades of the entire medieval era; others had converted earlier, including many of those who settled in the British Isles.

In many ways, in this pre-Viking era, Scandinavia remained more separated from the rest of Europe than did England; the Anglo-Saxon rulers enjoyed political links with the Frankish kings, and traded widely. The Scandinavian rulers were more distant, and to much of Europe appeared backward in many ways; even after the Vikings had become known to the rest of Europe, their homelands still remained culturally isolated from mainstream Europe, so much so that the eleventh-century German cleric Adam of Bremen described Jutland in the following way:

> And whilst the whole land of Germany is frightful with thick forests, Jutland is still more frightful, where the land is shunned on account of the poverty of its produce and the sea on account of the infestation of pirates. Cultivation is found hardly anywhere, hardly any place exists suitable for human habitation, but wherever there are arms of the sea, the country has very large settlements.

Given this desolate description, perhaps it is little wonder that migrations took place in the fifth and sixth centuries AD to the fertile lands of Britain, and that Norse settlers looked to England, France, the Mediterranean and Eastern Europe in the Viking Age. The Baltic island of Gotland, Beowulf's homeland, was actually wealthier than other areas of Sweden (of which it is a part) and Scandinavia. Consisting

The tribes who succeeded the Roman Empire in the fifth century AD included (from left to right) the Ostrogoths, the Franks, the Visigoths and the Sassanid Persians. The Goths and Franks wore similar armour and fought with similar tactics to Beowulf's Geats, whereas the Persians relied far more heavily on very well armoured cavalrymen and archers. (Chrysalis Picture Library)

of a great limestone mass, it had good farming land around the coast, and sheltered bays ideal for habitation. The inhabitants of Gotland exploited its strong strategic position to the full throughout the era of Beowulf and the Viking Age, and maintained their independence from the larger states which formed around them. This alone makes it inherently more likely that *Beowulf*, if written by the hero's own Geatish kinfolk, was already in existence before being committed to writing by an English descendant.

A major feature of the Beowulf tale focuses on kingship and the role played in this by gift giving and feasting. *Beowulf* clearly demonstrates the Germanic idea of loyalty – a warrior was expected to defend his king, act bravely in the face of danger, act upon the very word of his leader, and if necessary, die on the battlefield with him, in return for gifts, feasts, and lodgings. Beowulf and his Geats did this for their

King Hygelac, yet when Beowulf himself was king, his bodyguard deserted him in the face of a dragon – they were a poor body of warriors compared to those of earlier generations. Wiglaf sums this cultural expectation up in his speech before returning to Beowulf's side.

Beowulf also suggests how important a king's ancestors were in this age. Tales of ancient history were constantly recited in the Danish and Geatish feasting halls, to enforce the power of the ruling lineage. In keeping with this, high-powered rulers were buried in ostentatious barrows (such as those at Sutton Hoo in England and Vendel and Valsgarde in Sweden), as a reminder of their power and their successor's lineage. In early medieval Germanic and Scandinavian society, powerful ancestors were as important as a powerful army.

Essentially, the poem *Beowulf* sums up the foundations of strength and character that early Germanic and Scandinavian kingdoms were built on – honour and glory. A proud warrior would perform deeds for his king or warlord, expecting in return for this many prized gifts and perhaps – if he became an outstanding warrior – the bards to sing of his deeds. *Beowulf* captures the idylls of this culture perfectly.

In Battle

Beowulf and his followers were professional warriors, members of a chieftain's warband. They were present to fight for a chieftain or king, to give him power beyond his legitimacy, and to follow him wherever he requested – even into Valhalla and death. Battle poetry in the early medieval period was intended to glorify war and the warriors' actions. Therefore, much of the military information given within the poem is likely to be accurate for the time that the poem evolved – the audience would have included many warriors, and they would almost certainly have demanded that such details were described correctly both to please them and to glorify their true battle feats.

The period in which Beowulf is set is close to that of the historical King Arthur. In many respects, the two warriors would have had many similar ideas on how battles were to be fought, on how to reward their loyal followers, and of how to be a good leader and servant to their people.

The appearance of a seasoned, upper class warrior like Beowulf would have been similar to one of Arthur's companions. The main difference between Arthur and Beowulf on the battlefield, apart from the probable higher initial social standing (and therefore greater sized warband) of Arthur, was that Anglo-Saxon and Scandinavian warriors were traditionally renowned for fighting on foot instead of from horseback. Interestingly, while some modern commentators try to present Arthur as a foot warrior, arguing against the Britons' use of horses in war, several modern historians also argue for the use of mounted men by the Anglo-Saxons. High class burials at Sutton Hoo and in Northamptonshire have revealed princely burials complete with horses – so the old perception of the Saxon footmen (mostly deriving, it seems, from the eleventh-century Bayeux Tapestry) may well be wrong. Certainly, early Frankish armies on the Continent saw their nobility riding to battle and fighting from horseback, so the idea of their English and Scandinavian neighbours using similar tactics should not be as easily discounted as some historians believe. Indeed, it is more than plausible that when a warlord and his personal followers fought in small skirmishes against other personal warbands, they would have done so from horseback; when the fyrd or its equivalent were called out, it would have been preferable for the professional warriors to fight on foot in the shieldwall alongside these amateurs, bolstering the strength and morale of the army, instead of remaining isolated on horseback.

A warrior of Beowulf's generation would mostly have been paid for his martial services through gifts of weapons and armour; this is clearly demonstrated in *Beowulf* and other heroic writings. Therefore, the professional warrior in Beowulf's time would have almost certainly worn a metal helmet, chainmail hauberk, and shield (which increased in size between the sixth and ninth centuries). At his side would have resided a variety of weapons including a spear, possibly a sword, javelins, and possibly an axe or the seax dagger from which the Saxon name derived. Lower class warriors were less well equipped, being unarmoured, usually armed with spear and shield alone, occasionally supplemented by a sling or bow. As demonstrated in *Beowulf*, a warrior was rewarded by his king or leader with gifts of weapons, armour and jewellery; early Germanic society had no system of money or coinage, so presenting such valuable items was in lieu of

regular pay. Another way that warriors became equipped is
highlighted by Beowulf with his dying speech to Wiglaf –
Beowulf bequeaths his armour to him. This meant that
weapons and armour could be passed down from warrior
to warrior, ensuring that quality arms should never lay
dormant. This highlights the fact that well furnished, high
status burials including weapons and armour were even
more impressive than is usually imagined – fine weapons
and armour coming to the end of their lives along with
that of their owner.

In addition to the warrior's individual skills with spear
and shield, teamwork was important on the battlefield. In
battles larger than a small skirmish, the opposing warbands
would form into closely formed shield walls, each man
protecting the body of the warrior to his right with his
shield; to achieve this, a high degree of training and
camaraderie would be desirable. Close-knit groups of young
warriors were trained together, and the warband would
almost certainly have practised together on a daily basis.

We have a far clearer picture of the weaponry used by
warriors between AD 400–700 than of virtually any other
aspect of warfare during this period. This is partially
because metallic weapons are more frequent finds than
smaller, frailer, or non-metal items – their construction and
purpose means that they are more likely to survive in some
form on the archaeological record. Most pagan Germanic
cultures – including the early English kingdoms – buried
their dead with artefacts to take into the next world.
This religious belief has proved useful for modern

Beowulf: Warrior King of the Geats

The Fight at Finnsburh

The 'Fight at Finnsburh' is a fragment of an early medieval Germanic poem. The surviving copy has been dated through its language to the eleventh century, although this is certainly a later version of a traditional poem. Another part of the poem is spoken by King Hrothgar's poet in *Beowulf*, known as the 'Finn Episode' (Rodrigues, 1996: 9). The poem records an ongoing, tragic bloody feud between the Frisians and Danes, sparked by vengeance for a slain leader:

> The sword-flash gleamed,
> as if all Finnsburh were aflame.
> Never have I heard of worthier warriors,
> of sixty fighters better bearing arms,
> nor finer recompense for white
> mead made to one's own heroes than
> Hnaef to his young gallants gave.
> (trans. Rodrigues, 1996: LL35–40)

archaeologists, who have been able to study the weapons, armour, and more mundane everyday items left in the ground. From these (especially when combined with written sources and experimental archaeology and re-enactment), a fairly detailed picture of the pagan Saxon at war has evolved.

157

Warriors

A spear and shield are often referred to as the basic criteria required to fulfil a warrior burial by archaeologists. Härke points out that 44 per cent of Germanic inhumations in Britain during this period were accompanied by at least one spear and that 26 per cent of Germanic inhumation burials in Britain were accompanied by a shield (Welch, 1992). Perhaps significantly, 75 per cent of male burials in Beowulf's Gotland contained weapons from the mid-sixth century AD onwards – far above the average indicated by Härke. Although very little remains beyond the metalwork, we are able to deduce quite a lot about these weapons from the many hundreds of excavations in which they have been found. A typical set of warrior burials are those from St Neots, Cambridgeshire. Here, in the heart of early Anglo-Saxon settlement, between the Midlands and East Anglia, a number of burials representative of ordinary burial practice of the time were discovered in the early nineteenth century, as town building progressed (indeed, this period was a great age of archaeological investigation, as many towns and cities throughout Europe expanded at speed). The St Neots burials revealed a few cremation urns, along with brooches dating to the sixth century AD; several spearheads were present alongside the few inhumation burials that were found – indicating that the burials were those of Anglo-Saxon males – but could not be typologically identified at the time. Other, more famous and far more ostentatious burials are often considered typical of Anglo-Saxon furnished burials; however, as so few burials have been located and excavated in north-west Europe, it is more correct to see these as extremely high status burials, of the richest warrior kings. Such burials, such as Sutton Hoo and Benty Grange in Britain, and those of the Vendel culture in Scandinavia, include a great number of weapons, quite often body armour and or a helmet, many expensive or well regarded domestic items and occasionally horse trappings or a horse's skeleton. This puts into context the divide between the warrior king – and his companions – and the ordinary folk who followed their leaders to battle in times of strife, represented by the St Neots burials, armed with spears and probably shields.

Despite the continued mention of armour in the poem *Beowulf*, and the belief that material rewards made for better-armed warriors, we have surprisingly few items of personal armour in the archaeological record. In England, only four helmets from the early and mid Anglo-Saxon periods are known: the famous Sutton Hoo helmet (referred to in the chapter on Arthur), the Benty Grange helmet, the Pioneer helmet, and the Coppergate helmet from York. Of these, both the Benty Grange and Pioneer helmets have miniature metal boars on their crests – as mentioned in *Beowulf*. Several other helmets exist from Scandinavian sources, such as the Vendel helmets (discovered in four of the Vendel-Valsgarde burials), and Scandinavian burials on the whole suggest a better degree of armour and protection afforded to continental Germans and Scandinavians than their relatives had in England. Helmets had cheek and neck guards attached, and occasionally nasal guards were fitted. Chainmail or leather aventails may also

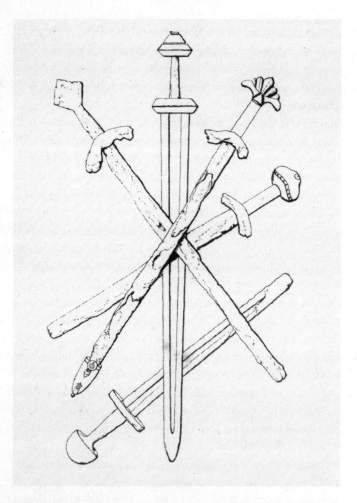

The sword was often endowed with mystical powers in Germanic mythology. This collection of Anglo-Saxon and Danish blades all measured between 2½ feet and 3 feet in length. (From Hewitt's *Ancient Armour and Weapons in Europe*, 1855)

have been fitted (as on the later Anglo-Saxon Coppergate helmet, from York). Spangelhelms were popular amongst Germanic peoples.

The Benty Grange helmet was excavated in the nineteenth century and is a spangelhelm. The excavator believed that it was covered with horn scales. The Pioneer helmet was excavated in Northamptonshire during 1997, and like the Benty Grange helmet, this helmet also had a boar crest. The Sutton Hoo helmet was excavated from a high status Germanic burial in Suffolk. It has an enclosed face like a Roman parade helmet and its style is derived from late Roman and Scandinavian Vendel designs. In combat the wearer almost certainly would have had to have been fighting a very static battle as the facemask would have greatly impeded vision. The Sutton Hoo helmet was highly decorated, despite its basic design being copied from a widely produced late Roman item. Study of Anglo-Saxon vocabulary and material culture has identified several other helmet-related words, including the acknowledgement of leather helmets (which would rarely survive archaeologically, and hence leave no evidence of use), the use of crests on helmets, cheek-pieces, visors and neck armour.

Less evidence exists for body armour. Fragments of chainmail have been found, and are alluded to in written and drawn sources, yet we have less physical, archaeological evidence. The idea that early medieval smiths were not skilled enough to make chainmail is simply not true – the earliest smiths to make mail were Celts, from whom the

Warriors

Romans learned the technique. Early medieval craftsmen were not less skilled in metalwork than the Celtic smiths of centuries before, and the method of construction (looping tiny hoops of metal through each other) would have been no mystical secret. Therefore, in all probability, the tiny rings of chainmail have just not often survived the ravages of centuries in the ground. Leather armour was also worn, and probably in the case of the Sutton Hoo leader, worn over a mail coat for added protection. Again, leather hauberks rarely survive in the archaeological record, so most evidence for them is conjectural.

Shields varied in size, generally becoming larger throughout the Beowulf period. Small shields, used in fluid skirmishes but less useful in the shield wall, were around 12 inches wide and designed to catch an opponent's weapon swing. Later, larger shields could be up to 3 feet wide, providing better all-round protection in a shield wall but being less manoeuvrable. All Anglo-Saxon shields were round, and often made of 'yellow' linden wood – as referred to in the *Beowulf* poem. Icons and designs would probably have decorated the warrior's shields – religious symbols may have been popular, and some sources suggest that two-coloured or multi-coloured shields, divided into coloured quarters or eighths, were used.

Spears were usually mounted on an ash shaft, between 6 and 8 feet long. The head of the spear could be between 4 and 8 inches long, some being pointed, some intended for slashing actions, and some referred to, in saga as well as known from excavation, as four-sided, mail-piercing heads.

Beowulf: Warrior King of the Geats

Germanic warriors in Britain and on the continent used
angons, although only a few of these weapons have been
found in Britain. These were prestige weapons with a thin
2-foot metal head and neck, mounted on a 6-foot wooden
shaft – the idea being that this would bend in an opponent's
shield, rendering the shield useless. Based on the earlier,
imperial Roman *pilum*, such weapons would have been
hurled shortly before impact between two groups of well-
armed warriors; the delay between discarding a shield and
either finding another or adjusting to fighting unprotected
could have been fatal in the hurried, frantic bustle of an
early medieval battle.

Swords were sometimes endowed with mystical qualities
in Germanic sagas. The very personal relationship between a
smith and the sword which he constructed, combined with
the high number of hours involved in producing such a
quality blade, meant that the sword was perceived as an
upper class weapon, and would only have been affordable to
– and wielded in battle by – the warrior elite. Anglo-Saxon
swords were about the same length as a Roman *spatha* –
around 3 feet. An ordinary farmer enrolled into a militia
would not have carried such a weapon – the symbolism
involved was akin to a gunfighter and his Colt Peacemaker
in the American West.

Axes are often thought of as being popular amongst
Anglo-Saxon warriors; and although this is true of the
Franks on the continent, who threw their *francisca* axes at
close range to break an enemy's formation, such axes are
uncommon in Britain. Several *francisca* axes are known from

graves in Frankish influenced Kent and on the Isle of Wight, but are less well known elsewhere. Hand-held axes are even rarer than the tapered *francisca* used for throwing.

Bows were known to the Germanic peoples in Europe, but appear to have been unfashionable in warfare in Britain, if not Scandinavia. Only six occurrences are known from Germanic graves in Britain and David Nicolle, speaking of the Anglo-Saxons, suggests that archers were of 'little social significance' (1984: 16). Slings were 'a popular weapon among poorer folk' (Nicolle, 1984: 24) in Germanic society. Beowulf draws a bow and kills a sea monster whilst searching for Grendel's mother; as this is an animal of a kind, perhaps this should more correctly be classed as a hunting weapon in the poem than a weapon of war.

An Anglo-Saxon duel between warriors armed with seax and spear. Such unarmoured warriors typify the ordinary fighting man of the early medieval period. (From Hewitt's Ancient *Armour and Weapons in Europe*, 1855)

Beowulf: Warrior King of the Geats

We have less idea of Anglo-Saxon clothing colouring than we do for the more colour-conscious Britons and Welsh. Early Franks supposedly wore green cloaks with red trim – although such uniform clothing was in reality unlikely. Striped and hooped patterns seem to have been popular, and as throughout much of the ancient and medieval eras, blue was a particularly hard colour to dye into clothing, and was therefore considered something of an upper-class colour.

Although Anglo-Saxon and Scandinavian armies at this time are often supposed not to have used horses in battle (although perhaps as transport to reach the battlefield), this may not be as solid a fact as once supposed. As noted above, a number of horses have been found in high status burials (again, these may only have been for transport), and horses are mentioned in *Beowulf*. Frankish nobles rode into battle, and were culturally similar to the Saxons and Scandinavians, and later Viking warriors certainly made use of mounted troops. Given that the early medieval period was dominated by heavy cavalry in north-western Europe, lasting right through to the fourteenth century, it is certainly possible that a warrior such as Beowulf would have been a competent rider and would have ridden into battle if the terrain and battle strategy made this a favourable way to fight.

We have little idea of the personal banners and standards of Anglo-Saxon and Scandinavian leaders. The archaeologically important seventh-century Sutton Hoo burial may have included a metal standard, although the form is hard to make out. The eleventh-century Bayeux Tapestry clearly shows the Anglo-Saxons of Harold rallying under a dragon banner very similar to late Roman *draco* windsocks; the Britons appear to have used such banners at the time of Beowulf, so it is reasonable to assume that such banners were used by their enemies too.

We have a fair idea of Anglo-Saxon battle tactics and army sizes, passed down to us from a few battle poems and (vaguely reliable) sources such as the *Anglo-Saxon Chronicle*. It may seem strange to think that Beowulf and his fourteen companions could be viewed as potential invaders by the coastal Warden of the Danes, yet, it would seem (from Anglo-Saxon law at least), that an army was defined as any group of armed men numbering thirty-five or more. At this time, warfare was based less on large, conscripted armies than on the personal bodyguards and companions of a leader, and it is likely that many small skirmishes between important leaders and their small warbands took place unrecorded in history; it is possible that items such as the Frank's Casket (named after its discoverer, not its cultural lineage) portray such an event. A good example of the ability of a small group of men to have an impact in a politically important arena is demonstrated by the events in Anglo-Saxon Wessex in 786; during this year, Cyneheard tried to overthrow the kingship with an army of eighty-five men, and was very nearly successful. Thus, the landing of Beowulf and his small band of well-armed Geats was rightly viewed with caution by the Danish coastal warden.

However, larger armies also existed – and would have fought the battles referred to in *Beowulf* for the control of land and nations. As kingdoms grew, the size of Germanic armies

Beowulf: Warrior King of the Geats

expanded in both Britain and Scandinavia; in times of strife, a warlord would call on the ordinary folk of his realm to bear arms alongside his personal warband; this gradually evolved into the well-organized *fyrd* of middle and later Anglo-Saxon armies. In the eighth century AD, armies probably averaged at about 700 men, comprising the warbands of the local chieftains all grouped together under the tribal king; later armies may have consisted of 2000 or 3000 men. The number of warriors recorded as having died in large battles cannot be accurately used as a source from which to ascribe army size – propaganda would have been used as much by chroniclers in the early medieval era as it can be by the media in the modern world. However, by the time of the better recorded Battle of Hastings in 1066, the Anglo-Saxon host had risen to around 8000 men, including the ill-trained fyrd of about 5500 warriors. Thus, King Hrothgar's pledge of a thousand thanes to the Geats in time of war would have been a massive boost to any army – 1000 well-armed and trained men would have been a significant force.

Beowulf, pure and simple, is a character of mythology only. Certainly warriors and kings like this great Geatish warlord would have existed, as Beowulf exhibits all the attributes necessary to succeed in early Germanic society – his devotion to his master early in his career and his devotion to his people after he had attained a kingdom. A great deal of debate has taken place with regard to the country of origin of Beowulf, but given the context of Britain and Scandinavia's relationship in the early medieval period, it may well be that the poem was worked upon first by Scandinavian bards and later by Anglo-Saxon bards in the British Isles. To become a great hero in the era typified by Beowulf, tactics and strategy fell into the background behind brute force and the ability to inspire one's followers; weapons, armour and battlefield tactics had not progressed further than clustering around the strongest friendly leader and fighting alongside him (to the death if need be for professional warriors following their leader). The need for a warrior as powerful as Beowulf to possess martial skills is demonstrated by the fact that his main enemies in the poem are not human, but incredible, mystical creatures – Grendel and his mother both have superhuman strength, and the dragon is renowned in folklore world-wide for its strength and intelligence. Beowulf's defeat of these creatures showed him to be worthy of the name 'King' in Germanic society; that he was also successful in battle against mere mortal foes is noted in the poem, yet the bards rightly did not feel that such victories deserved a place alongside the slaughter of fen monsters and dragons.

ROBIN HOOD
Greenwood's Master Outlaw

Robin Hood was a medieval English outlaw who stole from the rich and gave to the poor. Robin is mentioned in the 1377 *Vision of Piers Plowman*:

> If I should die this day, I'd still not keep awake. I can't sing my Pater Noster properly, as a priest should sing it, but I know the rhymes of Robin Hood and Ranulph, earl of Chester.
> (quoted in Saul, 1983: 224)

However, most of the earliest written stories of his exploits date from the mid fifteenth century. This does not, of course, preclude an earlier date for the foundation of the stories, it may just be that the tales were not committed to writing before this later date.

The first published collection of ballads about Robin, *A Lytell Geste of Robyn Hode* was printed around 1489. Tales of Robin's adventures continued to grow in popularity, and have been recreated for the cinema on many occasions; Hollywood has consistently portrayed Robin Hood as a noble outlaw, sometimes a little at odds with the earlier stories of the man. The earliest movie involving Robin starred Douglas Fairbanks in 1922, but many other actors have donned the green tights: Errol Flynn, Richard Greene, Sean Connery, Michael Praed, Jason Connery, Patrick Bergin, and Kevin Costner. This list of stars perhaps suggests the reasons why a medieval outlaw has gradually evolved into a gentleman rogue.

Perhaps surprisingly, the tale of Robin Hood seemingly dated as the earliest is not set in Sherwood Forest, which spread in the medieval period across the north-east midlands of England. Robin and his men are in Barnsdale in Yorkshire, and many other early stories locate Robin around this area and the Lancashire border.

Drawing based on a late fifteenth-century woodcut of Robin Hood.
(Author's collection)

Robin Hood: Greenwood's Master Outlaw

The *Geste* relates several of the tales of Robin Hood which were incorporated into later legend; the quotations used in this chapter have been taken from an early twentieth-century retelling of the tales, as much of the language and spelling in the *Geste* would be hard for the uninitiated reader to decipher. The most significant tale contained within the *Geste*, at least in terms of folklore and what may have happened in reality, revolves around a down-at-heel knight and a corpulent, greedy clergyman typical of those of Plantagenet England. One day, in the noble forest of Barnsdale, Robin was leaning against a tree, lost in thought, as his three companions – Little John (so named due to his great stature), Will Scarlet (who was Robin's cousin), and Much the miller's son – grew hungrily impatient for their dinner.

> Wherever Robin found himself
> He had a custom fine –
> Three Masses he would always hear
> Before he went to dine.
> (trans. Sue Bradbury, in Barber, 1999: 505)

Even so, he currently showed little sign of doing so. Little John questioned Robin as to when they should eat, pointing out that Robin had not eaten for so long.

> Robin aroused himself and smiled. 'Ah, Little John, me-thinks care for thine own appetite hath a share in that speech, as well as care for me. But in sooth I care not to dine alone. I would have a stranger guest, some abbot

or bishop or baron, who would pay us for our
hospitality. I will not dine till a guest be found, and I
leave it to you three to find him.'
(Ebbutt, 1910: 315)

Robin laughed at the crestfallen trio's facial expressions, as
they had not been expecting him to give them such a reply.
Robin wanted a guest for dinner, from whom he could then
demand a payment, thereby presenting Robin and his men
with an easy income from those with the money to spare. As
they prepared to leave, Robin reminded them of how to go
about their business. They were to do no harm to women
nor to any group in which a woman was travelling (in
honour of Jesus's mother Mary); they were to be kind and
gentle to husbandmen and toilers, to worthy knights and
yeoman, to gallant squires, and to children and helpless
people; bishops, prelates, and all other churchmen, and
sheriffs (especially the Sheriff of Nottingham), were to be
regarded as enemies to rob, beat and humiliate in any way
possible. When the trio had their 'guest', they were to meet
Robin at the famous great trysting oak in the forest.

Robin's parting words to the three were:

> 'Go ye all three, with bows and arrows in hand, and...
> As no man passes this way, you can walk up the willow
> plantation and take your stand on Watling Street; there
> you will soon meet with likely travellers, and I will
> accept the first who appears.'
> (Ebbutt, 1910: 316)

Robin Hood: Greenwood's Master Outlaw

So Much the miller's son, Little John, and Will Scarlet walked up through the willow plantation with their longbows and arrows, and placed themselves at a crossroads on Watling Street. No one was in sight, yet, as they stood looking, in the distance towards the forest of Barnsdale came a lone figure – a knight. As he drew near, the three yeomen observed him; he rode in a lacklustre way, as though he had lost all interest in life. His clothes were disordered and his head drooped sadly. Never before could the trio remember seeing so doleful a rider, but, sad as he appeared, he was a potential guest to take back to Robin and the meal table.

Little John ran out and grabbed the bridle of the knight's horse. The rider raised his head and blankly stared at Little John. In is turn, Little John doffed his hat, welcoming the knight on his master's behalf and telling him that he must accompany them to dinner. The knight cried 'Mercy', and asked who Little John's master was. Upon Little John's truthful reply, the knight replied:

> 'So Robin Hood is thy leader? I have heard of him, and know him to be a good yeoman… I had intended to eat my midday meal at Blythe or Doncaster to-day. But it matters little where a broken man dines!' (Ebbutt, 1910: 317)

Leading the woeful knight back to meet Robin, all three noticed that he wept silently, yet their courtesy – demanded by Robin himself – forbade them from outwardly showing notice of his distress, Arriving at the meeting place, Robin politely greeted his guest.

> 'Welcome, Sir Knight, to our greenwood feast! I have waited three hours for a guest, and now Our lady has sent you to me we can dine, after we have heard Mass.' (Ebbutt, 1910: 318)

Friar Tuck sang three masses, and then the group sat down to eat. There was a wide abundance of many of the good foods available in the forest – venison and game of all kinds, swans, fish and river fowl, bread and fine wine. At the end of the meal, the knight thanked Robin, saying that he had not eaten so good a meal for the previous three weeks. Then he exclaimed that if ever he passed this way again, he would do his best to repay Robin in kind. Robin was much aggrieved by this suggestion, explaining to the knight that he should pay before he left; a yeoman, he suggested, was never meant to pay for a knight's banquet. The knight pleaded that he had no money worth offering, blushing as he explained that he had no more than 10 shillings. Robin sent Little John to search the knight's saddle bags, and John returned to confirm the knight's story – he indeed had but 10 shillings. Thereupon, Robin announced that he would take not one penny from the knight, and, if his dinner guest so desired, Robin would lend to him more money, as a knight should have more than 10 shillings to his name. Inquisitively, Robin asked the knight how he had found himself in such a predicament, if he felt happy enough to explain.

Robin Hood: Greenwood's Master Outlaw

'Tell me just one word, which I will keep secret from all other men: were you driven by compulsion to take up knighthood, or urged to beg it by reason of some small estate; or have you wasted your old inheritance with fines for brawling and strife, or in gambling and riotousness, or in borrowing at usury? All of these are fatal to a good estate.'

(Ebbutt, 1910: 320)

The knight replied that his ancestors had been knights for over a hundred years, and that he had not lived wastefully, but soberly and sparely. He had a son whom, when he himself went on a Crusade with Prince Edward, he left in charge of his lands. The son was a brave and comely young man, twenty years old. Yet, when the knight returned from two years' hard fighting in the name of Christ, he found his son in great danger, for in a knightly tournament, he had slain a knight of Lancashire and a bold squire. The son would have died a shameful death if his father had not spent all of his money saving him from prison, for those who sought to try him were powerful men indeed. The money that the knight raised was not enough, and he had to mortgage his lands, pledging them to the abbot of St Mary's Abbey in York. The knight explained that he was riding to York when he was accosted by Robin's men.

The pitiful knight explained that the Abbot had lent him 400 pounds in return for his land, a sum far lower than the land actually deserved. Robin enquired what would happen if the knight failed to redeem his land, and the knight replied that he would leave England once more, journeying to Jerusalem and the Hill of Calvary, campaigning once more in the name of God and never again setting foot in his homeland. Indeed, the knight predicted that he had no likelihood of repaying the loan, and he had no intention of remaining in England to see strangers as the lords of his father's lands.

This sad story touched the hearts of Robin Hood and his band of simple yet kindly outlaws. Robin asked if the knight had any friends who would act as sureties for the repayment of the loan, to which the knight replied that he had none at all, save 'God himself, who suffered on the tree for us.' This reply slightly riled Robin, as it sounded too strongly of the kind of preaching that the corpulent monks whom he hated so spoke. He told the knight that he would lend him the money if a substantial surety could be guaranteed, as he could not afford to waste his money. The knight explained that he could make no earthly offer of surety, and in heaven, there was only 'our dear Lady'. This impressed Robin more than the knight's earlier preaching:

> 'Do you give Our Lady as your surety?... I would take her bond for any sum, for throughout England you could find no better surety than our dear Lady, who has always been gracious to me. She is security enough. Go, Little John, to my treasury and bring me four hundred pounds, well counted, with no false or clipped coins therein.'
> (Ebbutt, 1910: 322)

Robin Hood: Greenwood's Master Outlaw

Robin Hood on the Silver Screen

The legend of Robin Hood has proved irresistible to the producers of Hollywood and their smaller counterparts. Several retellings of the legend of Robin Hood were made for the cinema and for television in the twentieth century. The common method of adaptation in these media forms has traditionally seen much of the original tale discarded, only to be replaced by a simple good versus evil storyline – very much more 'abstraction' than 'adaptation'. However, Robin Hood has mostly escaped this fate, perhaps on television by virtue of the serial format, which allows on-going sagas to take place – very like the original method of telling by a bard or minstrel.

In the cinema, Robin Hood has been played by Errol Flynn, Patrick Bergin, Kevin Costner and even the comedian John Cleese (in the film *Time Bandits*); British television serials of the tale have seen Richard Green, Michael Praed and Jason Connery in the lead role. Usually dressed in green jerkin and tights, and often with a ridiculously pointed cap, Robin Hood cavorts around with agility, rescuing his love interest, Maid Marion, from the evil clutches of the Sheriff of Nottingham. Aided and abetted by his Merry Men – rarely failing to include the giant-sized Little John, fat Friar Tuck, ice cool Will Scarlett, and the often dim-witted Much the miller's son – Robin never fails to outwit the foolish Sheriff and his cast of supporting pantomime villains.

So well known has the legend of Robin Hood become that director Mel Brookes has spoofed it at the cinema (*Robin Hood: Men In Tights*) and even Disney has ventured into the retelling of Robin Hood's story as an animated cartoon, portraying Robin as a fox and King John as a

177

thumb-sucking lion – this latter perhaps a parody of the leopards (commonly perceived to be lions) on the Plantagenet coat of arms, paw raised perilously close to its mouth in the passant position.

Little John and Much, the competent treasurer of Robin's band, went to the secret place where all of the outlaw band's money was kept. They carefully selected the coins to take, making sure that each and every one weighed the correct amount and had not had its edges clipped of vital weight (and therefore value). On the suggestion of Little John, they also selected new clothes for the threadbare knight, including good boots and spurs, and also provided him with two horses, one for riding and one to carry his baggage and coffer of money. Both horses were splendid beasts, as befitted a man of knightly standing. Upon receipt of these, the knight quizzed Robin as to why he had done this for a complete stranger; Robin replied 'You are no stranger, but Our Lady's messenger. She sent you to me, and Heaven grant you may prove true.'

The knight enquired as to when and where he should repay Robin's kindness and loan. Robin said that they would meet again in twelve months' time, under the very same tree in the green wood. This, the master outlaw explained, would allow the knight time to regain his friends and gather his rents from his newly redeemed lands. He also offered the services of his loyal comrade, Little John, to act as the knight's squire on his trip to York, and to do the knight a yeoman's service, should he require it.

'In faith, good Robin, I had forgotten one thing. You know not my name. I am Sir Richard of the Lea, and my land lies in Uterysdale.'
'As for that,' said Robin, 'I trouble not myself. You are Our Lady's messenger; that is enough for me.'
(Ebbutt, 1910: 323–4)

As this interesting dialogue was being enacted, the very same abbot of St Mary's in York was rejoicing that the lands of Sir Richard were in his hands, and with him celebrated the local justice, with whom the abbot was corruptly in league. He had no pity for the knight, in fact he was rather pleased that the situation had led to him being able to exert the legal cruelty which was presented to him in this situation. Twelve months ago to this day, he had lent Sir Richard the 400 hundred pounds, and the abbot knew full well that unless the needy knight appeared with the money owed by noon on that day, the land would become the abbot's. Not all churchmen were so corrupt as the greedy abbot was, however, and a prior declared to him, as he rejoiced at what he stood to gain, that he should be ashamed of his behaviour. This had little effect on the abbot, who did nothing but scold the righteous prior.

As Sir Richard and Little John, in the guise of his man servant, approached the gates of the abbey, the porter recognized the knight. The porter took news to the abbot of the new arrival at the gate, which naturally upset him greatly, but the same news pleased the kindly prior, who now hoped that a cruel injustice could be avoided.

Warriors

Sir Richard was ushered in to see the abbot, and at once put a plan into action which he had hatched on the journey from Barnsdale to York with Little John, to teach the abbot a lesson in humility. Sir Richard announced that he had not one penny for the abbot, and begged to be granted a longer period to raise his monies. The abbot, now excited at the thought of keeping Sir Richard's lands once more, proudly exclaimed that he would allow no more than a minute beyond the appointed time, and that Sir Richard had broken his pledge, and therefore would forfeit his land.

Still kneeling, Sir Richard turned to the justice, and begged him to be his friend and plead with the abbot on his behalf. The justice replied that he would not, as his duty was to uphold the law, and Sir Richard currently stood outside of the law. With this, the cruel abbot swore an oath that the knight would never have his land as his own again. Sir Richard, acting that he was at the end of his tether and desperate to keep his land, threatened the abbot with violence. This suggestion of violence infuriated the abbot, and he shouted abusively:

> 'Out, thou false knight! Out of my hall!'
> Then at last Sir Richard rose to his feet in just wrath.
> 'Thou liest, Sir Abbot; foully thou liest! I was never a false knight. In joust and tourney I have adventured as far and as boldly as any man alive. There is no true courtesy in thee, abbot, to suffer a knight to kneel for so long.'
> (Ebbutt, 110: 326–7)

Robin Hood: Greenwood's Master Outlaw

As the quarrel rose in intensity, the justice intervened. He asked the angry abbot what he would offer the justice to force Sir Richard to sign a legal deed of release. As the abbot considered this, the justice explained that without this deed being signed, the abbot would never be able to hold the land in peace. This made the abbot's mind up, and he offered the justice 100 pounds, to which the justice greedily assented.

This was the time for Sir Richard to drop his false mask. He announced that the abbot would not so easily gain control of his land, and that the justice would not gain his 100 pounds so swiftly. He explained that even if the abbot were to pay 1000 pounds, he would never gain control of Sir Richard's estates. Then he signalled Little John to bring forth the coffer containing the money. Sir Richard counted out on the table 400 pounds and sternly told the abbot that if he had been more courteous, Sir Richard would have rewarded him well away and above the 400 pounds. Declaring that his lands were once again his, Sir Richard strode out of the hall with dignity, and rode home to his lands in Uterysdale; he and his family forever prayed for Robin Hood afterwards, never forgetting the master outlaw's generosity to them.

The abbot of St Mary's was bitterly disappointed and enraged. He had lost the wealthy lands of Sir Richard and had received only his 400 pounds as payment. This alone would not fund the extravagant lifestyle for which he so wished. Little John, on the other hand, returned to Robin in the forest and recounted the whole story, which mightily amused Robin and the others in his band. Robin and his men greatly enjoyed thwarting the schemes of such wealthy, overblown officials.

Warriors

When a year had passed, Sir Richard announced to his wife that he must return to Barnsdale to repay Robin Hood. He asked his wise wife what additional gift he should take to offer Robin, to show the true level of gratitude that he felt towards the man. His wife, thoughtful of the needs of such a man as Robin, suggested 100 bows of the finest Spanish yew, and 100 sheaves of arrows, peacock or goose feathered. This gift, she was sure, would be more than acceptable to Robin.

As Sir Richard rode to meet Robin, at the head of his well dressed retinue, he passed through a village where a fair had been set up. He stopped to watch a wrestling match, but soon saw that the wrestler who won every contest (a stranger to the village) would be defrauded of his prize, which consisted of a white bull, a caparisoned steed, a gold ring, a pipe of wine and a pair of embroidered gloves. This seemed so ill to Sir Richard that he decided to stay and defend the right of the wrestler. His troops kept the ring around the wrestlers in order, and the stranger was allowed to claim his prize and leave with it. Sir Richard, of course a kindly knight, bought the pipe of wine from him and allowed all of the villagers to drink from it, so as not to cause anger. By the time he had overseen the contest, though, it was nearly 3 o'clock in the afternoon, and he knew full well that his appointment with Robin had been at midday.

Robin had patiently waited under the tree as agreed, but, after an hour, he began to grow impatient. He expressed his fear to the ever present Little John that perhaps he had upset Our Lady Mary in some way, as she (through Sir Richard) had not returned his money. Little John reminded him that they should be patient and wait until sunset before assuming this, and was then sent out by Robin to find yet another 'guest' for the feasting table. Little John, Will Scarlet and Much set out to the willow plantation to Watling Street, as they had done a year before when they brought back Sir Richard. As they approached the road, they saw a little procession advancing towards them:

> Then, as they looked towards Barnesdale,
> Along the road they see
> A pair of monks, all dressed in black,
> Each on a good palfrey.
> (trans. Sue Bradbury, in Barber, 1999: 528)

Behind the two monks followed a train of fifty-two men and seven pack mules; the monks looked almost royal in appearance due to this great procession behind them. Little John commented that these monks had brought along their 'pay'. The more pragmatic Will Scarlet pointed out that they were but three against fifty-four men, yet even so, Little John stepped into the road followed by his two companions, telling them to:

> 'Look well to your bows, your strings and arrows, and have stout hearts and steady hands. I will take the foremost monk, for life or death.'
> (Ebbutt, 1910: 330)

Little John then shouted to the monk to stop where he stood, otherwise he would lose his life. The monk arrogantly challenged Little John, demanding to know who his master was, and, upon hearing that it was Robin Hood, announced that Robin was a foul thief and would come to a bad end. Outraged, Much drew back his bow and shot the monk through the heart, and watched him fall to the ground, dead. The other monk was taken to Robin, along with his pack mules, but the servants had all run away.

When they arrived to meet Robin, the master outlaw doffed his cap to his new guest, but the monk ignored him. Even so, the monk was obliged to hear three masses and was then sat at the feast. During the meal, Robin enquired from where the monk had come. The monk haughtily replied that he was the high cellarer of St Mary's Abbey in York – at which point Robin clapped his hands and announced that the packs on the mules surely held the money returned by the pledge of Our Lady Mary, which he had lent to Sir Richard. The monk denied this, but Robin saw this as an insult to the Virgin Mary, and angrily shouted the monk down. Robin asked the monk how much money was contained within the packs:

> 'The monk replied: 'Sir, I have only twenty marks in my bags'…
> Robin answered: 'If that be all, and you have told the truth, I will not touch one penny; rather will I lend you some if you need it; but if I find more, I will leave none, Sir Monk, for a religious man should have no silver to spend in luxury.'
> (Ebbutt, 1910: 331–2)

Robin Hood: Greenwood's Master Outlaw

When Little John opened the monk's packs, he emptied and counted out 820 pounds; he said to Robin that the monk had indeed been truthful. The monk, as Little John saw it, had 20 pounds of his own, but also had another 800 which Our Lady had sent Robin in return for his loan of the previous year. Robin thanked Our Lady, declaring her the best surety for a loan, as she had now paid it with kindness twice over. What Robin did not know was that the monk had been travelling to London, to obtain the consent of the king to reclaim the lands of Sir Richard of Lea once more; Robin, without knowing it, had saved the goodly knight again. The monk, minus his 800 pounds, was then allowed to depart – wryly commenting that a meal in Blythe or Doncaster would have cost him less.

Late in the afternoon, Sir Richard arrived to give Robin his money, explaining the honourable reason for his lateness. Robin thanked Sir Richard for protecting the innocent wrestler's rights at the fair, and for his generosity in sharing the wine with the villagers. He also refused the money that Sir Richard had come to repay him, as he felt that Our Lady had already delivered this via the monk. Robin and his men did happily accept the gifts sent by Sir Richard's wife, however. Sir Richard then returned to Uterysdale, and used his power and influence to protect the righteous outlaw band of Robin Hood. Robin continued to undertake good deeds for the poor and worthy, and never stopped his fight against the oppressive and tyrannical clergymen and Sheriffs.

Another aspect of the earliest tales of Robin Hood includes Little John entering the Sheriff of Nottingham's employment, disguised as a cook, whereupon he stole a plate. The Sheriff and his men gave pursuit, but were captured in the Greenwood by Robin's band – the Sheriff only being released after being forced to dine from the stolen plate and sleep rough for the night, and made to swear not to persecute the outlaw band.

Perhaps the best known part of the tale of Robin Hood is that of the archery competition; a tournament was held in Nottingham for the prize of a gold and silver arrow. Robin, accompanied in disguise by Little John, Will Scarlet, Much the miller's son, and Gilbert of the White Hand (another of Robin's followers), all shoot well in the competition right under the Sheriff's nose – and Robin wins the prize. The Sheriff realizes that only one man could shoot so well, and Robin narrowly evades capture in an epic fight.

A shooting competition also featured in *The Talkyng of the Munke and Robyn Hode*. This ballad, dated to the mid fifteenth century, saw Robin and Little John arguing over such an archery competition, whereupon they parted company and Robin was captured whilst attending mass in church by himself. Little John came to the rescue, and Robin offered his companion the leadership of their robber band; Little John, loyal to Robin, declined this offer. Much the miller's son again shoots a character in cold blood in this ballad – a page boy, so that the boy may not betray Robin's men. A lighter side of the Robin Hood cycle can be seen in *Robin Hood and the Potter* (dated to about 1500), a comic ballad in which Robin is beaten in a duel by a potter.

Robin Hood: Greenwood's Master Outlaw

In these early tales, Robin is overly and outwardly concerned with being a good Christian – acknowledging Jesus and Mary as his betters, and wishing to hear Mass before eating. This aspect has disappeared from modern retellings of the legend, notably in the television series starring Michael Praed and later Jason Connery, where Robin and his men were the 'Son's of Herne' – tying them in with the cult of the Green Man and medieval and ancient paganism. Perhaps this reduction of religious sentiment reflects the more secular culture of the later

Drawing based on the frontispiece to Wynkyn de Worde's version of the tales of Robin Hood, dating to the late fifteenth century. (Author's collection)

twentieth century in general, and certainly demonstrates how any given culture willingly modifies a tale so that its audience will comprehend and empathize with the characters more easily.

One early tale in the Robin Hood cycle involves the king dressing his men in Lincoln Green, and marching them through Nottingham, pretending to be Robin's men (this, apparently, was a jest on the king's part). The townsfolk flee in panic – which casts a curiously different idea to the usual representation of Robin's relationship with the ordinary folk. Why, if Robin was so popular, did the people flee from the men whom they believed to be Robin's band? Perhaps a strand of the tale now long forgotten explained this, yet now we can do little more than be mystified by it.

Of course, the Robin Hood cycle is yet another example of a tale which grew with time – probably incorporating the deeds of other folk hero brigands, whose names are now lost to us. Notably, Robin's allegiance to King Richard I (who actually ruled about 300 years before Robin became a popular folk legend) was incorporated, as was his rivalry with the Sheriff of Nottingham and Guy of Gisburne, and his love affair with Maid Marion. In essence, a whole literary cycle has sprung up around Robin Hood – in a very similar manner to that of King Arthur – incorporating many tales probably originally told about other medieval outlaws, yet adapted and interpolated into the legendary life of the presumably more popular Robin Hood.

In History

The truth behind Robin Hood's generosity and deeds is a tale cloaked in mystery, but diligent research by a number of historians has thrown enough light on to the matter for it to become an area of subjective debate.

In the three centuries after the Norman Invasion of 1066, England gradually developed a new administrative system, called feudalism. Some aspects came into being straight away within the lifetime of William I, yet others took far longer to filter through into practical use, or evolved from earlier systems. In late Anglo-Saxon England, under the umbrella rulership of a national king, the keeping of justice and peace was largely left to the powerful, individual landowners amongst their local people; in many ways, the community dealt with its own problems. In the Anglo-Norman system, royal authority was intended to be stronger, and was asserted throughout the kingdom, although for most of this period the king relied upon his localized barons and burghers to rule in his name as no standing army or police force existed to implement royal law (therefore the system was more similar to Anglo-Saxon administration than is often believed). Under the later Plantagenet rulers, a new, wealthy burgher class emerged, who had mostly gained their money and power from trade and economics; gradually, such men ruled where previously a nobly bred baron had acted in the king's name. Similarly, the clergy became wealthier, and with this wealth came corruption – indeed throughout much of England's history in the medieval and post-medieval periods, the Church has been one of the land's wealthiest organizations. Both churchmen and burghers were susceptible to corruption – their power came from their money, as opposed to coming from hereditary nobility, and money was therefore the way to their hearts. Many of the most powerful local men could be persuaded to act unjustly – yet in the king's name – if the price was right.

A natural opposition to such methods of local government grew, and occasionally, a group of people, quite often ex-soldiers or those with military experience, would act. M I Ebbutt saw such figures in a rather romantic light:

> It was therefore natural that in these latter days a class of men should arise to avail themselves of the unique opportunities of the time – men who, loving liberty and hating oppression, took the law into their own hands and executed a rough and ready justice between the rich and the poor which embodied the best traditions of knight-errantry, whilst they themselves lived a free and merry life on the tolls they exacted from their wealthy victims. Such a man may well have been the original Robin Hood, a man who, when once he had captured the popular imagination, soon acquired heroic reputation and was credited with every daring deed and every magnanimous actions in two centuries of 'freebooting'.
> (1910: 314)

Perhaps at this stage it should also be noted that the very composition of the human psyche dictates that at least a few people, no matter what their social situation, will strive and contrive to better their standard of living through illicit or immoral acts. Of course, what distinguishes Robin Hood and other medieval heroic outlaws from the likes of modern gangsters and criminals (and indeed those medieval outlaws less scrupulous than Robin and his men) is the fact that Robin and his fellows carried out their deeds to help the innocent and wronged.

Other Medieval Outlaws

Robin Hood was not the only character from British folklore to have been an outlaw. The Tale of Gamelyn features a younger brother who is deprived of the inheritance of his dying father by his eldest brother. Upon reaching adulthood, the youngest son – Gamelyn – is outlawed by his evil brother, and acts out many tales shared with the Robin Hood legend.

The Song of Trailbaston is a protest by a former soldier of the king, who claimed to have been unfairly accused of robbery and murder, fleeing to the forest and becoming an outlaw; the surviving copy of this poem has been dated to the mid fourteenth century (Ohlgren, 1998: xviii).

William Wallace – featured in Chapter Ten for his martial prowess – was famed early in his career as an outlaw-cum-freedom fighter, and is joined in this category by Hereward the Wake (who rebelled in the bloody aftermath of William I's invasion of England in 1066).

Warriors

But how did people actually come to be technically termed an 'outlaw' in medieval England, beyond this rather romantic and idealized viewpoint? If an accused person failed to turn up to the shire court to answer the charges set against them, the sentence could not be pronounced in the absence of the accused. However, the absentee would be declared an outlaw. This meant that a writ of *capias* was issued against the accused, and, if that person did not appear by a third summons or could not be found by the local sheriff, an exigent was issued. This exigent was a formal demand ordering the accused to attend court; if the accused still did not appear, he forfeited his goods and property to the king, and, after the fifth demand, was declared an outlaw. Until the outlaw presented himself at the court to which they had been summoned, they would remain outside of, and beyond the protection of the law.

English archers practising their art. This drawing, based on a medieval manuscript, may show a tournament of the kind that frequents the legend of Robin Hood. (Author's collection)

Robin Hood: Greenwood's Master Outlaw

The consequences of becoming an outlaw could be grave. Nigel Saul tells us that:

> ...until 1329 a man outlawed for felony could be killed with impunity. But in practice its severity was tempered. Outlawry applied only to the county in which it had been pronounced. So all an outlaw needed to do was flee from his own county to the next.
> (1983: 193)

Once outlawed, it was not unusual for the person concerned to start acting outside of the law themselves; if the law would no longer protect them or serve them, why should they serve it? Outlaws do appear to have been common in medieval England. For every man convicted in court, it has been estimated that about ten were outlawed. In Ebbutt's retelling of the Robin Hood tales, Robin himself describes some of the many and varied ways in which a normally respectable, socially high, or law-abiding person could find himself committing deeds to fall outside of the law through his own misfortune:

> '...were you driven by compulsion to take up knighthood, or urged to beg it by reason of the ownership of some small estate; or have you wasted your old inheritance with fines for brawling and strife, or in gambling and riotousness, or in borrowing at usury? All of these are fatal to a good estate.'
> (1910: 320)

Warriors

Returning to Robin Hood himself, the question must be asked as to whether or not he was a historical character. Like King Arthur (Chapter One), it is unlikely that we will ever know for sure. If Robin Hood did exist, he would have been found in northern England, probably in Barnsdale (lying between Pontefract and Doncaster in Yorkshire) rather than Nottinghamshire's Sherwood Forest. Sherwood was only introduced to later tales of Robin, the early *Geste* more reliably linking Robin to Yorkshire. Interestingly, and very significantly, the area of the Great North Road along which the *Geste*'s Robin operates was notorious in the medieval period and beyond for the robberies that took place there. Perhaps the strongest claim for a 'Robin Hood' is the man of that name, or Robin Hod or Robin Hobbehod described as a fugitive in a pipe roll from Yorkshire dating to the 1220s; his debt was owed to St Peter's in York (the Minster) so he may well have been a tenant of the Archbishop. As far as research has shown to date, this Robin is the only known outlaw and fugitive going by the name of Robin Hood or anything similar, and he was probably living fairly close to where the original tales of Robin Hood were set. Other candidates, of variable authenticity and not even always noted as being outlaws, include a Robyn or Robert Hood who fought for Thomas of Lancaster's army at Boroughbridge in 1322, a murderer from 1266 called Robin Hood (however, this Robin is only known from a later, Scottish source, and is already in the company of Little John), and a Robert Hood who broke the lord of the manor's fold at Alverthorpe in 1309.

Robin Hood: Greenwood's Master Outlaw

Robin Hood was not the only medieval outlaw made famous through folklore, and this perhaps suggests how common outlawry was in the medieval world. The acts of many became preserved in folklore as they stood against the perceived and very real corruption of the king's officials. In twenty-first century terms, outlaws such as Robin Hood crusaded on a very similar level and with a very similar manifesto to those who now stand up against powerful multi-national corporations. In modern terms, this means possibly going to prison or being heavily fined to bring notice to serious misdemeanours conducted by those who perceive themselves to be above the law; in medieval England, it could mean death.

In Battle

The sort of combat carried out by medieval outlaws should perhaps not be termed a 'battle'. Although many such men would have been experienced soldiers, and fought in set-piece battles in time of war, brief skirmishes would have been more common amongst brigands, and to lead a band and be successful in such small-scale actions required a different set of virtues to those used by the commanders of large medieval armies of thousands of men.

Some of the most relevant historically attested skirmishes of the type in which a historical Robin Hood would have involved himself occurred in Edward I's conquest of Wales. The medieval Welsh were less inclined to take part in a set-piece battle, where their poorly armoured spearmen and bowmen could be cut down in detail by combined archery and cavalry attacks (as happened at Orewin Bridge in 1282, for example). Instead, the Welsh conducted guerrilla campaigns against the invading English armies, and many hundreds of small skirmishes were fought between English patrols or garrisons and Welsh freedom fighters. Playing dirty was the order of such battles – in one recorded incident in 1257 (probably before 2 February), an English force awaited the local Welsh behind the walls of their fortified camp:

> Here the English in full battle array waited, only to be surprised by a new Welsh tactic. Llywelyn and his men stampeded a herd of cattle into the camp and this bold move was followed by the Welsh infantry who quickly expelled the English from their prepared position and then chased them the three miles back to Montgomery.
> (Remfry, 1998: 22)

Although the longbow was the most popular weapon with English and Welsh bowmen, the crossbow was far more popular on the continent. Many crossbowmen were professional soldiers, and were hired out extensively throughout Europe as mercenaries – Edward I included them in the force during his conquest of Wales. (From John Hewitt's *Ancient Armor*, 1860)

Robin Hood: Greenwood's Master Outlaw

To be successful in minor skirmishes, then, Robin Hood and his kindred outlaw contemporaries would have had to be able to think fast and improvise – much like the qualities demanded of a modern platoon commander.

The weapon most strongly associated with Robin Hood is, of course, the longbow. Between the fourteenth and sixteenth centuries, the longbow came to be feared and revered as a technology capable of winning the toughest of battles. The longbow was the symbol of medieval English martial power, yet its origins seemingly lay in Wales. A longbow is a specific type of bow. Others exist also: the simple self bow, which was effectively archery technology in its crudest form – essentially a straight, flexible staff spanned by sinew to provide enough torsion to fire a projectile; the more complex composite bow, which as its name suggests was constructed from several materials (a wooden staff reinforced with horn or antler); and the cross-bow, a weapon dissimilar to other bows due to its mechanical works and flat-level trajectory (essentially making the crossbow the forerunner to the rifle). Longbows evolved from simple self bows, becoming longer and therefore more powerful; examples recovered from the *Mary Rose* (which sank in 1545) were around 6 feet long and would have fired a projectile at quite some velocity. The *Mary Rose* longbows were, however, the pinnacle of evolution for the longbow, and it would be wrong to think of fourteenth-century longbows being quite as powerful.

Even so, a trained man could fire five or six arrows every minute, over distances of between 200 and 600 yards. John Morris, writing at the start of the twentieth century, noted that a skilled amateur of his own era could shoot as far as 286 yards, that Shakespeare's Old Double could shoot an aimed arrow 240 yards and an arrow in flight 290 yards, and Henry VIII – in an era when archery was in decline – would not allow bowmen to practice at less than 220 yards (1901: 103). Morris also noted that his contemporary amateur could fire an arrow that would penetrate four and a half pads of brown paper (each of 'forty-five stout sheets') at the short range of 7 yards (1901: 103).

The Wars of the Roses, which sporadically occurred throughout the latter half of the fifteenth century, witnessed the bloodiest battles on British soil, such as Towton in Yorkshire. Much of the death caused in these battles would have been due to the hail of arrows fired by longbowmen between the bodies of closely packed warriors as they struggled forward to clash in fierce melée. Earlier in the fifteenth century, and in the century before, the longbow had again proved its devastating effect against the French at Poiters, Crecy and Agincourt. Different shapes of arrow head were used for differing purposes – long, thin yet strong armour piercing heads were forged (known as bodkins), barbed examples were known for hunting (the barbs ensuring that the head would stay in an animal, even on the run through thicket), and an entire typology of designs somewhere in between these forms can be formulated from the medieval period amongst others.

The longbow was a powerful weapon indeed in the right hands; Gerald of Wales recorded the events of a skirmish at Abergavenny Castle:

Robin Hood: Greenwood's Master Outlaw

The Welsh shot at them from behind, and with the
arrows which sped from their bows they actually
penetrated the oak doorway of the tower, which was
almost as thick as a man's palm … William de Braose
also testifies that, in the war against the Welsh, one of
his men-at-arms was struck by an arrow shot at him by
a Welshman. It went right through his thigh, high up,
where it was protected outside and inside the leg by his
iron cuishes, and then through the skirt of his leather
tunic; next it penetrated that part of the saddle which is
called the alva or seat, and finally it lodged in his horse,
driving in so deep that it killed the animal.
(trans. Thorpe, 1978: 113)

Gerald of Wales then goes on to describe another horseman
who was pinned through both legs to his horse by Welsh
arrows, noting: 'It is difficult to see what more you could do,
even if you had a ballista' (1978: 113). The bows that the
Welsh used, Gerald notes, were not made of horn, sapwood
or yew, but were instead carved roughly from the dwarf elm
trees of the Welsh forests, and not completed to a smooth
finish or with any fineness.

Archery was a popular sport in England in the medieval
period. The competition that Robin Hood is often
portrayed as sneaking into and winning under disguise is
probably typical of many such tournaments that would have
occurred throughout the countryside at fairs and fetes.
Naturally, English monarchs were keen for their serfs to
practise their archery skills, and Henry I decreed by law that

any man who slew another by accident whilst practising with arrows would not be prosecuted for the crime. The medieval Englishman was also very proud of his mastery of the longbow – the now famous 'V-sign' insult reputedly stems from triumphant Englishmen waving their fingers at French armies to demoralize them – this was significant as longbowmen captured by the French had their two forefingers cut off to prevent them ever being a threat again.

Swords were common weapons in the medieval period; in the legends of Robin Hood – especially in the cinema – Robin often becomes embroiled in swashbuckling sword fights; the charismatic actor and wonderful showman Errol Flynn was allegedly very dangerous in such situations when under the influence of alcohol! Swords varied greatly in quality, according to the price paid for each weapon. The actual combat effectiveness would have been less affected by cost – a blade costing any price would be capable of doing damage – but cheaper weapons would have been more likely to break in the violent clash of a duel. The ability of a sword's owner to look after and care for his sword would have perhaps been more important to ensure its longevity.

Another weapon that has come to symbolize the legend of Robin Hood is the quarterstaff. This weapon was very basic indeed – a heavy staff with which to unbalance and beat your opponent into senselessness. The quarterstaff could also be used to parry opponent's lunges and blows, as the sturdy staff could deflect string blows without becoming badly damaged itself.

Clothing worn by outlaws, would, by the wearer's very

definition, be little different to those of an ordinary civilian; if of a noble background, likelihood would suggest that the outlaw would be better clothed than a companion of lower class. The legend of Robin Hood often refers to Lincoln Green clothing worn by Robin and his men – this would make sense as it would provide a crude form of camouflage in the forest environment.

For protection, leather and chainmail armour would have been favoured over plate armour; freedom of movement would have been important in combat and general activities to a brigand such as Robin, and the impediment of heavy, jointed plate armour would have far outweighed the protection which it afforded. In addition to the lack of flexibility provided by plates of metal, cleaning and upkeep of such items would have been impractical to those outlawed by society. Shields and helmets would similarly have been a rarity amongst brigands. Helmets would have impeded hearing or sight, and a shield – although valuable in melée – would greatly have cut down on one's agility. When shields were used, they were likely to have been circular in shape; although often presumed to have been antiquated by the medieval period, a small, round shield would have been easier to use and better balanced than a large, heavy kite or heater shield. Often in the legends of Robin Hood, we see a nimble Robin or one of his band staying one step ahead of the Sheriff's men at arms, who are slowed down and encumbered by their armour; Gerald of Wales describes something similar when speaking of the lightly armed Welsh:

Warriors

It is a remarkable fact that on many occasions they
have not hesitated to fight without protection at all
against men clad in iron, unarmed against those
bearing weapons, on foot against mounted cavalry.
They are so agile and fierce that they often win battles
fought against the odds. ... They use light weapons
which do not impede their quick movements, small
leather corselets, handfuls of arrows, long spears and
round shields.
(trans. Thorpe, 1978: 234)

The size of forces involved in skirmishes and policing action
at the time of Robin Hood would not have numbered, as in
the full sized battles of the time (such as those of William
Wallace in Chapter Ten), in the thousands. Instead, patrols
and garrison consisted of surprisingly few soldiers. For
example, the English forces at minor castles in thirteenth-
and early fourteenth-century Wales consisted of:

Cefnllys and Dolforwyn each by eight horse and
twenty foot, Dunawd by five horse and thirty foot, and
Radnor by four horse and twelve foot... The force
maintained by the sheriff, Roger Springhouse, at
Oswestry, consisted of two heavy and two light
troopers, three crossbows, and sixty foot...
(Morris, 1901: 172)

Such were the sizes of patrols entrusted with keeping the
peace in the British countryside in the medieval period.

Robin Hood: Greenwood's Master Outlaw

With such small numbers of men, those charged with enforcing the King's law sometimes resorted to novel tactics for foiling crime; Paul Martin Remfry notes an interesting method of preventing banditry occurring in Wales; Roger of Wendover recorded in 1228 that :

> the knights and soldiers of the garrison of the castle of Montgomery situated on the Welsh borders, sallied forth with the inhabitants of the district, to widen and render more safe a road near the castle, on account of the Welsh banditti who robbed and murdered travellers there. They therefore marched to the place with swords, axes, staves, and other weapons, and commenced cutting down the trees, hedges, and shrubs, to render the road wider for travellers.
> (Remfry, 1998: 7–8)

By removing the cover in which bandits could have lurked, the danger of the road was at least lessened; however, when the Welsh bandits heard of this occurrence, they attacked the hedge trimmers with great vigour, forcing them to retreat back to the castle.

Robin Hood is known in many countries as the gentleman robber who took from the rich to give to the poor; many latter-day folk heroes' exploits have been based on the Master of the Greenwood. Indeed, perhaps the original exploits attributed to Robin Hood were based on earlier or contemporary folk heroes. Robin Hood's

An English archer at rest. Drawing based on a medieval manucript.
(Author's collection).

legendary life has been opened to a far wider audience in the twentieth and twenty-first centuries that the earliest minstrels singing his name could possibly have imagined; the reason for this is cinema. The historicity of Robin may be doubted in as much as no especially well-suited, named candidate has yet been found; a few possibilities exist with names similar to Robin's and at a possible date, but no firm conclusions can really be drawn. However, the outlawed man was a feature of medieval English society, and even if no such 'Robin' did exist, others like him certainly did. Fieldcraft and ambush were more important to such robbers than expensive armour and powerful horses; the power of the longbow, combined with the skilled shot of a woodsman would have made any forest dwelling brigands more than a handful for local garrisons. The longbow in the hands of the Welsh and English was responsible for virtually all the great English victories against the Scots and French in the fourteenth and early fifteenth centuries.

MACBETH
Tyrant King of Scotland

The famous English playwright William Shakespeare irremovably etched Macbeth's place in legend. Shakespeare's tragedy *Macbeth* was first performed around 1606 and was first published in 1623. The main source Shakespeare used was Holinshed's *Chronicles*, published in 1577, so Macbeth was perhaps not a completely alien figure to all members of his audience. Shakespeare's work was clearly intended to generate political favour for him: Banquo, a character supposedly an ancestor of the Stuart kings, is sympathetically portrayed in order, we must presume, to please the king of England, James I. The use of English invaders to provide military support to a legitimate claim to the throne of Macbeth would no doubt have had popular appeal among London play-goers, given the on-going political turmoil between the two countries. The famous witches were an atmospheric addition to the tale introduced by Shakespeare himself, and had not featured in Holinshed's version – again this would have appealed to James I, who was convinced of the evils of witchcraft. The inclusion of witches would be topical in a play of this period.

Macbeth is set in a Scotland ripped apart by rebellion and

warfare; the king, Duncan, was under great threat from
invaders and internal revolt by the treacherous warlord
Macdonald, yet his army was rescued by two of his best
warlords: Macbeth and Banquo. On their way to meet King
Duncan, the two warlords were confronted by three witches
who prophesized that Macbeth would become Thane of
Cawdor and later king of Scotland.

> First Witch: 'All hail, Macbeth! Hail to thee,
> thane of Glamis!'
> Second Witch: 'All hail Macbeth! Hail to thee,
> thane of Cawdor!'
> Third Witch: 'All hail, Macbeth, that shalt be
> king hereafter!'
> (Act I, Scene III)

The witches also predicted that Banquo's sons would
become kings of Scotland. Both Macbeth and Banquo
dismissed the old hags' rantings, but almost straight away
news was brought to the two Scottish warlords that Macbeth
had been rewarded for his prowess in battle by being
proclaimed Thane of Cawdor. So it seemed the witches'
prophesy might be fulfilled given time.

> Macbeth [aside]: 'If chance will have me king,
> why chance may crown me,
> Without my stir.'
> (Act I, Scene III)

Warriors

King Duncan travelled to Macbeth's castle at Inverness to visit his new Cawdor, little knowing that Lady Macbeth had plotted his death after receiving news from her husband of his encounter with the witches. Lady Macbeth is portrayed as an ambitious woman who was determined that the witches' prophesy would be made to come true. *Macbeth* has been described as the Tragedy of Ambition.

Lady Macbeth overpowered Macbeth's natural loyalty to his king, and prepared an alibi for him. Macbeth fell under his wife's power, and murdered Duncan at Macbeth's castle in Inverness:

> Macduff: 'Awake! Awake!
> Ring the alarum-bell. Murder and treason!
> Banquo and Donalbain! Malcolm! awake!
> Shake off this downy sleep, death's counterfeit,
> And look on death itself!'
> (Act II, Scene III)

The alibi concocted by Lady Macbeth meant that suspicion immediately fell on Duncan's sons Malcolm and Donalbain, who then fled from Scotland to seek the protection of the English crown.

Macbeth was crowned in place of the late Duncan, yet felt strangely uncomfortable. Dwelling on the fact that the witches had predicted his rise to Thane of Cawdor and then to king, Macbeth also remembered that the witches had predicted that Banquo's sons would become kings. Despite Banquo being an old friend and ally of Macbeth, he set about organizing for the assassination of his former ally – again, the Tragedy of Ambition. Macbeth located the vilest assassins to commit this crime against his friend and close ally:

> Second Murderer: 'I am one, my liege,
> Whom the vile blows and buffets of the world
> Have so incens'd that I am reckless what
> I do to spite the world.'
> (Act III, Scene I)

Despite this boast, the murderers failed in their task, slaying Banquo but allowing his son to escape in a park near to the palace. Guilt and sleeplessness weighing on his mind, Macbeth then set out to find the witches once more, to have his future foretold. The witches set Macbeth's mind at ease by explaining that he would come to no harm and could not be defeated unless Birnam Wood came to Dunsinane Castle:

> Third Apparition: 'Be lion-mettle, proud; and take no care
> Who chafes, who frets, or where conspirers are:
> Macbeth shall never vanquish'd be until
> Great Birnam wood to high Dunsinane hill
> Shall come against him.'
> (Act IV, Scene I)

The witches also specified that no man born of woman would be able to deliver a fatal blow to Macbeth; they also show him a vision of the ghost of Banquo before disappearing. After this encounter, Macbeth scorned the witches, not yet knowing that what they had told him could come true:

> Macbeth: 'Infected be the air whereon they ride,
> And damn'd all those that trust them!'
> (Act IV, Scene I)

The Deception by Malcolm

Act V, Scene IV of Shakespeare's *Macbeth* sees Malcolm's army advancing to fight Macbeth, in country near to Dunsinane. Malcolm and Siward conjure between them a cunning plan of deception:

> Siward: 'What wood is this before us?'
> Mentieth: 'The wood of Birnam.'
> Malcolm: 'Let every soldier hew him down a bough
> And bear't before him: thereby shall we shadow
> The numbers of our host and make
> discovery
> Err in report of us.'
> Soldiers: 'It shall be done.'

Thus concealed, Macbeth's army is surprised and defeated by the wood that 'Comes toward Dunsinane', under which advance the warriors in the Anglo-Scottish army. There is no historical precedent for this act of the play, although concealing troops within wooden or built up areas was not an unusual tactic in ancient and medieval warfare. It is perhaps conceivable that Malcolm's army advanced on Macbeth's hill-fort stronghold from the direction of the wood to cover the advance – a wise strategy given that the view from the fort offered a wide, clear view of the surrounding countryside. If this is so, it would also explain why the wood from which Malcolm advanced lay to the north of Macbeth, instead of to the south, the direction one would usually expect an advancing army from England to attack; Malcolm may have worked his way around Macbeth's position to take advantage of the natural cover of the woods.

⚜

'The Devil, a wizard and witches', from Newes from Scotland (1591–2). Witchcraft was considered a very real threat when Shakespeare wrote *Macbeth*, and his inclusion of the three witches added a contemporary, thrilling twist to earlier versions of Macbeth's life. (From the collection of Joe Mersey)

However, Scotland was not faring well under the deceptive and tyrannical rule of Macbeth:

> Ross: 'Alas, poor country,
> Almost afraid to know itself! It cannot
> Be call'd our mother, but our grave: where nothing,
> But who knows nothing, is once seen to smile;
> Where sighs and groans and shrieks that rent the air
> Are made, not mark'd;'
> (Act IV, Scene III)

The powerful Thane of Fife, Macduff, travelled to seek out Duncan's exiled son Malcolm in England, in order to return the rightful king to the throne. On finding out the reason for Macduff's journey, Macbeth ordered the slaughter of Macduff's family, which was duly carried out:

> [Enter Murderers]
> Lady Macduff: 'What faces are these?'
> First Murderer: 'Where is your husband?'
> Lady Macduff: 'I hope, in no place so unsanctified
> Where such as thou mayst find him.'
> First Murderer: 'He's a traitor.'
> Son: 'Thou liest, thou shag-eared villain!'
> First Murderer: 'What, you egg!
> [Stabbing him]
> Young fry of treachery!'
> Son: 'He had kill'd me, mother:
> Run away I pray you!'

Macbeth: Tyrant King of Scotland

[Exit Lady Macduff, crying 'Murder!' and pursued
by the Murderers]
(Act IV, Scene II)

Macduff's journey had not been in vain, however, as he
persuaded Malcolm to march back to Scotland to reclaim his
rightful place on the throne. Lady Macbeth, distraught with
guilt, by now not only walked in her sleep, but also talked in
her sleep and betrayed her secret of the truth behind the
death of Duncan. Let down by his wife, Macbeth became
increasingly dependent upon the counsel of the three
witches, showing the true desperation of his position.
Cornered by the advancing army of Malcolm, the 'warlike
Siward' Earl of Northumbria and Macduff in the stronghold
of Dunsinane, Macbeth watched with dismay as the trees of
Birnam Wood advanced towards him – Malcolm had
ordered his men to cut down branches to hide their
advance. Before this, Macbeth had felt confident in his
position, despite being against three powerful foes:

> Macbeth: 'our castle's strength
> Will laugh a siege to scorn: here let them lie
> Till famine and the ague eat them up:'
> (Act V, Scene V)

Now though, with Malcolm's men advancing under the
branches of the wood, one of the witches prophesies of his
downfall was upon him, and Macbeth nervously watched his
army fall before the oncoming men of Malcolm and

Macduff. In the battle, Macbeth died at the hands of
Macduff – not himself born of woman but ripped out by
caesarean birth:

> Macbeth: 'I bear a charmed life, which must not yield
> To one of woman born.'
> Macduff: 'Despair thy charm;
> And let the angel whom thou still hast served
> Tell thee, Macduff was born from his mother's womb
> Untimely ripp'd.'
> (Act V, Scene VIII)

Macbeth's death, as accurately foreseen by the eerie,
prophetic witches, paved the way for Malcolm's return to
the throne, and Macduff felt justified in avenging the death
of not only his family but also the murder of Duncan:

> Macduff: 'Hail, king! for so thou art: behold,
> where stands
> The usurper's cursed head: the time is free:'
> (Act V, scene VIII)

Only in the very final scenes in the play does Macbeth
return to the courageous warrior that he once served
Duncan as, fighting bitterly to the end. Claiming the crown
through murder and deceit did not bring him any
contentment, and he could only watch as the kingdom fell
to pieces around him, and both his and Lady Macbeth's lives
fell to guilt and despair. Shakespeare's Macbeth must truly be

one of the great tragedies of world theatre, vigorous in the development of its plot and rightly famed for the character soliloquies within it.

In History

The small amount of knowledge that we possess about the historical Macbeth does not hold much in common with Holinshed's nor Shakespeare's dramatization. Scotland in the early medieval period appears, by all accounts (limited as these are), to have been a very violent place to live; despite this, Macbeth was recorded as a just and fair king.

Macbeth was born in 1005, the only child of Findlaech MacRuaridh. Findlaech was the Mormaer of Moray – the Scottish High King's ruler of the central Highlands; therefore, the historical Macbeth was far more powerful than the thane that Shakespeare famously presented. In the early eleventh century, Scotland had a rural economy with very little centralization of government, so Findlaech was potentially a very powerful man with his own autonomy of rule in the Highlands. The cultural basis was the clan, and alliances between clans were made often and broken almost as often; feuding between rival clans was common. As well as the Scottish inhabitants of the Highlands, Norse settlers had created their own earldoms, and raiding between the Scots and the Norse (as well as against their own kinsmen and the ever present threat of sea raids from the northern islands and

Scandinavia) were rife. To the south, the Anglo-Saxon kingdoms provided yet another threat to Scottish power.

In 1020 Macbeth's father was slain by his nephews in a feud. This may well have been a politically motivated killing, as Findlaech had entered into alliance with Moray's rival house of Atholl. One of the assassins, Malcolm, was elected to rule (this was perfectly acceptable in Scottish political tradition), and was succeeded at his death by his brother Gillecomgain in 1029. During this time, Macbeth lived under the protection of the Scottish king, Malcolm II, of whom his father had been a loyal supporter (Malcolm was of the House of Atholl).

Aged somewhere in the region of eighty years old, Malcolm II was concerned as to who would be his successor, and who would support an ageing king should conflict occur. He lowered the odds of being succeeded by an unwelcome ruler or being betrayed on the battlefield by eliminating those of whom he did not approve; Gillecomgain was one such candidate. Given Gillecomgain's role in his father's death, and bearing in mind that Macbeth lived under Malcolm II's protection, it is far from inconceivable that Macbeth may have had a hand in Gillecomgain's murder. Whether this was the case or not, Macbeth was duly elected as Mormaer of Moray in 1033 and continued his father's alliance with Malcolm II's House of Atholl.

Malcolm II died at Glamis on 25 November 1034, and his eldest grandson, Duncan MacCrinan, was elected as High King in December of the same year. Previously, Duncan's experience of rulership had been limited to a petty kingdom in Scottish-controlled Cumbria, so he may not have been the strongest man available to keep order among the feuding clans. Duncan was a strong follower of Atholl, yet unlike Malcolm II, was described as a vicious tyrant (perversely similar to the Macbeth of Shakespeare's play) who waged war against the Norse in the Isles and Highlands and the Anglo-Saxons to the south at the same time. With hindsight, history has often proved against a leader who fights on two fronts at the same time, yet Duncan personally led an army into Northumbria whilst his nephew Moddan assaulted the Norse district of Caithness (the north-eastern tip of the Scottish mainland), ruled by a fearsome Viking, Thorfinn.

Duncan was a poor leader on his campaign into Northumbria; he was recorded as sending his cavalrymen to charge the fortified walls of Durham, from which the Anglo-Saxon defenders duly slaughtered them. This completed, the Anglo-Saxons proceeded to sally forth from the fortified burgh and complete the Scottish defeat by routing the Scottish footmen, too. The survivors retreated back into Scotland, whilst the unfortunate dead had their heads displayed on the walls of Durham as a warning against any further assault. In the north, Moddan's campaign faired little better, and the two retreating Scottish forces reunited on home soil.

Not learning any lessons from his first two campaigns, Duncan proceeded to take the remainder of his Scottish army north again, hoping that his own presence would help to defeat Thorfinn. This combined assault by land and sea once more ended with defeat, Duncan being defeated at sea off Deeness. Moddan, commanding the land forces, made camp whilst awaiting the support of Irish auxiliaries to arrive for him. The Scottish army was surprised in a night attack as the men slept; unable to rally his men in time to make a stand, Moddan's army was defeated in its tents, and Moddan himself was beheaded with a single blow from Thorfinn's foster father, Thorfell. Again Duncan rallied his tattered and defeated army, and led them once more to defeat by Thorfinn in August 1040.

The Vikings

In the year AD 793, Norwegian Vikings sacked the monastery at Lindisfarne on the north-eastern coast of England. From this date, until well into the medieval period, Scandinavian influence on Scotland and in Ireland grew to dominance; England and Wales were also affected, and the ruling families of England included Scandinavian blood (even, it can be argued, through the Norman kings – as the Normans themselves had Norse origins). Although not as well known as the violent raids that sometimes took place, Viking influence was spread most successfully by establishing trading routes, naturally followed by a native absorption of Scandinavian culture; this, backed up by Norse armies, proved to be a very effective form of cultural expansion throughout the British Isles.

In Ireland notably, but also in Scotland and to a lesser extent in England and Wales, Scandinavian influence could clearly be seen in the art of war. Before Norse influence, Ireland was regarded as a military backwater, where warriors fought in a ritual manner with small weapons and a lack of body armour. With Norse influence, the Irish quickly adopted the use of heavily armoured axemen as the backbone of their armies, supported by the lightly armed traditional warriors; such armies continued throughout the medieval period, until the reign of Elizabeth I in the mid sixteenth century. Scottish armies saw similar changes, as heavily armed and armoured footmen came to dominate the battlefield (this continued in the Scottish Highlands and Isles until well into the sixteenth century). In England and Wales, warriors adopted the axe as a weapon.

Domestically, archaeologists have been able to define what it would have been like to have lived in the Viking era, with the findings of excavations in Norse-influenced British towns being examined in great detail. York is the most famous of these settlements, and the results and theories resulting from excavation work have been vividly brought to life in the Jorvik Viking Centre.

After the defeat of August 1040, accounts of Duncan's life vary. Some accounts show that Duncan fled the battlefield and was killed later, others believe that Duncan's death was on the battlefield – at the hands of Macbeth. If Macbeth did slay Duncan, what could the circumstances have been? Duncan had been very unpopular – a ruler who proved to be a warmonger, and a bad one at that, was bound to have been resented by his people. It is possible that Macbeth fought for Duncan as a loyal supporter of Atholl, but at the final defeat did what he felt was best for the Scottish people to end the misery caused by continual war. Perhaps more likely – especially given the events directly after Duncan's death – Macbeth fought on the same side as Thorfinn's Norsemen, and had abandoned his sorely tested loyalty to Malcolm II's House of Atholl. Moray and Atholl were traditionally enemies, and it seems only to have been a personal bond between Macbeth's father and the High King Malcolm II that brought Macbeth's initial loyalty to Malcolm, so a modern reader should not be too surprised if Macbeth did actually fight against Malcolm's kinsman and successor, Duncan. Also, Macbeth may have been riled by Duncan's accession to the High Kingship, which Macbeth could easily have felt entitled to himself; an alliance with Thorfinn would therefore have been beneficial to Macbeth's political career.

Beneficial it was, because after Duncan's death Macbeth was pronounced High King late in 1040. Thorfinn fared equally well, as he became established as the Norse ruler of Caithness and Orkney with no opposition from the Scots under Macbeth's command, so this may well further point to a treaty between the two, mutually benefiting from the removal of Duncan.

Contemporary chronicles refer to Macbeth as a liberal and productive ruler; given Duncan's terrible reign, virtually any successor would have appeared an improvement. However, between 1040 and 1045, Macbeth set about rebuilding the countryside and repairing relationships with his neighbours to the north and south. However, the neighbours were not so keen to keep peace amongst themselves, for in 1041 Thorfinn, probably with permission (or possibly even aid) from Macbeth, began to raid Anglo-Saxon Northumbria from a base camp in Strathclyde, an area under Macbeth's rule. The Northumbrian earl Siward attacked and repelled the Norse raiders, and forced them out of his earldom. In 1042, Thorfinn returned, not only with his army of Caithness and Orkney Norsemen, but with Scottish and Irish supporters too. Despite Macbeth's hope for a peaceful reign, this situation would have appealed to him – as well as securing Thorfinn's loyalty and allegiance (through Macbeth's agreement to allow raiding from Scottish soil and the use of his warriors), the Scottish High King could be assured that his southern border was a well defended military zone with his own warrior's presence there, and that if the Norse raiding went well, his border could conceivably creep further south into English territory. Thorfinn struck this time through Cumbria, avoiding Siward's Northumbrians who had previously bloodied his nose, and striking instead at the Mercians – who he defeated in battle twice on this campaign.

In 1045 the only record of internal revolt against Macbeth was recorded. Crinan, the father of Duncan, was killed along with 180 of his Atholl warriors in battle against Macbeth near Dunkeld (to the north of Perth). This decisive defeat – stemming from a revival of the Moray-Atholl rivalry – allowed Macbeth a further nine years of stability. During these nine years, Macbeth visited the Pope in Rome (which would have sealed his fate in Shakespeare's mind as a villain!), and maintained courtly and trading contacts with most of the kingdoms of Europe. To the north, however, Macbeth's ally Thorfinn encountered problems when Rognvald Brussisson of Norway disputed his claim to the Orkneys. Thorfinn managed to defeat his rival at sea in the Pentland Firth and on land at Stronsay.

The son of Duncan lived in exile in England, gaining support under the new English king Edward the Confessor, who had been crowned in 1043. Duncan's son was named Malcolm, and under English law, Malcolm's claim to the Scottish throne was legitimate and to English minds had to be upheld and supported; perversely, under Scottish tradition, Malcolm had no claim on the Scottish throne at all. In 1054, an English and Danish army commanded by Siward was ordered to march into Scotland and lay claim to the Scottish throne for Malcolm. Siward, as Thorfinn had found to his cost over ten years before, was a fearsome fighter, having delivered the head of a treacherous earl to his king in a show of support.

The *Anglo-Saxon Chronicle* recorded the event:

> 1054: Eorl Siward went with a great force into Scotland, with both ship-forces and land-troops, fought with the Scots, put to flight the king, Macbeth, killed all the best in the land, and brought back much plunder, such as no man had ever obtained. But his son Osbern, and his sister's son Siward, with some of his housecarles and also the king's, were killed there on the day of the Seven Sleepers.
> (Savage, 1997: 181)

Macbeth: Tyrant King of Scotland

As the *Chronicle* records, Siward lost his son and part of his personal bodyguard (the huscarles); for him, this invasion of Macbeth's territory was becoming personal. Malcolm accompanied the army invading his country on his behalf, and many of the warriors from Atholl (his father's land) rallied to his cause. The army headed for Scone – where the High Kings were crowned – as Malcolm hoped to be crowned almost as soon as Macbeth was defeated.

The Anglo-Scottish force of Siward and Malcolm clashed with Macbeth's Scots and Norsemen at Dunsinane, which lay between Perth and Scone. Although the battle did not end in outright victory for either army, Macbeth reportedly lost 3000 warriors compared to his enemy's 1500. It was here that Siward lost his son and nephew, and was forced to retreat from Scotland without placing Malcolm on the throne. The price of defeat was too great for Siward, and the following year, whilst sick with dysentry, he threw himself fully armed from the walls of York, rather than die on his sick bed 'like a cow on straw'.

Edward the Confessor had not decided to support Malcolm's claim to the Scottish throne out of the kindness of his heart, nor indeed to uphold what the English perceived to be the right of succession. Although this was a useful grounds for invasion, Edward hoped to place Malcolm on the throne as a puppet ruler. As the English army retreated, without placing Malcolm on the throne, without killing Macbeth, and with the loss of a number of the royal troops who accompanied Siward, the chances of this looked slim. Instead, Malcolm was officially recognized as King of Cumbria, and his comrade Tostig Godwinsson was appointed earl of Northumbria in the wake of Siward. Macbeth retained control of much of Scotland, and the good qualities which he had shown in his previous years as High King retained much of the support for him.

Over the next three years, Malcolm and Tostig plotted and campaigned the downfall of Macbeth, and on 15 August 1057, Macbeth was slain by Malcolm. The battle which led to this is traditionally believed to have occurred at the ancient stone circle of Peel Ring, at Lumphanan in Mar; in the course of a campaign, Malcolm's Anglo-Danish troops had pushed Macbeth into retreat beyond Scone, and the Atholl clan probably rose in support of Malcolm. This forced Macbeth further north into the friendlier territory of Mar, yet even so, this could not prevent Macbeth's defeat and death.

Malcolm did not immediately take the High Kingship unopposed. Macbeth's step-son Lulac was elected at Scone and resisted and frustrated Malcolm's army for the next seven months. Lulac was slain in March 1058 by treachery, and King Malcolm III was crowned on 25 April 1058. Thorfinn, Macbeth's former ally, died in 1059 – possibly whilst campaigning on behalf of Macbeth's family against Malcolm.

Macbeth's rule brought greater unity to Scotland than it had ever previously experienced, and with Malcolm III's introduction of a feudal system similar to that which he grew up under in England, the country was drawn more and more into European politics, as opposed to remaining on the 'Celtic Fringe'. With the Norman invasion, Malcolm was drawn into conflict against the Anglo-Normans by 1079 (Scotland was a stronghold and haven for Anglo-Saxon exiles after the Battle of Hastings), and was killed by William Rufus in 1093.

In Battle

In the eleventh century, warfare in Britain was an unsophisticated test of muscle and weaponry. Warriors would have been armed and armoured much in the same style as the warriors depicted on the Bayeux Tapestry, which is an excellent source for warfare in mid to late eleventh-century Britain. Indeed, Macbeth enlisted a small number of Norman knights into his army in the 1050s – they themselves were fugitives from an anti-Norman backlash on the Welsh Marches of England. All of Macbeth's Norman followers were slain in battle in 1054.

Horsemen from an Anglo-Saxon manuscript, *c* AD 1000. (From Hewitt's *Ancient Armour and Weapons in Europe*, 1855)

Ian Heath sums up the cosmopolitan nature of a Scottish army of Macbeth's era very succinctly:

However, Scots spearmen would have been heterogeneous to say the least, with lowland spearmen and Strathclyde Welsh little different from the Saxon fyrd, highlanders and Scots spearmen and javelinmen little different from the Picts, Gall-Gael of very Irish appearance, and well-armoured Viking types probably riding to and from the battlefield. Percentages are impossible to establish, though clearly the latter would have provided the nucleus of the army and lowland spearmen probably the greatest proportion.
(1980:15)

A warlord and his close bodyguard would have been well armed and heavily armoured. As depicted on the Bayeux Tapestry, and in many contemporary manuscripts, the professional warrior of the mid eleventh century wore a chainmail hauberk, a helmet with added chainmail protection around the neck and cheeks (some helmets may have had iron cheek pieces – such as the earlier Coppergate helmet from York), and carried a shield for protection. This shield would probably not have been the kite shield famed from the Bayeux Tapestry, but more typically a round or sometimes oval shield; the kite shield is generally accepted as having evolved in order to protect a horseman's leg, and would appear to have its origins in the Norman and Frankish kingdoms. To inflict damage on enemies, Macbeth and his warriors would have carried a variety of weapons, including the war axe, sword, and spear. It is a commonly held perception that Celtic warriors were less well armoured than their Anglo-Saxon and Scandinavian opponents, but there is no reason to believe this in the case of the professional warriors in Scotland, who would have benefited as much as their southern and eastern contemporaries from sturdy armour. Lower class warriors were in all probability poorly equipped, though, and even up to the period of the Battle of the Standard in 1138, wild unarmoured Galwegians and Highlanders charged headlong into battle against better armed Anglo-Norman soldiers; darts or javelins were hurled by these fearsome Galwegians shortly before making contact in melée.

One or two interesting warrior types may have been part of the armies of Macbeth and his contemporaries, in addition to the ordinary spearmen and cavalrymen. In many Icelandic and Norse sagas, evidence exists of 'berserkers' – warriors who, in a battle frenzy, went into battle unarmoured. Many strange rumours have surrounded such warriors – some claim that they were clad in wolf fur clothing, others suggest that they fought entirely nude. Perhaps they have more in common with the warriors of the British battle poem *Y Gododdin*, which suggests that the warriors went to battle under the influence of mead (a strong, sweet ale). In the *Heimskringla*, we are told that berserkers fought in bodies of twelve men, although this was on longships. Paddy Griffith has amusingly yet perhaps realistically likened the Viking berserker to a Glasgow gang leader, who clads himself in threatening symbols, such as death's heads and Motörhead badges; much of the rest of the berserker mythology, he feels, is just that – spurious and unhistorical (1995: 136). Bowmen were common in Viking armies, unlike the contemporary English armies, if our historical sources are to be believed. The bows used in this era were not the powerful longbows of the later medieval period, but, as demonstrated on the Bayeux Tapestry, could still be potent weapons with which to distract enemy formations. It is perhaps likely that such missile weapons were more common in Scottish armies than in those of their English enemies, due to the undeniable influence of Viking warfare on the Scots.

The war axe, on a long shafted handle, was to become a peculiarly Scottish weapon in the medieval period and beyond. It evolved from the single-handed Norse weapon commonly associated with Viking raiders, but in Scottish and Anglo-Danish hands, the handle of the axe seems to have been lengthened, and usually wielded in two hands – in a similar fashion to that shown on the Bayeux Tapestry's Anglo-Saxon Huscarles. Inevitably, a two-handed weapon, although giving increased power to the blow, meant that the user's shield became useless, leaving the bearer susceptible to injury in combat or under missile attack. During the eleventh century, the downward- and rearward-facing 'beard' of the Scandinavian axe was superseded by an upward- and forward-facing horn; this would eventually evolve into the Lochaber axe famed in Scotland long after the end of the medieval period.

Scandinavian influence was also to be seen on helmets in Scotland during this period. The popular image of the Viking horned helmet did not exist in reality – this was a

Macbeth: Tyrant King of Scotland

Ancient Sea Warfare

Even before the Vikings arrived in the waters around the British Isles, sea warfare was already well established. The Romans knew of both the Picts and the Scots-Irish as sea raiders, and the Roman writer Vegetius recorded camouflaged Roman ships in the fourth century AD; many ships in the Classical period were accompanied by contingents of marines (warriors trained to fight at sea). The earliest reference to a sea battle in the British Isles is that between the Cenel Loairn and the Cenel n Gahrain in AD 719 (Foster, 1996: 102).

As ships and boats were used in the main to transport warriors to a battle on land, battles which took place at sea in the Viking Age closely resembled land battles. Ships did not carry rams or have main armaments like the ships of later navies, and instead relied upon pulling close to their opponents and bombarding the crew and structure with arrows (and perhaps fire). When suitably subdued through such an attack, the triumphant ship's marines would then board the enemy ship and remove any remaining threat – while keeping as many of the enemy crew alive as required to man the ship if it was to be taken as a prize. Marines did not wear heavy armour (the threat of going overboard and drowning must have been a very real one), instead wearing perhaps only a helmet and leather jerkin. Shields would have been useful in defence but would have proved cumbersome when boarding an enemy ship, and spears and short swords would have been useful in the eventual assault.

figment of the overactive Victorian imagination – but 'spectacled' helmets, with reinforced metal work around the eyes, and spangelhelm style helmets were introduced into the British Isles around this time. Spangelhelms had been seen in Britain towards the end of the Roman era, but it seems likely that helmets became quite rare between the end of the Roman Empire and the establishment of Scandinavian influence in the British Isles.

An eleventh-century king and his personal retinue, including a shield-bearer. Only the king wears chainmail body armour. (From Hewitt's *Ancient Armour and Weapons in Europe*, 1855)

Macbeth: Tyrant King of Scotland

The most common weapons, amongst professional
warriors and peasants alike, would have been spears and
javelins. Indeed, the spear was the mainstay weapon of most
armies throughout the ancient and medieval periods. The
Scottish spear during Macbeth's era would not have been
the lengthy pike made famous by the Scots Common army
under leaders such as William Wallace and Robert Bruce, but
a shorter, 8-foot long pole with a blade between 6 and 8
inches long mounted upon it. Some spears were exclusively
for stabbing at opponents with, whereas some blades were
designed to slash at an opponent also – almost an early form
of halberd. Some early medieval poetry, mostly Germanic
and Scandinavian, make mention of four-sided spearheads,
designed for piercing armour; it is likely that the
Scandinavian influence on eleventh-century Scottish armies
meant that these weapons were also used by Scots warriors.

Leather armour would have been used by Macbeth's
warriors, in conjunction with chainmail armour, and its use
would have extended to the construction of shields. Perhaps
fewer warriors would have been so well armed as is
traditionally considered in Viking Age Britain – an Irish
chronicle entry referring to the Battle of Clontarf between
the Irish and Vikings in 1014 records that only 1000 or 2000
Vikings wore chainmail armour; the rest presumably wore
either leather armour or were protected only by their
shields. Although some warriors, including those most
heavily influenced by the Norsemen and English, would
have carried large shields, Scottish shields appear to have
been smaller, rounded leather 'target' shields. Chieftains and

professional warriors could have had well decorated shields, but it is also possible that – given the likelihood of a shield being irreparably damaged on the field – many warriors went into battle with roughly finished or undecorated shields, not wishing to expend the time decorating a potentially discardable, throwaway item. Many different decorative patterns and colours would have been used on Scottish, Anglo-Saxon and Viking shields at this time; the Pictish love of complex art may have been taken up by their unified Scottish grandchildren, and an old Irish reference mentions that the Scottish High King's chiefs at Scone were 'of the bright shields' (Karunanithy, 1998: 21). Celtic Irish and Welsh sources, which are both curiously better documented than their Scottish brethren, record shields of white, red and white, dark red, dark blue, dun, purple, red-brown, green, and yellow speckled; one should imagine that contemporary Scottish warriors would have been arrayed with a similarly colourful mix. A fanciful nineteenth-century frieze in the National Portrait Gallery in Edinburgh depicts Macbeth with a kite shield emblazoned with an intricate Celtic cross and knot work; kite shields had been used in England from the beginning of the eleventh century, but we do not know how quickly their use spread to Scotland – certainly the medieval Lewis chessmen carry them, but a great number of the English on the Bayeux Tapestry are not depicted as carrying such shields, preferring the older, traditional round shield of a foot warrior.

Although predominantly foot armies, the Scots of Macbeth's era undoubtedly included some mounted warriors. Pictish carvings show mixed armies of spearmen and horsemen, and it is known that the militarily inept King Duncan sent horsemen against the defences of Durham; Macbeth's Norman followers would almost certainly have fought from horseback, and would probably have influenced their companion Scottish nobles to fight as heavy cavalry too. The tenth-century battle of Brunanburh apparently saw the use of English horsemen, against the usual tradition of Anglo-Saxons fighting on foot. Cavalrymen at this period, whether heavily armoured in chainmail, helmet and with shield like the later Normans were depicted on the Bayeux Tapestry and on the Pictish carved stones, or more lightly armoured with only a shield for protection, would have advanced on their opponents and flung javelins. Charging horsemen with couched lances do not seem to have existed in the British Isles at this time, and it is far more likely that mounted warriors would have hurled javelins from a distance, and if heavily armoured, perhaps followed this up with attack using sword or axe.

Clothing for the warriors of Macbeth would have varied greatly according to class; poor, conscripted warriors would have worn a variety of dull or natural coloured tunics and leggings, mostly in a variety of browns and off-whites. The ubiquitous chequered Celtic cloth was probably used, although not in the distinctive tartan patterns of the Highlander (these were not formalized until several centuries later). Upper-class warriors and nobles may have worn brighter colours; the northern British epic *Y Gododdin* mentions sixth-century nobles wearing red and white (red

and purple were traditional colours implying nobility
throughout much of Europe), and early medieval Irish laws
noted that kings were allowed to wear seven colours
(including purple and blue), upper classes were allowed five
colours, and the lower classes two colours (yellow, white and
black being common). Writing in 1582, George Buchanan
noted that the favourite colours of the highland Scots, both
in his own time and earlier, were blue and purple. Although
there is no firm evidence to support this, it is possible that
these two colours may have been popular at the time of
Macbeth. Viking colours popularly included red, blue, green,
white, black and grey. On the whole, Scandinavian warriors
appear to have been quite vain regarding their appearance –
they bathed and changed their clothes regularly, and it seems
that they may even have worn eye make-up.

Armies were much smaller than those of later medieval
battles; tactical prowess was also at a minimum during the
era of Macbeth. As in the wars of Arthur, Beowulf, and
countless other heroes of this age, battle would have been a
test of brawn and arms instead of a warlord's use of tactics
and manoeuvre. The eleventh-century battle would have
mostly been a short and bloody affair, over in perhaps thirty
minutes to an hour, and taking the form of disorganized
skirmish – likened by some commentators to a modern riot.
The most common formation of armies in early medieval
Britain was the shield wall. Used from the late Roman
period right into the later medieval era, the shield wall
comprised a body of tightly packed warriors, each using
their large wooden shield to protect their own body and

those of their comrades; such a formation would have required a fair degree of co-ordination to make any kind of manoeuvre whilst maintaining a defensive wall. This therefore explains the lack of tactical prowess on the part of army commanders, who would have almost certainly have spent most of their time attempting to keep their shield walls intact. The Anglo-Saxon battle poem 'The Battle of Maldon' gives a vivid description of such fighting:

> Thus stoutly stood the resolute
> fighters in battle, fervidly strove
> to be the first with spear there
> to wrest life from a fated man,
> warriors with weapons. The slain fell to earth.
> (Rodrigues, 1996: LL 122–6)

Scandinavian and Anglo-Saxon allies were enlisted into Scottish armies; they usually provided a backbone of heavily armoured infantrymen around which a formidable fighting force could be built. Macbeth is also recorded as having a number of Norman allies, who would probably have fought as their relatives did at Hastings twelve years later – as heavily armoured, javelin-casting horsemen.

In addition to the small, professional body of warriors that permanently resided with a warlord of Macbeth's rank, such a leader would be able to call upon the freemen of the realm to bear arms in times of national danger. This law was very similar to the system governing the fyrd in England and the later medieval system of feudal hosts. The warriors called up

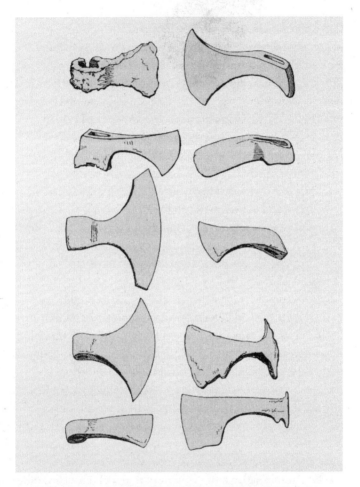

A collection of early medieval axe heads showing both Frankish and Danish influence. The axe was quickly adopted as a weapon of choice in Scotland, England and Ireland after early experience of the weapon in the hands of Norse warriors. (From Hewitt's *Ancient Armour and Weapons in Europe*, 1855)

under such systems could swell the ranks of an army to several thousand men, but were mostly poorly armed and armoured. Such a warrior's role on the battlefield was to provide a spear hedge in line formation, preventing the enemy from destroying the army before his own professional warriors – his martial and social superiors – could do the same to the enemy force. Having said this, the English equivalent, the fyrd, could be fairly effective as a fighting force. For example, the fyrd managed to defeat invading Scandinavian raiders in four out of seven recorded battles between the years AD 840 and AD 851. The quality of such a force could therefore be fairly influential on the outcome of any battle, and if a warlord were able to motivate such peasant militias into cohesive fighting forces, success could be met with.

The battle of Brunanburh in AD 937, between a combined Scots and Norse-Irish force and an English army saw each side putting around 18,000 men on the battlefield. The later battle of Stamford Bridge (between the English and Norse as a prelude to Hastings in 1066) saw forces of around 8000 to 10,000; Hastings itself, fought between the English and Normans in 1066, saw around 2000 huscarles and 5500 fyrd opposed by 2000 cavalry and 5000 infantry. Such large armies were relatively uncommon however, and for armies of individual kingdoms around 2000 or 3000 would have been far more common, unless all commoners were also called to arms. The battle of Dunsinane reportedly saw the loss of 3000 Scots and about half that number of their enemy; if these figures are accurate, Dunsinane would

have been one of the larger battles fought in early medieval
Britain (estimating the casualties to be around a quarter of
the total number of combatants). One Viking army in
Scotland was recorded as being commanded by eight kings
and twenty earls – each of whom controlled 1000 men; such
a significant force would only have been raised and capable
of sustaining itself on a very large campaign, but it is possible
that the number of earls and kings is correct, but that each
controlled a significantly smaller retinue. The documented
battle between the English and the Danes at Maldon in 991
was fought between a raiding army and a locally raised
force, similar to the wars of Macbeth before the involvement
of Siward; both armies at Maldon probably numbered
around 2500 men. The 180 men recorded as dying with
Crinan in 1045 were probably his personal retinue of
professional warriors; many of the smaller skirmishes which
comprised a campaign alongside the major battles would
have been fought by such small forces – and as proved in
Crinan's case, could be equally deadly to even the highest
ranking warlords.

Longboats were a convenient means of transporting large
numbers of warriors quickly and efficiently; the average
Viking boat carried between sixty-five and eighty-five men,
and large raiding fleets would probably have consisted of
between ten and thirty ships. Orvar Odd's Saga refers to a
force of fifteen ships, each crewed by 120 men, as very great.

Evocative visual images of battles in Scotland between the
demise of the Roman Empire and arrival of the Norsemen
can be seen on the carved Pictish stones still found around

A well-armoured eleventh-century warrior, typical of the professional fighters present in the armies of both Macbeth and his enemies. (From *L'Art Pour Tous, Encyclopedie de l'Art Industriel et Decoratif*)

the countryside and in museums. Although of a slightly earlier date than the wars of Macbeth, these decaying visual records of historical events present the viewer with peculiarly Scottish aspects of battle. One carving shows spearmen clustered together in what has often been interpreted as an early form of Scottish pike formation; more accurately, it shows a body of spear-armed infantrymen, like those of any other army of this period, gathered together for mutual protection. Other carvings show a variety of horsemen, some heavily armoured (and sometimes adorned with helmets bearing a remarkable resemblance to the Coppergate helmet of York), and others wearing only a tunic for protection. Most carry spears, and some carry shields or swords.

Another useful source of information on warfare in Britain at this time is the Anglo-Saxon battle poem, 'The Battle of Brunanburh'. In AD 937, King Constantine of Scotland and Olaf Guthfrithson – one of the last Norse kings of York – invaded England together, and were defeated by the Anglo-Saxon forces under the command of Athelstan. On the battlefield lay the bodies of five dead kings, seven of Olaf's earls, and the 'aged Constantine, the hoary-headed warrior' lost his son. It is probable that each army comprised around 18,000 men; for this period, forces as large as this were unusual, and clearly represent a massive investment by both sides in terms of manpower and politics – such large alliances between kingdoms were not common. Simeon of Durham claimed that there were 615 boatloads of Vikings at the battle, whilst another source mentions 4000 Vikings and

Macbeth: Tyrant King of Scotland

30,000 Scots. Whatever the actual numbers, both sides drew up in two large bodies – seemingly a common tactic in early medieval Britain, and the Scots were routed first, allowing the free Saxon command to crash into the flank of the Vikings, destroying that too.

William Shakespeare has, without question, immortalized the name of a relatively obscure Scottish ruler through a play based only remotely on historical fact. Contradicting the picture that Shakespeare painted (itself based on Holinshed's text) Macbeth appears to have been a worthy king, fiercely independent of English intervention. Warfare was endemic to life in the north of the British Isles at this time, and Macbeth acted as any worthy ruler in the defence of his people and territory. Later tales of Macbeth were constructed by those wishing to condemn his politics (Shakespeare, for example, would have wished to incriminate any pro-Scottish, anti-English monarch due to the political situation of his own lifetime), and discredited him as a leader. Warfare in Macbeth's time was very unsophisticated and relied on personal bravery and strength; a warlord would have needed to inspire his men to victory through his own martial deeds, rather than keeping a cool head and out-manoeuvring his opponents. The Viking influence among professional warriors in eleventh-century Scotland dominated over earlier Caledonian and Pictish methods, and Scottish warfare and politics suffered many external intrusions from English and Scandinavian leaders.

HIAWATHA
Deliverer of the Nation

enry Wadsworth Longfellow's 1855 narrative poem
is loosely based on Native American folklore, but
placed itself in a firmly accessible position for
nineteenth-century American–European readers.

Unlike the other characters featured in this book,
Hiawatha was not renowned as a warrior, but as a
peacemaker – a far more worthy role in the eyes of a modern
reader as well as that of a Native American storyteller, it
would seem. The backdrop to Hiawatha explains his inclusion
in this book, however, as it involves the warring North
American tribes and a highly important event in the history
of North America – the arrival of the Europeans.

Longfellow's poem represents Hiawatha as the son of the
West Wind ('Mudjekeewis') and Wenonah. In a series of
twenty-two verses and a prologue, or 'cantos', Longfellow
retells Hiawatha's life from his early years in the forests,
through to his final, ostentatious departure to the Island of
the Blessed.

Hiawatha was born into a nation that had only recently
started to consider that conflict among its tribes might have
been detrimental to advancement. Gitche Manito, the

Hiawatha: Deliverer of the Nation

Great Spirit, 'He the Master of Life', had called the warring
tribes together: the Delawares, the Mohawks, the
Shoshonies, the Blackfeet, the Pawnees, the Omahas, the
Choctaws, the Camanches, the Mandans, the Dacotahs, the
Hurons, and the Ojibways all came together to hear him
speak his council:

> And they stood there on the meadow,
> With their weapons and their war-gear,
> Painted like the leaves of Autumn,
> Painted like the sky of morning,
> Wildly glaring at each other;
> (1993: 7)

Gitche Manito announced that he was tired of the tribes
fighting one another, of the dissent and vengeance, and
proclaimed that:

> 'I will send a Prophet to you,
> A Deliverer of the nations,
> Who shall guide you and shall teach you,
> Who shall toil and suffer with you.'
> (1993: 8)

This Prophet was Hiawatha, son of the West Wind
'Mudjekeewis'. Mudjekeewis himself was a great and
accomplished warrior, who defeated many mythical beasts in
combat; his son Hiawatha demonstrated different strengths –
those of a wise man and orator of knowledge.

Warriors

Hiawatha grew from childhood in the woodlands; he spoke to animals and learned his field craft quickly as an accomplished hunter:

> Forth into the forest straightway
> All alone walked Hiawatha
> Proudly, with his bow and arrows;
> And the birds sang round him, o'er him:
> 'Do not shoot us, Hiawatha!'
> Sang the robin, the Opechee,
> Sang the blue-bird, the Owaissa:
> 'Do not shoot us, Hiawatha!'
> (1993: 23)

Hiawatha had been well provided for by his father, the West Wind. He had magical mittens – called Minjekahwun – with which he could crush rocks. He had enchanted moccasins in which he could stride a full mile with every pace.

> Swift of foot was Hiawatha;
> He could shoot an arrow from him,
> And run forward with such fleetness,
> That the arrow fell behind him!
> (1993: 26)

Perhaps more importantly, Hiawatha was aware of the beauty of the land around him, and learned more from his father the West Wind when he travelled to see him:

Hiawatha: Deliverer of the Nation

'Go back to your home and people,
Live among them, toil among them,
Cleanse the earth from all that harms it,
Clear the fishing-grounds and rivers,
Slay all the monsters and magicians,
All the giants, the Wendigoes,
All the serpents, the Kenabeeks,
As I slew the Mishe-Mokwa,
Slew the Great Bear of the mountains.'
(1993: 32)

On his trip home, Hiawatha stopped to buy some arrows in
the lands of the Dacotah; Hiawatha's eyes focused on the
arrow-maker's daughter, the dark-eyed Minnehaha
('Laughing Water'):

Who shall say what dreams of beauty
Filled the heart of Hiawatha?
(1993: 33)

Hiawatha set about the tasks laid down to him by his father
the West Wind, defeating opponents such as Mishe-Nahma
('The Great Sturgeon') and the cunning Pau-Puk-Keewis
('The Storm Fool'). He wooed and won the heart and hand
of the arrow-maker's daughter Minnehaha, the 'Handsomest
of all women' (1993: 69).

Eventually, Hiawatha's work could be seen to have effect;
enemies from the animal kingdom had been tamed, the
harvests had been secured through Hiawatha's actions against

them, and peace was gradually spreading across the land as
people became more content with the quality of their lives:

> Buried was the bloody hatchet,
> Buried was the dreadful war-club,
> Buried were all warlike weapons,
> And the war-cry was forgotten.
> There was peace among the nations,
> Unmolested roved the hunters,
> Built the birch canoe for sailing,
> Caught fish in the lake and river,
> Shot the deer and trapped the beaver;
> (1993: 94)

Hiawatha also had to battle against the Evil Spirits, who were
unhappy at the unity his actions were bringing. Unable to
reach Hiawatha in person, they instead killed his dear friend
Chibiabos in a hunting accident; Hiawatha was protected from
the spirits by the native medicine men, who built him a Sacred
Lodge to seek sanctuary in while mourning his friend's death.
After the soul of Chibiabos was purged, Hiawatha travelled
among the Native Americans, teaching the use of medicine
and the 'sacred art of healing' (1993: 112). Despite Hiawatha's
knowledge of medicine, Minnehaha died in a famine:

> And his bursting heart within him
> Uttered such a cry of anguish,
> That the forest moaned and shuddered,
> (1993: 145)

Hiawatha: Deliverer of the Nation

Henry Wadsworth Longfellow

The poet Longfellow is single handedly responsible for introducing Hiawatha into the heart of the emerging (Europeanized) American folk cycle of the nineteenth century.

Born in 1807 in Portland, Longfellow studied at Bowdoin College in Brunswick. His skill with languages became apparent during his studies, and he was sent to Europe in preparation for the appointment of Chair in Foreign Languages. Although offered a post at Harvard upon his return to the United States, Longfellow had acquired a love for travel and instead went abroad again. In 1835, with the premature death of his wife, Longfellow finally returned to the United States and took up the post of Professor of Modern languages and Literature at Harvard between 1836 and 1854.

As well as *Hiawatha* – published amidst great popularity in 1855 – Longfellow also penned *Ballads and Other Poems* (1841), and *Tales of a Wayside Inn* (1863). The latter included the well known 'Paul Revere's Ride'.

In old age, Hiawatha observed the coming of the Europeans to his land. The white faces of the newcomers, and the hair-covered chins made Hiawatha's people whoop with derision. Hiawatha did not laugh himself, instead realizing that he had foreseen this event in a vision. He advised his people to welcome the strangers with friendship, as that had been the

advice given to him by Gitche Manito. Yet Hiawatha foresaw
something else in his vision also:

> 'The darker, drearier vision
> Passed before me, vague and cloud-like.
> I beheld our nations scattered,
> All forgetful of my counsels,
> Weakened, warring with each other,'
> (1993: 153)

In his vision, Hiawatha's people were swept westwards, 'Like
the withered leaves of Autumn.' (1993: 153). With the arrival
of the white settlers and his advice to befriend them, and his
work in uniting his own people before this arrival, the task
for which Hiawatha had been sent was now complete.
Society had progressed to a civilized state and the people
had learned the ways of peace, so he could now depart to
the Island of the Blessed.

> On the shore stood Hiawatha,
> Turned and waved his hand at parting;
> On the clear and luminous water
> Launched his birch canoe for sailing,
> From the pebbles of the margin
> Shoved it forth into the water;
> (1993: 159)

And then Hiawatha sailed west into the sunset and onward
to the Island of the Blessed, hoping that the advice and

wisdom that he had given to his people would help them to avoid his vision of destruction.

Longfellow used the semi-historical character of Hiawatha as the basis of an essentially Romantic European tale, which, whilst retaining some elements and characters of Native American myth, was aimed to be read by European Americans more used to the writings of Byron, Tennyson and the Brontës than the orations of Native American storytellers. The tales that Longfellow based his poem on, though, were actually derived from Algonquian myths from the Hare Cycle.

Before Longfellow's hijacking of the character, Native American mythology told its own stories of Hiawatha. In these tales, Hiawatha was closer to his historical, sixteenth-century counterpart – an Onondaga chieftain and Amerindian teacher. He planned a peaceful union between all of the tribes of the Iroquoian and Algonquian cultures who had been involved in intertribal conflict for many years. Hiawatha's plans were strongly opposed by a great warrior and shaman named Atotarho – whose head was covered with snakes for hair, and whose anger was so fierce that anyone who caught his stare would immediately fall dead with fear. As Hiawatha and Atotarho argued at a tribal council, Atotarho summoned a great white bird from the sky, which swooped upon Hiawatha's daughter and slew her.

Hiawatha left Atoharho's council meeting when this happened, sure that there was no point in trying to reason with his bloodthirsty opponent. Travelling up river in a magical white canoe, Hiawatha arrived at the settlements of the Oneida tribe, the chieftain of whom, named Dekanawida, greatly appreciated Hiawatha's wisdom and quickly became a staunch friend and ally. Together, Hiawatha and Dekanawida converted the Mohawk and Cayuga tribes to Hiawatha's vision of unity. Atotarho, having seen these strong-willed tribes converted, conceded, joining Hiawatha's confederacy, which formed the League of the Long House. Hiawatha, his work complete in bringing peace and unity to the Iroquoian and Algonquian tribes, sailed away across the Great Lakes in his magical white canoe to the Land of the Souls in the far west.

The idea of the Noble Savage developed throughout the nineteenth century, exemplified through works such as Mary Shelley's *Frankenstein*, in a world where the 'civilized' European societies were coming into contact with other cultures. These cultures were 'savages' to most European minds, and debate sprang up surrounding the idea that a non-European education could create more than just a savage creature, and may indeed have developed something which could not be paralleled – a presence of mind uncorrupted by Western thought. Longfellow's heroic Hiawatha adds to this debate, as the poem charts the progression of Native American civilization through the hero's actions, from its beginnings through to the beginning of colonialism.

In History

In many respects, Native American mythology can be compared to Celtic legend. Just like the stories told by the Iron Age Celts, Native American mythology relied upon oral tradition rather than the written word, and incorporated many similar and colourful images and tales of brave warriors and wise shamans, wizards or bards.

Longfellow successfully moved his Native American character away from the stereotype that was emerging of the early Americans in the mid nineteenth century, which continued to be a popular view well into the twentieth century. This stereotype was, according to Daniel Aaron's thoughtful introduction to Hiawatha, namely:

> …the stoic warrior, the sententious orator, the cunning and treacherous savage brandishing a bloody tomahawk (1993: xii)

The earliest Native Americans left their mark on the continent 60,000 years ago, migrating from the temperate plains of Central Asia through Siberia and across the Chukotka peninsula into North America – via modern-day Alaska. The Stone Age nomad hunter-gatherers gradually moved south down the Columbia River into the warmer lands of the modern southern States, and began hunting the buffalo which would provide a staple food well into the late nineteenth century.

Famously, the Native Americans were banded into as many tribes as there were 'stars in the sky'. The area of what is now New York State in the north-eastern United States was the homeland of the Iroquois (pre-European cultural division in North America was decided by linguistic group). The Iroquois principally consisted of six tribes – the Seneca, the Oneida, the Onondaga, the Cayuga, the Mohawk and the Tusorora – but also encompassed some of their neighbours – the Huron, the Erie and the Susquehanna. The Iroquois faced on-going struggles against their neighbours, notably the Huron tribes. The early seventeenth-century population of the Iroquois was proposed to be around 20,000 at a conservative estimate.

In 1497, John Cabot became the first known European to set foot on North American soil – Newfoundland – since the Viking adventurers several centuries before. Contact between the natives and explorers occurred throughout what is now Canada and the northern area of the United States. French, British, Spanish and Portuguese explorers ventured on to the mainland, and in 1535–6, Frenchman Jacques Cartier sailed up the St Lawrence River and formed a fragile alliance between the European settlers and the Native Americans. From this time on, through the eighteenth-century conflict in Canada between Britain and France, right up to a number of border actions by the famous Canadian 'Mounties' in the late nineteenth century, relationships between the natives and Europeans fluctuated between uneasy peace and extreme violence. Despite the settlement by Europeans, 'colonization in North America looked very much less impressive than that further south,' (Roberts [ed] 1996: 270) until the start of the eighteenth century.

By the time that the first Europeans arrived, Iroquoian culture had begun to prosper, and had advanced well beyond the hunter-gather society of early America. Their villages had developed stockaded defences (described by early

Hiawatha: Deliverer of the Nation

European observers as 'castles'), and legend has it that the first French explorers who encountered the Iroquois were served popcorn and maple syrup – Hiawatha's people being responsible for introducing this culinary delight into European culture.

The original Native American hero Hiawatha – whose name was first recorded as Heowenta or Haiowatha in the sixteenth century – was a Mohawk or Onondaga leader who was born in New York State. The name Hiawatha translates as 'He Who Seeks the Wampum-belt' (Spence, 1914: 382) – wampum being beads made of shell according to Longfellow's 'Vocabulary' of the 1855 poem. Hiawatha was originally known to the European colonists from Iroquois folk tales, and may once have been considered a purely mythical character.

In fact, it seems that Hiawatha was a real Native American leader, influential in the foundation of the Five Nations League (also known as the League of the Long House). The Five Nations League was an alliance of feuding Iroquois tribes – the Mohawk, Seneca, Cayuga, Onondaga and Oneida; Hiawatha was to bring these five enemies together to create a strong political unit, which lasted from the mid sixteenth century at the latest to 1775. The Native American legend of Hiawatha reflects the lasting memory of this momentous feat in the history of the previously warring tribes of the north.

Longfellow not only changed the mythology surrounding this celebrated Native American bringer of peace, but also moved Hiawatha's homeland to Minnesota. In fact,

Warriors

Longfellow's hero is essentially a combination of two characters from Native American folklore – Hiawatha and Manabozho. According to tradition, Manabozho was 'a demi-god of the Ojibways' (Spence, 1914: 223), and it was he, not Hiawatha, who undertook many of the adventures in Longfellow's poem.

Probably born around 1500, and active until about 1570, Hiawatha travelled through the Mohawk Valley, bringing the tribes to whom he orated into his peaceful Iroquois League:

> ...a new order of brotherly feeling between the peoples, not necessarily peace for all men, but rather a union of relatives.
> (Nagelfell, 1995: 10)

It has been suggested that Hiawatha's Five Nations League operated by a system of voting and election, decided by unanimous voting, and that disputes were adjudicated by arbitration instead of the former, more bloodthirsty method of warfare. This would be in keeping with the traditional form of governance in Native American tribes – a council of elders and chiefs (called 'sachems' or 'sagamores' by French witnesses) who sat to decide on tribal matters. Perhaps Hiawatha succeeded where others had failed due to his skills of oration and persuasion. If so, Lescarbot's observations are of particular interest when he states that:

> They have no special chiefs with absolute command, but rather pay honour to the eldest and bravest, whom

they appoint captains by way of honour and respect,
(quoted in Heath, 1999: 137)

However Hiawatha's League had initially worked. By the
time the Iroquois came into contact with colonial statesmen,
the Europeans were impressed with this display of unity and
civility, quite unlike the culture experienced in previous
contact with the natives of North America:

> When the Iroquois…were found by the French and
> Dutch they occupied the western part of what is now
> New York State, and were at a much more advanced
> stage of culture than most of the Indian tribes. They
> tilled the ground, cultivating maize and tobacco, and
> were skilled in the arts of war and diplomacy. They
> were greatly strengthened by the Grand league, or
> 'Kayanerenh Kowa', which, as has been said, was
> founded by the chief Hiawatha, and were much the
> most important of the North American tribes.
> (Spence, 1914: 224)

The League was also united in warfare against non-Iroquois
enemies, allowing the Iroquois to grow and flourish as a
nation; when Samuel de Champlain wrote of the region in
the early seventeenth century, the Iroquois and their Huron
neighbours were the region's two most powerful tribes, yet
had been at war for around fifty years.

By 1715, a sixth tribe joined the league – the Tuscarora –
and the union became known as the Six Nations. Perhaps,

given the general European view of Native Americans from the earliest contact to the end of the nineteenth century, it is little wonder that as time passed, the historical Hiawatha became a mystical, supernatural leader famed for undertaking impossible tasks. Hiawatha, therefore, was an ideal figure for Longfellow to hang his Native American hero's mantle on.

Yet the historical figure whose name Longfellow borrowed for his work seems to have been a very important figure in the history and cultural advancement of the Native Americans. As Lewis Spence proclaimed in the early twentieth century:

> ...one prefers to think of this Iroquois statesman as a real man, a bright particular star in a dark sky of savagery and ignorance.
> (1914: 228)

In Battle

Sources for Native American warfare mostly survive as European or colonial American accounts of battles against them. What becomes immediately apparent, and is of great significance when discussing warfare in the era of Hiawatha, is that the development of Native American warfare seems to have been virtually stagnant between the first accounts of Europeans in battle against the natives and the final accounts of The Plains Wars of the late nineteenth century. Accounts of Native American tactics and weapons in the sixteenth century have much in common with those of the nineteenth century before gunpowder weapons became widespread among the native tribes. Therefore, as early accounts are few and far between, our knowledge of warfare in Hiawatha's time can, within reason, be supplemented with accounts from later centuries.

Native American warriors have been described as the best light cavalry in the world; but they were much more than just light cavalrymen:

> In the art of guerrilla warfare the Indians have always shown exceptional skill. Armed with bow and arrow, a war-club, or a tomahawk, they carried on a fierce resistance to the incursions of the white man.
> (Spence, 1914: 63)

Raiding, ambushes and surprise attacks on enemy villages were the most common tactics used by the Iroquois and their foes. The Iroquois and Hurons would also face their enemies on the open battlefield, but many of their smaller, less powerful opponents shied away from such battles, not being able to field a large enough army to make a decent fight of it. Lescarot spoke of the tactics of the Native Americans thus:

> Their wars are carried on solely by surprises, in the dead of the night, or, if by moonlight, by ambushes or subtlety.
> (quoted in Heath, 1999: 138)

Shamans and Medicine Men

In Native American mythology only the Shaman (more popularly known as 'Medicine Man') had the power and vision to communicate with the spirit gods. He acted as a mediator between these spirits and the mortal people of his tribe, and could speak to the souls of the dead; the Shaman was also the guardian of oral folklore, the healer of the ill, and the mystical prophet of the tribe's future. In so many ways, the Native American Shaman fulfilled many of the legendary roles performed by the Druid of Celtic tradition or the soothsayer of the early Classical world.

The initiation ceremonies and learning involved to become a Shaman began when an ordinary mortal 'received the call'. This call – a religious vision or happening – allowed the mortal to begin their initiation in the rites of Shamanism. The Shaman began by enacting a symbolic death and resurrection, indicating a new way of life; physical and mental changes placed the initiate Shaman between the worlds of the spirit gods and the mortals – he would see the spirits of the universe and leave his own body in the form of a spirit, journeying through the Underworld and the heavens. In this journey, the Shaman was taught how to address and communicate with the many Otherworld spirits whom he met, so that he could contact them when he returned to his tribe as a fully initiated Shaman.

A Shaman was also skilled in hypnosis and exorcism; as Lewis Spence noted, 'The Indian assigns all illness or bodily discomfort to supernatural agency' (1914: 136-7), and as such, the Shaman fulfilled an important clinical and physiological role in Native American society.

Hiawatha: Deliverer of the Nation

Raids were carried out in the summer or autumn, to make use of the dense foliage covering the countryside. Canoes were used strategically as transport, because water was often an easier terrain to travel over quickly than broken ground to all pre-industrial societies. Fieldcraft and woodcraft were important to war parties, who reportedly travelled in each other's footsteps so as not to betray the number of warriors in the group. Reconnaissance of common travel routes (both land and river based) was an effective way to spot enemy penetration, and to counter this, war parties would travel only by night once within a few days' march of their enemies.

Full-scale battles also occurred. These took place by daylight, to prevent them becoming too chaotic for the commanders to control. On such occasions, the warriors would draw up into close order formations, fighting much like pre-feudal European armies in a series of wild charges and missile assaults. Some reports show battle tactics to have been well planned in advance of the action, with individual warriors or units being told exactly where or exactly whom to fight against.

In battle, Native American warriors could fight as individuals or as part of a group; they could also fight with stealth or vigorous strength. Infiltration of enemy positions was a speciality, with warriors optimizing their use of the terrain, only breaking cover to fire weapons or charge an enemy in hand to hand combat. Wild charges at close range, preceded by missile fire, were another favoured tactic. Both tactics lasted through the succeeding centuries, and were recorded in detail by the witnesses of nineteenth-century battles, such as the Fetterman Massacre and The Battle of the Little Bighorn.

Warriors

Bow fire seems to have been used to lay down a barrage of fire, as opposed to a few well-aimed shots. Even so, marksmanship must have been high – these skills were honed down through hunting – and individuals would probably have been able to act as 'snipers' if so required. When arrows ran out, the warriors would charge into hand to hand combat with their tomahawks and spears, shouting out defiant war cries to lower the enemy's morale:

> It is a shrill and piercing note, sounded long, and with a swell, on the highest key of the voice, with the most rapid vibration possible, made by the striking of the flat of the hand or the fingers against the lips.
> (Catlin, 1875: 76–7)

In 1600, the estimated size of the Iroquois tribes was around 20,000 in total; from this populace, the tribe could muster a grand total of around 2500 warriors. The main enemy of the Iroquois – the Hurons – could muster around 500 less warriors, from a population of 30,000 according to Champlain. Of course, many raiding parties would have consisted of a number of warriors counted in the tens or perhaps hundreds rather than a whole tribe being mustered. The nineteenth-century observer George Catlin wrote of the warfare that he observed while living among Native American tribesmen:

> Warfare amongst those people is generally conducted by small parties who volunteer under a war-chief, to avenge

some wrong or cruelty inflicted by their enemy; and
when a few scalps are taken, sufficient for retaliation, they
generally return, make a great boast, and entertain the
villagers with the scalp dance and other ceremonies.
(1875: 75)

The oratory skills of a war party leader wishing to raise his
warriors for such a raid must have been almost as strong as
the spoken wisdom of Hiawatha if credence is given to one
such speech:

> 'Hear my voice, ye warlike birds!
> I prepare a feast for you to batten on;
> I see you cross the enemy's lines;
> Like you I shall go.
> I wish the swiftness of your wings;
> I wish the vengeance of your claws;
> I muster my friends;
> I follow your flight.
> Ho, ye young men that are warriors,
> Look with wrath on the battlefield!
> (quoted in Spence, 1914: 70)

Fortification played a part in Iroquoian strategy. Villages were
encased by stockades, and sometimes even moats. These must
have amounted to significant obstacles to attacking native
war parties, as even European expeditions against such
villages encountered difficulties storming them, even with
the added destructive qualities of cannons.

Warriors

Obviously, costume among the many tribes of Native
Americans varied as much as the national dress of different
European countries; according to the Bureau of American
Ethnology, Hiawatha's people would have been dressed as
follows:

> ALGONQUIAN–IROQUOIS. Northern – Men:
> Robe, shirt-coat, long-coat, trousers, leggings,
> moccasins, breech-cloth, turban. Virginia – Men
> and women: Cloak, waist-garment, moccasins,
> sandals (?), breech-cloth (?). Western – Men: Robe,
> long dress-shirt, long leggings, moccasins, bandolier-
> bag. Women: Long dress-shirt, short leggings,
> moccasins, belt. Arctic – Men: Long coat, open in
> front, short breeches, leggings, moccasins, gloves or
> mittens, cap or headdress. Women: Robe, shirt-dress,
> leggings, moccasins, belt, cap, and sometimes a
> shoulder mantle.
> (quoted in Spence, 1914: 58)

Of course, this traditional dress would not have been
uniform; some Algonquians (who lived in the same
geographical locale) were known to walk naked, and dress
would certainly have changed depending upon the climate.
In warm weather, especially for energetic activities such as
hunting and fighting, warriors may have worn no more than
a breechcloth. Most clothing was manufactured from deer,
otter, moose, lynx, bear, beaver or seal skin, either
incorporating the fur or as finished, smooth hide. Red and

black appear to have been popular clothing dye colours. When trade contacts were established with the European settlers, a few items of European clothing were worn by Native Americans.

Tattooing and painting were common forms of decoration amongst the Iroquois; these could be geometric or striped patterns, or images of animals or spirits. Yellow, blue, red and black were common colours for decoration among many Native American warriors. Facial, throat, chest and limb skin decoration was common; feathers and silver and copper jewellery were also frequently observed by European adventurers. Writing in the nineteenth century, although probably very little different to the natives of the sixteenth century, George Catlin noted that:

> Each warrior has some peculiar and known way of painting, by which he is recognized by his fellow-warriors, at a distance at which they would not distinguish him from his comrades from the natural differences, so great is their resemblance in the open air when naked and in action.'
> (1875: 72)

The most common weapons amongst the Iroquois and their enemies were bows, war clubs (or tomahawks), and perhaps more unusually, javelins. All of these weapons could be used on foot or from horseback, as suited the Native American style of fluid battle.

Warriors

The Battle of the Little Bighorn

The most famous, and probably best documented, battle involving Native American tribesmen was the Battle of the Little Bighorn, which led to the defeat of George Armstrong Custer and several companies of the Seventh Cavalry in 1876. A colossal mound of oral history, interviews with participants, and theoretical analysis has been accumulated in the years since the battle took place. Richard Allan Fox Jr's reports on the excellent excavation and modern studies of the battle site – which happens to be the best example of battlefield archaeology in the world to date – have added much to our knowledge.

Although several centuries after warfare in the age of Hiawatha, a number of tactics and activities occurred in Custer's defeat which would have been vividly familiar to those whom Hiawatha persuaded to join him in peace:

Repeatedly he shot at soldiers on Custer Hill, jumping up to fire, then falling down to crawl ahead again.
(Standing Bear's actions, quoted by Fox, 1993: 356)

...the soldiers all were running toward the Hunkpapas (Sioux) on foot... The Hunkpapas said: 'Hokahey!' and charged at them. The soldiers were running downhill and the Hunkpapas were charging. When they saw us, the soldiers swung down... The Hunkpapas ran right up to the soldiers and encircled them from all sides.
(Iron Hawk's testimony, quoted in Fox, 1993: 203)

Hiawatha: Deliverer of the Nation

The warriors... were shifting from shelter to shelter, each... trying to get close enough to strike a coup blow... upon a living enemy.
(Kate Bighead's testimony, quoted in Fox 1993: 199)

Iroquoian bows were reportedly about 5 or 5½ feet long, and constructed from red cedar, ash, maple, fir and elm wood. Arrows were around a yard in length, and tipped with stone or bone flakes, although iron or brass heads were used if the metal was available through trade, and some arrows had only fire-sharpened wooden tips. Arrows could be delivered either in volleys, perhaps preceding a wild charge, or aimed individually by warriors skilled in the art of the bow through hunting with the weapon. It was a long time before gunpowder weapons were able to match bows in terms of rate of fire, range and accuracy – it can be argued that the British army did not match the firepower of its Agincourt ancestors until the adoption of the magazine-loading, rifle-barrelled Lee-Metford at the end of the nineteenth century. The bow was also an extremely useful weapon in the kind of close quarter forest skirmishing common amongst the Iroquois and their enemies.

Tomahawks were usually constructed entirely of wood, although stone blades could be found – as could steel blades by the end of the seventeenth century. According to William Wood, who wrote in 1634, the war club comprised:

staves of two and a half feet long, and a knob at one
end round and as big as a football.
(quoted in Heath, 1999: 138)

Other reports described the tomahawk as a wooden mace,
or likened them to swords (these clubs presumably being of
the bladed variety). Although Mudjekeewis, a powerful
spirit, was a fictional character in Longfellow's *Hiawatha*, his
use of a tomahawk against the great bear Mishe-Mokwa
demonstrates the effectiveness of the weapon:

> Then again he raised his war-club,
> Smote again the Mishe-Mokwa
> In the middle of his forehead,
> Broke his skull, as ice is broken
> When one goes to fish in Winter.
> (1993: 11)

Javelins or throwing spears were also used. William Wood
referred to the Mohawks as using javelins tipped with seal
teeth, although we cannot be sure how accurate his
observations were. Such weapons could probably be used in
the hand as a close-combat weapon.

Shields were the most common piece of defensive
equipment used by the Iroquois. Made of leather or wood,
the Iroquoian shield usually had a rounded top edge;
leather shields were normally round, and wooden shields
were usually rectangular. Rectangular shields appear to
have been quite large – the French referred to them as

pavises, which were large European shields designed to cover the majority of the body from missile attack. Unusually amongst the Native Americans, Iroquoian warriors were sometimes recorded as having worn body armour. Champlain's *Voyages et descouvertes faites en la Nouvelle France* of 1619 includes a drawing of an Iroquois warrior in armour of woven cotton and wood; this was apparently protective against arrows but (unsurprisingly) not resistant to firearms. Armour could cover the torso only, or include leg and arm protection too, although this would surely have severely restricted movement in the fast and frantic skirmishes common amongst the Iroquois and their opponents. Despite this, armour appears to have been fairly widespread in use.

European and European–American accounts of Native American warfare often noted the mutilation of the casualties on the battlefield; this may have involved some degree of aggression, but is more commonly associated with spiritual rites, as reflected by Richard Allan Fox Jr's study of the later Little Bighorn battlefield:

> Archaeological results, in instances where sufficient human remains existed, testify to decapitation and dismemberment … Maimed enemies could not confront you in the hereafter. Also, certain marks on a body showed the ethnic identity of the one who had killed an enemy.
> (1993: 221)

An empassioned oration at a tribal gathering. (Author's collection)

Hiawatha: Deliverer of the Nation

Scalping is also known to have taken place; contemporary settlers at the time of Hiawatha recorded such events as a post battle ceremony, along with head taking. Scalps and heads were taken as trophies to the triumphant warriors' home villages.

The arrival of Europeans was to change the face of Native American warfare only very gradually. Although the introduction of gunpowder led to the gradual abandonment of the now ineffective body armour, traditional tactics and weapons prevailed in Native American armies. Gunpowder weapons were adopted to supplement bows and war clubs, but it was not until the nineteenth century that these weapons took over as one of the main armaments of Native American warbands. The weapons that had been used for centuries beforehand were well suited to the style of warfare carried out by Hiawatha's people and their descendants, evolved from hunting practices, and stood the natives in good stead for repelling the European settlers successfully for another 200 years.

Due to the nature of European colonization in North America, it is perhaps unsurprising that few deeds of pre nineteenth-century Native American warriors have popularly survived into present times. Longfellow's creative poem – itself dating to the nineteenth century – has meant that at least one early chieftain remains well known, by name if not by historical deed. Perversely, the actions of the historical Hiawatha potentially make him the most significant and impressive of the heroes featured in

this book; his unification of a
large swathe of warring tribes
stands out above and beyond the
factual deeds of any other historically
attested character in this book. Although
Hiawatha is renowned for bringing peace,
the violent background to his rise to power
qualifies his people for inclusion in this
collection of warriors; Native American
warfare was more subtle than European
warfare in many ways – rouses, ambushes and
stealth were thought of in high regard
compared to the European's favoured battle
tactic of the straight, standing fight. Although
it seems that Native American tactics stayed
comparatively stationary between the arrival
of the Europeans and the eventual demise of
the Plains Tribes, it should be noted that, even
in the latter stages of the nineteenth century
the Native Americans were considered skilled
opponents.

An early Native American tomahawk. This example has a stone
head; tomahawk typology later
evolved to include metal heads.
(Author's collection)

ROLAND
The Frankish Paladin

Roland was the hero of early France; he was the most famous of Charlemagne's Paladins, and has been put forward as the 'Christian Theseus' and the 'Achilles of the West'. The legendary Roland was the Count of Mans, and his mother was the sister of Charlemagne himself. Legend tells us that Roland was 8 feet tall.

When Roland was killed in the valley of Roncesvalles in AD 778, in the Pyrenees, with him died the flower of Frankish chivalry. Roland is the hero of *The Song of Roland*, and countless stories of his chivalric behaviour grew in the medieval period – not unlike King Arthur in England. One such folk tale, Pulci's *Morgante Maggiore*, tells of Roland converting the giant Morgante to Christianity.

The Song of Roland was written in the eleventh century, often being ascribed to the Norman writer Trouvère Théroulde. This tells the story of the death of Roland and all of Charlemagne's Paladins.

The Emperor Charlemagne had been campaigning in Spain for seven years, and had conquered the land in its entirety except for Saragossa, which was ruled by the

Warriors

Muslim Saracen king Marsile. Marsile lived in fear of
Charlemagne, as he did not wish to be converted to
Christianity by the Frankish king. Gathering a council
around him, Marsile reclined on a seat of blue marble and
asked the advice of his wisest advisors:

> 'The emperor of sweet France, Charlemagne,
> has come into this country to destroy us.
> I have no army fit to give him battle,
> nor have I men who might put his to rout.
> Since you're my wise men, give me your advice,
> so I may rest secure from death and shame.'
> (Harrison, 1970: LL 16–21)

One of Marsile's most cunning advisors, Blancandrin, was
the only counsellor to speak; wise in counsel and brave in
war, he was a loyal servant and vassal to his lord the king.
He suggested that a pledge of loyalty and service should
be sent to Charlemagne, along with a promise of Marsile
becoming a Christian himself, but still ruling in Spain as
the Frankish vassal, thereby retaining his kingship. Upon
hearing this, Marsile dismissed the council with thanks,
but retained ten of his most renowned barons (chief of
whom was Blancandrin), and asked them to travel to
Charlemagne in Cordova, bearing olive branches of peace,
to tell the Christian leader that he himself would become
Christian. Marsile intended to travel on to Aix shortly
afterwards, to meet with Charlemagne and receive his
Christian faith and law.

Roland: The Frankish Paladin

Charlemagne was in an orchard with his Twelve Peers
(the best of his warriors and advisors), at the head of an
army of 15,000 Franks when the messengers from the
Saracen king arrived. These ambassadors greeted the Franks
with all honour, and Blancandrin passed Marsile's message
on to Charlemagne – the Saracen king would become
Charlemagne's vassal king in Spain and a Christian.
Charlemagne raised his hands in thanks to God at this news,
yet, ever wise, asked how he could trust Marsile's words –
the words of his greatest opponent. Blancandrin offered
twenty hostages to Charlemagne, including his own son, and
then told Charlemagne that Marsile was now marching to
meet with the Frankish king at Aix, to be baptised.

Charlemagne held counsel with the Twelve Peers, to tell
them of this development, that Marsile would become a
Christian and a vassal of the Franks if the Frankish army left
Spain under his rule. The assembled Franks advised their
leader to beware of this promise.

Roland, one of the Twelve Peers, advised to fight Marsile
to the end, besiege Saragossa, and avenge the Franks who had
died in the war against him. The other Franks remained
silent, except for his step-father Ganelon, who hated Roland
– he advised Charlemagne to follow up the Saracen's offer,
and that any man who said otherwise had little value for the
lives of the Franks. The aged Duke Naimes spoke up to agree
with Ganelon – and then added that one of Charlemagne's
men should be sent to agree the terms of peace with Marsile.
The impetuous Roland wished to be sent on this mission, as
did the wise Archbishop Turpin. However, Charlemagne

chose Ganelon to travel, in honour of his wise counsel.
Ganelon did not wish to risk his life on so dangerous a
mission, yet had little choice but to obey. So Ganelon rode
away and shortly caught up with the Saracen ambassadors
who had delivered the original news to Charlemagne.

Roland Prepares for Battle

Count Roland rode into the Spanish pass on Veillantif, his good, fast-
gaited horse: the armor that he wears becomes in him well. The baron
rides forth, brandishing his lance: its upraised ferrule moves against the
sky, a pure white pennant laced upon its shaft, whose golden fringes
flutter at his hands. He is well built, his features frank and smiling; his
comrade comes along, not far behind: the men from France consider
him their champion. He gazes fiercely toward the Saracens, engagingly
and humbly toward the French,
(Harrison, 1970: stanza 91)

Roland is not a tragic hero, but a martyr. A tragic hero must display
flaws in his character, whereas a martyr participates in a higher reality
far beyond that expected by human reason or sense. A martyr is a
human embodiment of Christ – a Christomimetes – who earns his
martyrdom though an act of self sacrifice which allows him to become,
for the briefest of moments, a reincarnation of Christ.

Roland: The Frankish Paladin

Conversation was struck up between Ganelon and
Blancandrin on the journey into Spain. Both were wary yet
skilful statesmen, who guarded much in their outwardly
friendly conversation – yet Ganelon let slip his hatred of
Roland. Suddenly, Blancandrin addressed Ganelon in
whispered tones – if Ganelon would betray the greatly
feared warrior Roland and lead him to his death, King
Marsile would reward him greatly. The treacherous Ganelon
agreed to this readily.

Ganelon was led to meet Marsile, and was complemented
by the Saracens for his bold entrance into the hall of his
enemy. Demanding a pledge of secrecy, Marsile revealed to
Ganelon that he felt Charlemagne was now old and weak; the
Frank praised his emperor, and proclaimed that as long as the
Frankish emperor had his Twelve Peers to rely upon, he could
come to no harm. Ganelon also proudly stated that the Franks
were the world's best living warriors, to which Marsile
countered that he could bring 400,000 men to battle against
the Frankish host of 20,000. Ganelon advised against this,
saying that only wisdom could overcome the Franks. Offering
advice, in return for the death of Roland, Ganelon suggested
that Marsile should send Charlemagne vast amounts of
treasure, and the pledges that he had offered – thus the Franks
would leave Spain, 'Haughty Roland in the rearguard' (Ebbutt,
1910: 133) accompanied by the bold Oliver, whence, the
treacherous Frank exclaimed that the Saracens should:

'Send out a hundred thousand of your pagans
to make the first assault upon them there.

> The men from France will be thinned out and
> crippled –
> I do not say your side will not have losses –
> but nonetheless, attack them once again;
> there'll be no way for Roland to escape.
> And then you shall have done a knightly deed:
> throughout your lifetime you'll have no
> more war.'
> (Harrison, 1970: LL588–95)

Marsile was overjoyed with the traitor's advice, and richly rewarded Ganelon for his treachery.

Ganelon returned to Charlemagne, who had, in respect of the forthcoming treaty, retreated as far as Valtierra (closer to France). Ganelon advised the emperor that Marsile had put to sea 300,000 warriors who would not renounce their faith, and that these sea-borne warriors had been drowned in a tempest only 4 leagues from land – a punishment surely inflicted by God on the heathens. Marsile would, Ganelon said, obey Charlemagne's commands in all respects, to which Charlemagne announced that Ganelon had succeeded well in a difficult embassy, and would be suitably rewarded.

As the Frankish army retreated towards the Pyrenees, through which they would re-enter France as decreed by the truce, none except Ganelon knew what awaited them. The Saracen host had also marched, and was encamped in woodland not far from the Franks. That night, as both armies slept, Charlemagne had a dream of terrible omen –

in the dream, Ganelon seized the imperial spear of ash
wood and broke it, so that the splinters flew far and wide.
In another dream, Charlemagne saw himself at Aix, attacked
by a leopard and a bear which tore off his right arm; a
greyhound came to his aid in this dream, but Charlemagne
saw no more of the struggle, and slept unhappily for the rest
of the night.

The next morning, the Franks prepared to cross the
Pyrenees; Ganelon suggested that Roland led the
rearguard, and this was consented to. Roland donned his
armour, his helmet, strapped on his famous sword Duranda,
and hung around his neck his flower-decorated shield.
Knowing the rearguard to be the most dangerous part of
an army to ride with on a retreat from hostile territory,
Roland was both pleased (as he might well earn more fame
on this journey) and wary at the same time. Duke Naimes
had advised Roland to take with him half of the entire
army, but Roland refused, and rode with just his 20,000
men. Beside Roland rode the famous Peers – Oliver the
Bold, Archbishop Turpin, and Count Gautier. When the
rest of the army had set out, Roland followed at a suitable
distance, to prevent the main army being caught at a
disadvantage on the march should the unlikely event of
hostilities break out. Gautier was sent by Roland with 1000
men to search the mountains around the rearguard's path
of march – these brave Franks were all to die at the hands
of the Saracens before the main battle, and only Gautier
himself survived to join Roland in his later stand against
the odds.

King Marsile had pursued the Franks so quickly that his
van soon saw the banners of the Frankish rearguard waving
in the distance. As battle drew near, eleven Saracen chieftains
took a vow to slay Roland and thereby spread the faith of
Mahomet throughout the Frankish world:

> 'Death to the rearguard! Roland shall die! Death to the
> Peers! Woe to France and Charlemagne! We will bring
> the Emperor to your feet! You shall sleep at St Denis!
> Down with fair France!'
> (Ebbutt, 1910: 137)

The Franks soon noticed the advancing Saracen hordes, and,
guessing that betrayal was afoot, Roland addressed his men:

> 'Our duty is to hold this pass for our king. A vassal
> must endure for his lord grief and pain, heat and cold,
> torment and death; a knight's duty is to strike mighty
> blows, that men may sing of him, in time to come, no
> evil songs. Never shall such be sung of me.'
> (Ebbutt, 1910: 137–8)

Oliver climbed a hill and looked back into Spain. He
perceived a huge heathen army advancing, their helms and
hauberks gleaming in the sun. 'Alas we are betrayed! This
treason is plotted by Ganelon, who put us in the rear!'
(Ebbutt, 1910: 138) Seeing the odds against which they
would fight, Oliver bade Roland to blow his war horn, so
that the main Frankish column would hear and return to

their aid. Roland dismissed this as cowardice, and said that he himself would defeat the Saracens with his sword Duranda – 'Death we choose, but not dishonour!' (Ebbutt, 1910: 139).

The Frankish knights dismounted to be absolved and blessed by Turpin, who bid them all to strike hard against the heathen foe. Roland turned to his companion Oliver and announced that he was certain that they had been betrayed by Ganelon, who had sold their lives in return for some reward. He proclaimed that the payment would be made by their swords, and, when Roland, Oliver and their men had fallen in battle, Charlemagne himself would avenge them. With those, words, the Frankish host spurred their horses towards the Saracen hordes.

The battle at Roncesvalles turned into a bitter, deadly melée, as Franks and Saracens swirled and crashed against one another, shouting battle cries proclaiming their faith, invoking gods and saints, and wielding their swords and spears with the utmost skill and courage. Lances, javelins, scimitars, daggers and swords carried out their fatal work, and helmets and shields were clove into pieces on the battlefield. Roland slew the nephew of King Marsile, who himself had sworn to his uncle that he would bring Roland's head to the king's feet – delivering 'the right hand Charlemagne' to the Saracen leader. Oliver killed Marsile's brother, and each of the Twelve Peers gained the upper hand and defeated their opposite numbers amongst the twelve champions of Marsile. Roland dashed around the battle, appearing wherever their warriors needed most encouragement and martial support; Duranda flashed across the battlefield, striking home with every blow.

The Saracens died in the hundreds, building into thousands as the day progressed. Finally, all the Saracen host lay dead bar one man, who fled from the battlefield badly wounded. The Franks were the masters of the field, surrounded by carnage and gore, with their broken swords and lances, pierced chainmail coats, bloodstained banners and lance pennons, staring at the corpses of their comrades who had fallen at their side. Turpin praised the army aloud, proclaiming them heroes of the Christian faith, and exclaiming that no king under heaven's gaze had more worthy men than Charlemagne.

It was upon this weary host that the main army of the Saracens advanced. King Marsile, wily as ever, had only sent part of his huge force against the small Frankish rearguard earlier in the day. When the wounded survivor fled to him, urging the King to attack whilst the redoubtable Franks were disorganized and worn out, Marsile led the main part of his army into the valley. Now, 100,000 Saracens bore down on the Franks, in columns of 50,000 men at a time, blowing trumpets and sounding horns.

The Franks observed, and readied themselves for more bloodshed. Turpin exclaimed:

> 'Rather let us die victorious,
> Since this eve shall see us lifeless! –
> Heaven has no room for cowards!'
> (Ebbutt, 1910: 142)

Roland: The Frankish Paladin

The two forces clashed once more, the odds further
against the Franks than ever before. Yet they fought on,
without retreat or flight, for they knew that on that day
they had been marked for death. The mighty struggle
between the two forces seemed to affect nature itself: in
France tempests raged and thunder, hail and rain fell in an
outpouring from the skies; a terrible darkness spread over
the land, occasionally being lit by the crash of lightning.
People whispered in terror that it seemed as though the
end of the world was nigh, for they did not know the
truth of what was happening in the Pyrenees as Roland
and Marsile's armies clashed. Roland's men were tired and
disordered from their first encounter with the Saracens,
and as the battle against Marsile's fresh combatants
progressed, more and more of the exhausted Franks fell.
Roland, Oliver and Turpin continued to smite down yet
more of their enemies, as the other Peers and their
retainers died around them. As the fiery prelate Turpin
struck down a bold emir, there were but sixty Franks left
alive and fighting, including Roland, Oliver and Turpin
himself.

A third host of Saracens appeared and surged forward to
engulf the small band of Frankish heroes. Roland cried
aloud to Oliver:

> 'I must mourn for our fair country
> France, left widowed of her barons.
> Charles my King, why art thou absent?'
> (Ebbutt, 1910: 144)

Warriors

With that exclamation, Roland lifted his war horn Olifant
to his lips intending to blow it so that Charlemagne and the
main army would hear it along the mountain pass. Perhaps,
Roland thought, he would return with the Frankish army to
aid this small band of intrepid warriors. Oliver angrily
chastised him:

> 'That would bring great shame
> and reprobation down on all your kin,
> and this disgrace would last through their lives!
> You wouldn't do a thing when I implored you,
> so don't act now to win my gratitude.
> No courage is involved in sounding it;
> already you have bloodied both your arms.'
> (Harrison, 1970: LL 1705–1711)

The quarrel continued, Roland wishing to blow his horn as
the battle flowed against them. Earlier, he had claimed that
to blow his horn would be a sign of cowardice, and of this
fateful decision and its outcome Oliver reminded him:

> 'Tis thy fault;
> Valour is not kin to madness,
> Temperance knows naught of fury.
> You have killed these noble champions,
> You have slain the Emperor's vassals,
> You have robbed us of our conquests.
> Ah, your valour, Count, is fatal!'
> (Ebbutt, 1910: 144–145)

Roland: The Frankish Paladin

Turpin attempted to calm the quarrel, pointing out that the lives of the gallant dead could not be saved by such arguing, yet to sound the horn would allow Charlemagne to return and avenge their deaths, and for their bodies to be collected and returned to France for burial in Christian soil. Turpin's sense was victorious and Roland blew the horn so loudly that Charlemagne heard it from 30 leagues distant. Roland gave a second mighty blast on the horn, blowing with such strength that the veins of his temples burst. Charlemagne exclaimed that his rearguard must be in battle, as Roland would only sound his horn in such a manner if the lives of Franks were threatened, yet Ganelon sneeringly pointed out that Roland would be too proud to sound his horn in danger. He added with sarcasm that no one would be foolish enough to attack a man as great as Roland, and that doubtless he must have been neglecting his rearguard duty to go hunting. However, when Roland blew his horn a third time, out of breath and producing a feeble yet still audible sound for Charlemagne to hear, the king was convinced by Duke Naimes that Roland must have been in some trouble – probably betrayed by the one who now trying to dupe the king of Roland's fate – Ganelon.

Charlemagne called for Ganelon to be held under arrest. Ganelon suffered the humiliation of being held in custody by the kitchen staff, who chained him and beat him as the whole army retraced their steps, mourning 'Ah, if we could find Roland alive what blows we would strike for him! Alas! It was too late! Too late!' (Ebbutt, 1910: 146)

Back at Roncesvalles, Roland wept for the dead warriors

around him, as the Saracens advanced cautiously. 'Death is duty now' he declared, and so saying, rushed into battle, slaying King Marsile's only son. With fury, he drove the Saracen hordes before him like the hounds drive the deer. Turpin applauded this brave act, and commented that he hoped that monks would pray for the sins of such fighters.

In wrath, King Marsile himself assaulted Roland; the attack was in vain, and Roland struck the lordly Saracen's right hand off. The king fled back to Saragossa, while his main host, seized with panic at the king's departure, fled the battlefield too. However, the Caliph, Marsile's uncle, rallied his men and took these 50,000 once more against the tiny band of Roland's rearguard.

Roland cried aloud to his followers, Champions of the Cross as they were: 'Now shall we be martyrs for our faith. Fight boldly, lords, for life or death! Sell yourselves dearly! Let not fair France be dishonoured in her sons. When the Emperor sees us dead with our slain foes around us he will bless our valour.' (Ebbutt, 1910: 147–8). With this, the intensity of the battle increased to fever pitch. The Caliph rushed at Oliver, and struck him down from behind by running a lance through his body. Roland rushed to his friend's aid, but Oliver, seeing only a hazy figure drawing near through his now dimming, dying eyes, mistook Roland for an enemy and clove his helmet in two with a mighty blow. Roland recovered from this blow and clasped Oliver as he died, falling facing the east. This was symbolic – in Christian burial, the body is laid out facing east to await the resurrection.

Roland: The Frankish Paladin

Turpin and Roland now stood together, and were joined
by Count Gautier, whose scouting party had all been slain.
Even so, like the loyal vassal he was, Gautier came back to
Roland's side to die with his lord. Gautier died as Saracen
arrows rained down upon the surviving Franks. Having been
bloodied before, the Saracens kept their distance, attacking
only with these missiles. Some bravely advanced and
wounded Turpin with spears from beyond his sword's reach.
Turpin, knowing himself to be mortally wounded, charged
headlong into the pagan host, and killed 400 warriors before
he fell; Roland now fought on alone, blowing his horn once
more when a lull occurred in the fighting. Charlemagne
heard this rapidly dying blast, and urged his army onward:

'I know by the sound of Roland's horn he has
not long to live!'
(Ebbutt, 1910: 149)

His men sounded their trumpets in return – 60,000 of them
– so that Roland and his enemies would know they were
coming. In one last effort to slay Roland before his rescuers
arrived, 400 Saracens banded together to kill him; Roland
rushed at them, mounted on his trusty steed Veillantif, and
the previously confident Saracens fled before him. Alone on
the field, Roland dismounted to tend to the dying Turpin,
whereupon some hidden Saracens threw javelins, killing
Veillantif and piercing Roland's armour. Fighting back waves
of pain, Roland dragged the bodies of his fallen comrades
the Peers to Turpin, so that they might be blessed; in doing

so he collapsed, exhausted and badly wounded. Slowly and in great pain Turpin struggled to his feet and took Roland's horn, Olifant, to gather water from the stream for Roland; he fell dead, his maimed body unable to exert such effort.

Roland lay on the bloodied ground clutching Olifant and his sword Duranda, praying to his guardian angel Gabriel. A lurking Saracen saw him, and crept forward to steal the beautiful sword, but fell dead as Roland pounded his head with his war horn. Summoning up his remaining energy, Roland attempted three times to break Duranda on a stone, so that it would not fall into a Saracen's hands. Yet the sword would not break, but was instead thrown into a poisonous stream. Then, having done all he could, Roland collapsed to the ground and died. He made sure that he fell face down, so that Charlemagne would know that he had died victorious.

Soon after the Frankish relief force rode into the valley, and saw for themselves the battlefield, where not a foot of ground remained uncovered by bodies. Weeping at the sights which met them, the Franks carried out their vengeance the next day in battle against the Emir of Babylon, who was Marsile's ally. Charlemagne then went on to capture Saragossa, only to find that Marsile had committed suicide at the news of the Emir's death.

The Frankish army buried the dead with all honour on the battle site, but carried Roland, Oliver and Turpin to France, where they were buried in the great cathedral of Blaye. Ganelon was tried, found guilty and torn apart by wild horses, his name remaining a byword for treachery evermore. And Charlemagne prayed for Roland, who had, in his own sacrifice, saved Charlemagne and the Christian Franks from Marsile's plot:

> 'The Lord have mercy, Roland, on thy soul!
> That thou mayest rest in flowers of Paradise
> With all His glorious Saints for evermore!'
> (Ebbutt, 1910: 154)

One legend has it that Roland escaped the slaughter in the valley, but died of hunger and thirst seeking to cross the Pyrenees. This version is less inspiring in the heroic tradition, and when Wace wrote that Norman minstrels sang parts of the Song to William's troops to spur them on at the Battle of Hastings, we can be almost certain that the version used there spoke of his heroic sacrifice and death in battle.

As we have seen, parallels may be drawn between the virtues extolled by Roland and King Arthur. Like Arthur, Roland had a famous sword; this sword, named Duranda, was said to have belonged to Hector (see the chapter on Achilles). The sword, like Roland's horn Olifant, had been won from the giant Jutmundus. It had in its hilt a thread from the Virgin Mary's cloak, a tooth of St Peter, one of St Denys's hairs and a drop of St Basil's blood. When Roland received his fatal wound in battle, he attempted to break Duranda on a rock so that it could not fall into pagan hands. The quality of the sword was such that it would not shatter, so instead he hurled it into a poisoned stream, where it was to remain forever. This shows obvious parallels with Arthur's sacrifice of Excalibur, and both tales would appear to combine the ancient, pagan practice of sacrificing weapons and objects of value to water gods, with overt Christian sentiments being added by medieval authors.

In History

L ike several other heroes featured in this book, the romantic legend of Roland has developed from a single, simple entry in a contemporary chronicle; referring to the battle of Roncesvalles in AD 778, it was recorded:

> In which battle was slain Roland, prefect of the marches of Brittany.

After the fall of the western Roman Empire in the fifth century AD, many cultures flooded into Roman Gaul to fill the power vacuum. One such tribe was the Franks, a formidable race that controlled the majority of modern France firstly through the Merovingian dynasty, and later through the Carolingian dynasty. The Carolingian dynasty traced its origins back to an early seventh-century AD alliance between Pepin the Old and Bishop Arnulf of Metz. The power of the Merovingian king was waning by this time, and a shift in power towards the 'Mayors' occurred. These 'Mayors' were landowners who came to dominate the power centres of early medieval France; Pepin was Mayor in

Roland: The Frankish Paladin

Austrasia (the north-eastern region of the Frankish state) and his daughter married the son of Bishop Arnulf. This was the beginning of the Carolingian dynasty, which became so powerful that, within a century, they controlled the army and held sway over the Merovingian king.

The Franks had built their kingdom despite facing opposition on all sides: to the north were pagan Germans and Scandinavians (the Franks had converted to Christianity earlier in the Merovingian period), to the south were the Visigothic and Arab kingdoms of Spain and north Africa, and to the east were the Lombards and many other Germanic peoples. To the west, over the English Channel, there appears to have been peace with the Anglo-Saxons, but the Britons (Bretons) who had settled in western France still had to be subdued; it was against the latter that the historical Roland may have made his name as a warrior. The Carolingian leader Charles Martel had defeated a Muslim army at Poitiers in AD 732, and his son Pepin took the fight across the Frankish borders, campaigning against pagans in the north, Christians in the west (in Italy), and Muslims to the south. Pepin had deposed the last Merovingian king in AD 750, and had been crowned the first Carolingian king in the following year; he also had to campaign within his own borders against those who disputed legitimacy of his claim to the throne. In AD 754, Pope Stephen III travelled to France to proclaim Pepin and his sons Roman Patricians – this made them duty bound to protect Rome and support the Pope against the Lombard rulers of the majority of Italy. As may be imagined, this lead to Carolingian expansion in all directions, and when Charlemagne became sole king in AD 771, he continued this policy more aggressively than his predecessors. This was the background against which Roland rode to his death.

The Historical Charlemagne

Charlemagne remains the most famous leader of early medieval France. An empire builder and crusader, he was only thirty-six years old at the time of Roland's death. In *Vita Karoli Magni*, Einhard describes him vividly:

> He was large and robust of body, tall in stature but not disproportionately so, for his height was seven times the length of his foot...his hair beautiful and white, and his expression gay and cheerful, so that he appeared dignified and imposing when seated as well as when standing...his voice was clear, although less powerful than the size of his body might lead one to expect.

Charlemagne is also described in *The Song of Roland*, obviously in exaggerated language, but language that nonetheless typifies the high regard in which Charlemagne was held by later French poets:

> No man who ever sees and comes to know him
> will fail to say the emperor is great.
> I cannot praise or laud him to you so

Roland: The Frankish Paladin

that he will not have yet more worth and honor.
His mighty courage – who would itemize it?
God made such heroism shine in him
that he would rather die than fail his barons.
(trans. Harrison, 1970: LL530–536)

In AD 778 Charlemagne was returning from one such expedition into Spain, after battling the Muslim warlords who ruled there. His army had captured Pampeluna, but was forced back before Saragossa, and did not cross the Ebro. The route that Charlemagne took naturally led through the Pyrenees. When the main army had navigated its way through the passes, the rearguard was ambushed and surprised by a large force of Basques and Gascons – skilled mountain fighters adept at hit and run attacks. The Frankish rearguard was driven into a valley and slaughtered to a man; the legend of Roland replaces the Basques and Gascons with Saracen warriors – allowing Roland and his companions to become Christian crusaders, fighting not for land but for religious idealism. At the end of the historical battle, the victorious Basques and Gascons plundered the Frankish baggage train and then melted away into the countryside – a far less grandiose point of victory than the one the Saracens thought they had achieved through their religious triumph in the poem. The revised *Annals of the Kingdom of the Franks* recorded the action of the battle and the Frankish anger with their opponent's tactics with anger, thus:

Warriors

> Although the Franks were manifestly superior to the
> Basques in both weapons and courage, yet they were
> rendered their inferiors by the steepness of the terrain and
> the character of the battle, which was not fought fairly.
> (quoted in Hooper & Bennett, 1996: 16)

As befitted a chivalric hero, Roland was transformed in
legend to become the nephew of Charlemagne; in reality, he
was not of royal blood. Charlemagne himself becomes older
and grander in the *Song of Roland* than he actually was at the
time of Roncesvalles. Ganelon – the poem's traitor – is
likened in many ways to the Biblical Judas, and the mighty
Saracens replace the more historically and religiously less
alien and antagonistic Basques as the victors of the battle
against Roland.

We know a little more of the battle from a mid
nineteenth-century poem called the *Song of Altobiscar*. We
are told that the Basques occupied the high ground above
the valley and hurled rocks down among the Franks. The
disorder caused by such a man-made rock-fall allowed the
mountain men to run amok with the Franks, charging
down from high and attacking with speed and ferocity as
the Franks struggled to control their horses and form shield
walls. Even so, the attack saw the destruction of the
Frankish host.

Roland was the prefect of the Breton March; the areas
under the control of the Carolingian Franks spread widely
across Europe, and the king's law and interests were upheld
locally by trusted prefects such as Roland. In many ways, this

system was an early development of feudalism, and was later mirrored by medieval rulers, as shown in Chapter Five about Robin Hood. Such a prefect would be responsible for mustering the army from his own region, and for maintaining the fortifications which defended the region from invasion – strong forts joined by roads. We know little of Roland beyond the mention of his death at Roncesvalles, although a man holding his post would have been considered a king in any society contemporary to his apart from the Frankish empire, such was the quantity of land he was responsible for ruling.

The men of medieval France and neighbouring European countries grew to learn their chivalric ways from works such as the *Song of Roland*. The scenes of Roland proclaiming 'Death is duty now' and other heroic statements must have been at the forefront of many knights' minds as they rode into battle at places such as Poiters and Agincourt where they suffered such bitter defeats at the hands of the English.

In Battle

Conflict between the Frankish empire and her enemies took place on many fronts, and the men that followed Charlemagne and fell with Roland were in many ways the forerunners to William the Conqueror's knights nearly 300 years later. The main strike force of the Carolingian Franks was a heavily armoured mounted wing, equipped in a style which was to evolve into the Norman

cavalry shown on the Bayeux Tapestry. Again, like the later
Normans (whose lineage descended from both Norse and
Frankish peoples), this mounted strike force was supported by
infantrymen armed with spears and missile weapons.

Many medieval cultures have been described as being
societies organized for war, yet the Carolingian Franks were,
as succinctly noted by Timothy Reuter, more a society
'largely organized *by* war' (Keen [ed] 1999:13). Throughout
the reign of the Frankish kings, large forces were sent into
battle against peoples along the Frankish frontiers – whether
in punitive raids or to subordinate new lands.

This society organized by war left some quite detailed
records of its military organisation and development; the
nineteenth-century antiquarian John Hewitt described the
obligations laid down by Charlemagne to his subordinates:

> ...in the capitularies of Charlemagne especially, we get
> a glimpse of the improvements in northern warfare. 'Let
> each count,' commands the emperor, 'be careful that the
> troops he has to lead to battle are fully equipped; that
> they have spear, shield, a bow with two strings, and
> twelve arrows, helmet, and coat-of-fence [chainmail].'
> We here see the soldiery adding to their defensive
> appointments the casque and lorica, and to their
> offensive arms the bow and arrows.
> (1996: 8)

Whether each man went into battle so well equipped is
debatable, yet it would seem likely that the personal retinues

of high ranking commanders would have been so armed. The heavily armoured Frankish cavalryman was the early medieval equivalent of a modern battle tank; rounded shields, helmet, chainmail, leather or ringmail (a leather jacket with rings or scales of metal stitched on) hauberk, and possibly padded or armoured leggings made the mounted warrior almost invincible. Scale armour was often shown in contemporary manuscripts, although archaeological finds of such material are few and far between. For offensive duties, the cavalryman would have been armed with a lance and/or javelins, and probably a well made longsword; the bow, as pointed out by Hewitt, may also have added to this armoury. Frankish swords were renowned as among the best in Europe; they were pattern welded and well balanced. The Frankish sword was a cutting, slashing weapon, ideal for using from horseback.

Not all of the Carolingian cavalrymen would have been so well equipped; many of the lesser warriors rode to battle equipped only with lance, javelins and a shield to fight with. In contemporary manuscripts, the number of unarmoured horsemen often far outweighs the number of well armoured ones. Many of the provinces controlled by the Carolingians sent such lightly armoured cavalrymen to fight for their overlords when called upon; Gascons, Bretons, and Old Saxons (from mainland Europe as opposed to from England) fought in such a way, often as skirmishers ahead of the main force.

The dress of Charlemagne himself was recorded in a contemporary description by the Monk of St Gall; Roland and his fellow Peers would have been similarly attired:

his iron breast and his shoulders of marble were
defended by a cuirasse of iron.
(quoted in Hewitt, 1996: 8)

From a ninth-century record, we have a good idea of how
expensive it was to arm and armour a Carolingian heavy
cavalryman:

Helmet – 6 cows
Chainmail – 12 cows
Sword and scabbard – 7 cows
Greaves – 6 cows
Spear and shield – 2 cows
Horse – 12 cows
(source: Heath, 1980)

Only the higher class landowners would have been able to
afford such equipment outright, so this list demonstrates the
benefits of a number of landowners being grouped together
to equip one warrior. The list above would be the equivalent
in cost to forty-five cows. From the list, one warrior so
equipped would have cost the equivalent of raising twenty-
two levies armed with only a spear and shield. Even so, the
Frankish rulers preferred the well equipped, better trained
horseman to a vast army of untrained levies likely to break
and run at the first contact with an enemy.

The Carolingian kings and some of their immediate
predecessors attempted to make their cavalry arm the
strongest fist of their army and cut down the numbers of

infantry present. At the beginning of Charlemagne's reign, the majority of the army were still infantrymen, but the use of mounted warriors grew throughout his reign. The overall effect of this was to allow a smaller yet better armed and trained force to take to the battlefield. Instead of all able bodied men being called up to fight, small groups were encouraged to provide just one well armed warrior – in effect, one capable soldier replacing four or five badly trained and ill equipped ones. Such organization can be seen in many armies in the late twentieth and early twenty-first centuries, often classified as 'rationalizing'. The idea of using cavalrymen as the main strike force of an army probably came to the Franks from their campaigns against fast-moving raiders on their borders – Avars, Vikings, Arabs, Magyars and Lombards all proved to be tricky opponents for foot-based armies to bring to battle. By AD 864, Charles the Bold decreed that all Franks who owned a horse should bring it to muster, and a chronicle of AD 891 mockingly mentioned that the Franks did not even know how to fight on foot. Around a hundred years after Roland's lifetime, the seeds for such an army were sown in his time.

Although the Franks' enemies and neighbours such as the Arabs, Lombards and Avars used stirrups, the early Carolingians showed little interest in this piece of riding equipment. Stirrups did eventually become standard equipment by the end of the ninth century, and helped pave the way forward for the development of the chivalric heavy cavalry of the high medieval period.

The Battle of Tours, AD 732

The Battle of Tours was a landmark victory for the Franks over their
Muslim enemies in the eighth century AD. The Franks fought on foot
under the leadership of the Austrasian Frank Charles Martel (the son of
Pepin), and the Muslim cavalry swarmed forwards, being thrown back
from the Frankish shield walls time after time. The battle was fought
over two days, and according to Arabian chroniclers, was won by the
Franks when word spread among the Muslims that their camp was
being plundered by a flanking Frankish force. Although this turned out
to be a false rumour, the sudden and rapid movement of a number of
key Muslim cavalry units to protect their camp to the rear was
interpreted as a retreat, and the rest of the army turned and retreated
too. As the Muslim general, Abderrahman, attempted to rally his men,
he was struck down:

> All the host fled before the enemy, and many died in the flight.
> This deadly defeat of the Moslems, and the loss of the great
> leader and good cavalier, Abderrahman, took place in the
> hundred and fifteenth year [of the Moslem calendar].
> (quoted in Creasy, 1851: 169)

Many ordinary foot soldiers would have gone into battle
armed with nothing more than a spear and a shield. Shields
would have been around 3 feet wide, and spears up to 8 feet

long. A handful of javelins may have replaced spears for some warriors, providing missile support from the shield wall. Some may have been well protected (a few contemporary illustrations show helmets and chainmail being worn), as the Frankish rulers of the Carolingian era were attempting to make the levy more effective on the battlefield, although Heath asserts that:

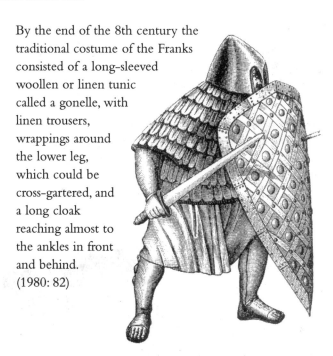

> By the end of the 8th century the traditional costume of the Franks consisted of a long-sleeved woollen or linen tunic called a gonelle, with linen trousers, wrappings around the lower leg, which could be cross-gartered, and a long cloak reaching almost to the ankles in front and behind. (1980: 82)

A ninth-century Frankish footman, clearly shown in scale armour. (From Meyer's *Konnerlations-Lexicon*, 1895)

Warriors

Tunic colours were often white or blue, although a selection of reds, browns and yellows were also worn. Purple, however, was reserved for royalty. Shield colours appear to have been quite bright and decorative; manuscript illustrations often show quartered shields, accompanied occasionally by what appears to be reinforcing studs mounted geometrically in the shield's surface. The seeming obsession which the Carolingian Franks had with being the successors of Rome may suggest that imperial red was a favoured colour for shields, although we do not know for sure.

Bowmen played a significant role in Frankish warfare, though unlike many of their opponents from the east, Frankish archers went to battle on foot rather than fighting from horseback; the bow became regulation equipment for Frankish warriors in AD 802. Written evidence suggests that bowmen were of a lower social standing than mounted warriors, as in most European armies. But while they could turn the course of a battle with their showers of arrows, archery does not appear to have been a particularly popular pastime among the Franks. Some Carolingian archers were heavily armoured, one illustrated in a manuscript from AD 924 wore a scale hauberk and a helmet with an aventail.

As noted above, by the time of Charlemagne, a fledgling feudal system of levying and muster had appeared in the Frankish Empire. At the emperor's call, his lords would bring their men to muster at a pre-determined site, drawn and funded from the lord's land-owning and servile populace and equipped as outlined above. Failure to appear could result in a fine or confiscation of the guilty lord's holdings.

Roland: The Frankish Paladin

Vuksic and Grbasic aptly sum up the forces available to
Charlemagne to wage war without having to call up a levy:

> Charlemagne also had a standing force organized into
> independent units (*scarae*), numbering several hundred
> men, under the local administration and command of a
> count (*graf*). These units guarded the borders of the
> state and garrisoned important forts; they could also be
> used for police duty. Several border counties were
> joined in administrative provinces called *marcae*, under
> the rule of a *comes marcae*, or *markgraf*.
> (1993: 60)

Roland would have been one such *markgraf*. The king was
also protected by a personal retinue of noblemen, known as
the *scola*. These would have been formed of the heavily
armoured cavalrymen described earlier in this chapter, and
those nobles lower than the king – yet still important –
would have had their own versions of this retinue.

As the Frankish empire spread across several countries, a
mustered army could be multi-cultural. For a late eighth-century
campaign against the Avars, it was noted that the Frankish army
included Franks, Old Saxons, Alemanni, Bavarians, Lombards,
Frisians, and Thuringians – a fairly complete muster of all of the
important Germanic tribes of north-west Europe; the
commanders of such armies were usually Frankish, though.

Drawing on a diverse cultural background allowed the
Frankish commanders to go to battle with large forces of
men. At the Battle of Toulouse in AD 721, the Franks could

allegedly suffer 1500 casualties while still winning; at Tours in AD 732, the army facing the Franks possibly numbered 70,000 or 80,000 strong, yet the Franks were able to contest and defeat such a huge army. Army sizes are often given in rounded figures, often in multiples of 600 (Reuter, in Keen [ed] 1999: 28), numbering in the thousands. Realistically:

> Ferdinand Lot suggested a maximum size of 5000 for armies of the Carolingian period, the German Karl-Ferdinand Werner argued a generation later for a maximum of 15,000–20,000, drawn from a reservoir at least twice that size.
> (Reuter, in Keen [ed] 1999: 28)

Verbruggen estimated a Carolingian army as numbering between 2500 and 3000 horsemen, and 6000 to 10,000 infantrymen. A very valid point to be made here (and applicable for some other armies at this time besides the Franks) is that armies were drawn from pool, and would comprise of a number of warriors considered suitable for the task, from several hundred to perhaps a maximum of 10,000 or 15,000 men; speculatively, an average army may have numbered around 2000 fighting warriors.

With such large armies, the Franks developed an efficient commissariat system; each man was required to carry enough rations for three months on the frontier, and supply trains were also noted. These ox-drawn waggons would carry supplies such as flour, port, wine, and corn mills, as well as tools for constructing fortifications and camps.

A ninth-century Frankish cavalryman. (From the late nineteenth-century *L'Art Pour Tous, Encyclopedie de l'Art Industriel et Decoratif*)

Warriors

The tactics used by the Carolingian cavalry on the battlefield varied according to their enemy. An account of AD 782 records the Franks as charging headlong at a full gallop into their Saxon enemies, only to meet with defeat. The criticism aimed at this Frankish force suggests that a more normal tactic would have been a careful approach, probably hurling javelins, and standing off until the enemy had become disordered enough to charge successfully. Under such circumstances, a wild charge of horsemen could be formidable.

Against horse archers and other light troops with missiles, the Frankish cavalry used their shields to protect themselves against bow fire, and then charged into contact at the first opportunity; this would scatter lightly armed troops, and leave the Franks at an advantage in the ensuing confusion.

The sources which we have for the battle of Roncesvalles suggest that the Frankish force, when surprised by the Basque ambush, dismounted and formed a shield wall. This would have been dictated by the steep and broken terrain, which would put mounted warriors at a disadvantage. Though less mobile on foot, the Frankish tactics were sound, if ultimately ending in defeat, as the light troops which characterized Basque armies and similar hill forces would usually struggle against a densely packed body of armoured infantrymen. The Byzantine *Tactica* records that:

> …in a cavalry action a hard-pressed force might dismount and stand back to back in a shield wall to face the enemy.
> (quoted in Heath, 1980:42)

Roland: The Frankish Paladin

Perhaps at the death of Roland, weight of numbers took its toll, or the benefits of Basque surprise prevented the Franks from forming into a defensive body effectively.

Large bodies of levied infantrymen would be capable of little more than forming a tightly packed shield wall, and fending off any attacking force. From behind such a formation, archers and javelinmen could fire arrows into their enemies, reducing their numbers and damaging the enemy's morale.

It is rumoured that the victorious Norman army at the battle of Hastings in 1066 were inspired to victory by the epic actions of France's most chivalrous warrior, Roland. *The Song of Roland* appears to have drawn on an actual event and historical character, embellishing the little known event into a matter of national importance. Roland and his companions showed the characteristics requisite among all aspiring knights of the later medieval age, and their battle against a non-Christian enemy was significant in light of the Crusades. Religion plays an important part in Roland's tale, attempting to place Christianity as the premier religion while frowning upon the underhand tactics of the Franks' Muslim enemies. Compared to many of the other heroes in this book, Frankish warfare was extremely well organized and on a much larger scale than comparable battles in the British Isles, for example. The cavalry formed a well armed and armoured elite, with support from levied troops when required. The Frankish military system was the basis of the later Norman system, and thus should be seen as the forerunner of medieval arms and warfare. Therefore, the historical Roland and his compatriots – although probably not as chivalrous as legend was to dictate – do deserve some credit for playing a formative role in the development of the medieval knight.

CUCHULAIN
The Hound of Ulster

Cuchulain was the Hound of Ulster – ancient Ireland's greatest warrior. Ebbutt noted that Irish mythology holds plenty in common with Greek mythology; if this is to be agreed with, then Cuchulain is undoubtedly the Achilles of Irish myth. In true Irish tradition, however, tales of Cuchulain contain elements of humour and pathos missing from the folk tales of many other nations. Irish mythology is also a very colourful group of folk tales, often recorded in beautiful language with extra attention paid to visual descriptions.

The legendary Gaelic bard and warrior Ossian referred to Cuchulain as Cuthullin in the third century AD; Ossian's work was translated between 1760 and 1763 by Scotsman James Macpherson, but later authors have claimed that Macpherson's work was mostly created by himself, with some use of ancient sources. Even so, many tales of Cuchulain have passed down through Irish oral tradition. Perhaps the single most important author to bring Cuchulain to modern audiences was Lady Isabella Augusta Gregory, who devoted much of her time after the death of her husband in 1891 to the study of Irish folklore and

307

mythology. Encouraged by W B Yeats, she spent the end of
the nineteenth and early years of the twentieth centuries
retelling these stories in her own trademark dialect of
Kiltartan – developed from Irish and traditional Elizabethan
speech mannerisms, and spoken by the peasants around
Lady Gregory's home near Coole, Galway. Lady Gregory's
Cuchulain was a literary success, selling through four editions
in ten years, and remaining among the most important
translations of Irish saga over 100 years later. Many
intriguing episodes, probably separate myths in their own
right, have been incorporated into the Irish myth cycle
and Cuchulain's legend in particular, and what follows
contains the most common elements of the life of the
Hound of Ulster.

Cuchulain was the nephew of King Conchobar of Ulster,
one of the most powerful kings in a unified Ireland ruled by
several kings and queens. His mother, Dechtire, was the
king's sister, and it is often said that Cuchulain's father was
not a mortal man but Lugh of the Long Hand – a powerful
Celtic god.

Cuchulain was brought up by his uncle the king, with the
help and support of his wisest and most able counsellors.
The huge promise that Cuchulain showed as a child was
demonstrated when, at the age of only five, he beat the clan's
other, older boys in all manner of athletic and martial
exercises and events. Cuchulain took his name at an early
age – as a small boy he accidentally slew the ferocious
watchdog of the smith Culan and took the dog's place for a
period of penance. On his seventh birthday, Cuchulain

assumed the arms of a warrior, many years in advance of the usual age for a youth to become a fighter. Cuchulain did so as he overheard the druid Cathbad foreseeing that any youth who took up arms on that day would be destined for a most unusual and special life:

> 'If any young man take arms to-day, his name will be greater than any other name in Ireland, but his span of life will be short.'
> (Ebbutt, 1910: 185)

Cuchulain, therefore, loved fame above longevity, and in the life that he led, he certainly emphasized this trait. His reputation soon spread over all Ireland, where people learned of him as the great warrior who accomplished great martial feats at an age when he should have been in nursery. By the time he was seventeen, Cuchulain was peerless among the champions of Ulster and the rest of the island. When the time came for Cuchulain to wed, the men of Ulster searched across the whole of Ireland for a woman suitable to be his wife. Whilst the other warriors were away on this quest, Cuchulain started to search for himself, starting at the dun of Forgall the Wily, a powerful druid. Forgall had two daughters, one of whom, named Emer, was the most beautiful woman in the entire country. She became Cuchulain's own choice of bride. Emer was less enamoured with Cuchulain's wooing to start with, despite his great skill in such matters, and instead set him a series of tasks and trials to complete within a year. This was partly to test his worthiness as a suitor, but also to satisfy her father who was as yet not prepared to consent to the union. When Cuchulain returned at the end of the year, triumphant in all of the deeds set for him, he rescued Emer from the confinement that her father had bestowed upon her, and won her as a wife. The pair married in Armagh, the capital of Ulster, and lived under the protection of King Conchobar.

Cuchulain – The Celtic Warrior Idyll

Cuchulain's wife Emer, desperate to prove that her husband was the greatest champion of all Ireland, summed him up in glowing prose of an heroic age:

> 'It is he is not a hound that is weak; there is blood on his spear, there is blood on his sword, his white body is black with blood, his soft skin is furrowed with sword cuts, there are many wounds on his thigh…he is the strong protector; his chariot is red, its cushions are red; he fights from over the ears of horses, from over the breath of men; he leaps in the air like a salmon when he makes his hero leap…he breaks down armies in the hard fight…he finds joy in the terror of the ignorant.'
> (Gregory, 1973: 59)

Queen Maeve similarly summed up everything that was considered to comprise a proud and powerful man in her description of Cuchulain. Like so many other aspects of traditional Irish myth, the description paints a vivid picture in prose:

Cuchulain: The Hound of Ulster

'Like the sound of an angry sea, like a great moving wave,
with the madness of a wild beast that is vexed, he leaps
through his enemies in the crash of battle, they hear their
death in his shout. He heaps deed upon deed, head upon
head; his is a name to be put in songs. As fresh malt is
ground in the mill, so shall we be ground by Cuchulain.'
(Gregory, 1973: 66)

One of the chiefs at Conchobar's court was a true
troublemaker, always conspiring to make mischief for others.
His name was Bricriu of the Bitter Tongue. Bricriu
approached King Conchobar, and invited the king and his
royal bodyguard – known as the Red Branch of Ulster – to
a grand feast at Bricriu's new hall; Bricriu felt that this
would present him with many chances to create strife. The
King of Ulster and his men were not fools, however, and
knew well Bricriu's capacity for creating trouble; the king
refused Bricriu's offer unless he made an oath to leave the
hall before the feast began, only remaining present long
enough to receive and welcome his guests. Bricriu, being so
experienced in his role as a troublemaker, had foreseen this
possibility, and readily agreed to it before retiring to his hall
to prepare the feats and his mischief.

However, before Bricriu left Armagh, he went to praise
the hero Laegaire. He questioned Laegaire as to why he
should not be Champion of Ireland forever; Laegaire replied
that, if he could, he would be. Bricriu confided to the hero

that, if he followed the trickster's advice, he certainly would
be the Champion of all Ireland. Bricriu explained that
King Conchobar and his retinue were coming to a feast at
his hall; Bricriu would be laying out a Champion's portion
on the feasting table, and that any man who claimed that
would certainly be acclaimed the Champion of the land.
Laegaire, he suggested, should bid his chariot driver to
claim Laegaire as being worthy of the Champion's portion,
and gain the approval of King Conchobar through this
nomination.

> 'Some men shall die if my right is taken from me,'
> quoth Laegaire; but Bricriu only laughed and
> turned away.
> (Ebbutt, 1910: 187)

Bricriu next went to meet Conall Cearnach, Cuchulain's
cousin, one of the important chieftains of the Red Branch.
He addressed Conall the Victorious as he had Laegaire,
describing him as the 'defence and shield' of Ulster, who no
opponent dare face in battle. Bricriu asked of Conall the
same as he had of Laegaire – why should he not be the
Champion of all Ireland? Bricriu then explained that a
Champion's portion would sit at the feasting table, and that
Conall should ask his chariot driver to nominate Conall to
sit at it.

Having roused the ambition of both Laegaire and Conall,
two of the most powerful warriors in Ulster, he then went
to meet Cuchulain, and set about flattering this hero too:

Cuchulain: The Hound of Ulster

'…all the men of Ulster acknowledge that your
bravery, your valour, and your deeds are beyond their
own. Why, then, would you leave the Champion's
Portion for some other one of the men of Ulster, when
not one of them would be able to keep it from you?'
(Gregory, 1902: 55)

Cuchulain, suitably stirred, said that any man who tried to
keep him from the Champion's portion would lose their
head. With that, Bricriu travelled back to his home, where
he made preparations for the feast – and quarrelling – to
come.

Soon, King Conchobar and his men came to Bricriu's hall
in Dundrum, and, once seated, Bricriu left as agreed. His
parting words were to say that the Champion's portion at his
feast was well worth having, and to let the best hero in the
whole of Ulster eat it. All three chariot drivers claimed the
meal for their master, and King Conchobar could come to
no decision. He decreed that the Champion's portion would
be shared between the three on that night, and that they
should travel to King Ailill and Queen Meave of Connaught
to hear their wisdom on which should be named Champion.

Ailill and Meave – much concerned by the initial
approach of three warriors of such great reputation – set
about organizing a series of challenges with the help of the
Fairy People of the Hills of Cruachan. First, they sent three
magical, monstrous cats into the hall where the three
Ulstermen slept. Conall and Laegaire sprang with all their
strength and dexterity into the hall's rafters, yet Cuchulain

stood against the cats and fought them away. After standing guard all night, Ailill suggested that the other two Ulstermen should concede:

> 'Are you not content to yield the Championship to Cuchulain?'
> 'Indeed no,' said Conall and Laegaire. 'We are used to fighting men, not monstrous beasts.'
> (Ebbutt, 1910: 194)

The next day, King Ailill sent the three heroes to his foster father, Ercol. Ercol tested them sorely – first he sent Laegaire into the night to fight the witches of the valley. Laegaire returned, defeated, and having had his armour and weapons stolen. Conall faired the same against the witches, yet Cuchulain, goaded by his chariot driver for fighting badly against women, beat them all and returned with their cloaks. Conall and Laegaire still would not concede defeat. Ercol's next test was to fight each of the champions in turn himself. He defeated Conall, and beat Laegaire so fully that Laegaire fled in panic to Meave and Ailill; Cuchulain arrived later, with the defeated Ercol tied to his chariot. Even so, the other champions would not concede, and Meave and Ailill tricked each into thinking he had won, sending them back to Conchobar before they discovered this.

Finally, Laegaire, Conall and Cuchulain travelled to Kerry where the magician Curoi lived. Each of the three fought a shadowy giant, Cuchulain being the only victor, and then Curoi asked them to return to Armagh, to await his

Cuchulain: The Hound of Ulster

decision. After many weeks, when all the men of Ulster were feasting – with the exception of Cuchulain who was not present – a gigantic stranger strode powerfully into the hall:

> It seemed to them as if none of the men of Ulster
> could reach half his height. He was frightful to look at;
> next to his skin he had an old cow's hide, and a grey
> cloak around him… Ravenous yellow eyes he had, and
> in his right hand an axe weighing fifty cauldrons of
> melted metal,
> (Lady Gregory, this edition 1973: 73–74)

He introduced himself as Uath, the Stranger, and announced that he had come to find a man who would meet an agreement with him. Conchobar enquired as to this agreement, and Uath gestured to his mighty axe:

> 'The man who will grasp it to-day may cut my head
> off with it, provided that I may, in like manner, cut off
> his head to-morrow.'
> (Ebbutt, 1910: 200)

Uath excepted Conchobar from this challenge, due to his royal blood and dignity, but defied any of the heroes of Ulster to take up his challenge. Laegaire sprang up and immediately accepted; Uath knelt and Laegaire delivered a scathing blow, removing Uath's head with one hack. The gathered crowd gasped in awe as Uath's headless body rose up and strode from the hall, head in its hands.

The next night Uath returned, his head restored to his body, to deliver his blow to Laegaire as promised. Laegaire's bravery had failed him, however, and he failed to turn up to meet his challenger at all. The Ulstermen were ashamed, so Conall took up the challenge. Delivering a blow as good as Laegaire's, he too hewed off Uath's head, and again the headless man strode out of the hall carrying his head. Returning the next night, he discovered that Conall's heart had failed him too.

Uath, again taunting the cowardly Ulstermen, challenged the remaining warriors. Cuchulain was present on this occasion, and took up the challenge. Cuchulain's mighty blow beheaded Uath, yet once more, the stranger strode from the hall. The next night, Cuchulain sat awaiting Uath's return, sorrowful, but determined to keep his word. The hall doors crashed open, and Uath strode in. The Hound of Ulster knelt before Uath and awaited his fate. The axe fell – but by Cuchulain's side – and as the brave Ulsterman looked up, he no longer saw the hideous Uath, but instead the smiling face of Curoi, who had made his decision based on the three challengers' reaction to his apparition as Uath. To Cuchulain, and the rest of the assembled warriors, he announced:

> 'The championship of the Heroes of Ireland is yours from this day forth, and the Champion's Portion at all feasts; and to your wife I adjudge the first place among all the women of Ulster.'
> (Ebbutt, 1910: 203)

Cuchulain: The Hound of Ulster

The Ulster men accepted this decision with delight. Even Laegaire and Conall swore to abide by it, having been shamed in front of their fellow kinsmen. After his desire to be Champion of all Ireland was satiated, Cuchulain served his kinfolk well. Cuchulain guarded the southern passes into Ulster, falling upon invading or raiding enemies unawares, routing all before him and allowing the people of Ulster to live in peace; on one occasion, he defeated an army of eighteen *tuatha* (warbands) numbering over 50,000 raiders from Queen Maeve's kingdom.

Many of Cuchulain's deeds as the Champion of Ulster were against Maeve. In battle against her warriors, Cuchulain was known to launch himself into a battle frenzy:

> He became a fearsome and multiform creature such as never was known before. Every particle of him quivered like a bulrush in a running stream... The beats of his heart sounded like the roars of a lion (Rolleston, this edition 1994: 209–210)

And his blood boiled, forming a smoky mist shimmering around him. In such a frenzy, Cuchulain was recorded as having killed a hundred men single handedly. Cuchulain also fought against the mighty Loch Son of Mofebis; in this duel, Cuchulain had to stain himself a beard with berry juice, so that his enemy would not accuse him of being a mere boy and refuse to fight. As they fought, the fearful female sorceress Morrigan came against Cuchulain in several shape changing forms, yet he beat both her and Loch. Further victories were had against Maeve's allies, including the esteemed Calatin and his twenty-seven sons.

Cuchulain also travelled to the Fairy Land, and adventured out on many mystical quests, facing a number of colourful human and monstrous foes. Amongst the strangest of these were a party of demons who resembled the waves of the sea.

Cuchulain's downfall came through his honesty and respect of the law. In battle against the children of Calatin, Cuchulain was confronted by a number of bards. A true hero could never refuse a bard's request, and the bards demanded of Cuchulain his spear, with which they slew his chariot horses. Again the bards demanded his spear, and they:

> threw the spear, and it went through and through Cuchulain's body, and he knew he had got his deadly wound; and his bowels came out on the cushions of the chariot,
> (Lady Gregory, this edition 1973: 255)

Knowing that death was near, Cuchulain dragged himself to a lake and quenched the thirst brought upon him by near death. As he lay dying, his head was cut off, as was his sword hand. Cuchulain's body was taken to Tara, where he was buried under a great mound. Cuchulain, Hound of Ulster, was no more.

Cuchulain: The Hound of Ulster

In History

I reland, in common with other Celtic areas, did not commit its history into writing until the early medieval period. If Ossian really did make note of Cuchulain in the third century AD, we know that his historical place must fall at or before this date. However, I think it is more likely that Cuchulain's supposed place in history falls far earlier in the Celtic Iron Age; Conchobar, Cuchulain's uncle and guardian, was said to have died on the day of Christ's crucifixion, although this reference seemingly follows the attempts of later storytellers to bestow Christian overtones on pagan figures.

The earliest settlement of the British Isles and Ireland is still somewhat shrouded in mystery. Although we know of a great number of archaeological sites from the Neolithic period and earlier, and have a few tantalizing sentences from Classical travellers, relatively little is known of pre-Celtic society. The Celts from whom Cuchulain was descended probably settled in or traded in Ireland in the third century BC as part of the La Tène cultural movement; yet the early and dominant Hallstatt culture which sprang up in the seventh century BC 'scarcely touched' Ireland (Barry Raftery, in Ryan [ed] 1991: 107). Whatever the circumstances, the arrival of Celtic people in Ireland occurred at the same time as the arrival of the Irish Iron Age, and it seems very unlikely that the two phenomena were not connected. Historians of different ages have seen the arrival of immigrants in different ways – possibly as aggressive invaders (a common school of thought in the post

Warriors

Second World War studies of the 1950s) at one extreme, and possibly as peaceful traders acting as cultural sponges and diffusers (favoured notably in the more peace-minded 1960s and 1970s). This is common not just in the archaeological theory behind Celtic studies, but in most people movements considered by archaeologists and historians. The reality probably lies somewhere between the two extremes. However, at the start of the nineteenth century, Ebbutt had more lurid visions of the arrival of the Celts to Britain:

> When the stronger and more civilized Celt came he drove before him these little dark men [meaning Iberian Picts, in Ebbutt's own words], he enslaved their survivors or wedded their women, and in his turn fell into slavery to the cruel Druidic religion of his subjects.
> (1994: xii)

Archaeological evidence identifies contact between the Mediterranean and Ireland during the Early Iron Age; one of the most evocative fragments of evidence is the skeleton of a Barbary Ape, which was excavated at Navan in Armagh – suggesting that sea trade occurred and that the ape came from such a ship. Tacitus, writing at the close of the first century AD, spoke of Ireland:

> the interior parts are little known, but through the commercial intercourse and the merchants there is better knowledge of the harbours and approaches.
> (quoted in Ryan [ed] 1991: 112)

Cuchulain: The Hound of Ulster

As Ireland became visible to the Classical World, more of its
society and culture were recorded – through admittedly
discriminating eyes. A Celtic language was spoken throughout
the country, and powerful kingdoms had emerged. Perhaps the
most surprising aspect of later Iron Age Celtic culture to the
uninitiated, not least caused by the heroic emphasis placed
upon warriors epitomized by Cuchulain, is the highly
structured way in which society operated. Different strata of
society had their own well defined place, and laws were laid
down to allow the Celts to live peaceable lives, aside from
small-scale raiding and minor feuds. Rolleston, writing early
in the twentieth century, felt confident enough in the stability
of Celtic culture to comment upon the five distinct factors
which he felt summed up pre-Christian Celtic life – popular
superstition, philosophic creed, worship of personified deities,
demi-scientific teaching by the Druids, and well organized
secular teaching of literature and learning (1994: 89–90). This
viewpoint is inevitably simplistic, but does list a number of
crucial aspects of Celtic life; Rolleston's list would have been
more complete if he had added Celtic art and craftsmanship,
domestic and agricultural skill, and a stratified and stable social
strata. When we consider the archaeological evidence
alongside that written by Classical authors, it is hard to
conclude that Celtic life was really as barbaric and unpleasant
as the Romans and Greeks so often portrayed it. Propaganda
is not an invention of the twentieth century.

We have a fair idea of how Celtic society was structured,
and of the warrior's place in this society not only from the
literary observations of biased Classical writers (whose

evidence we must use with caution), but also from the laws
of later Celtic societies. The medieval Celts were justifiably
proud of their ancestors, and complex oral (and later literary)
testimony recorded much of the attitudes and social
structure of earlier Celtic life, from which we may build up
a general picture of Celtic life.

The role that a warrior like the mythical Cuchulain
would play in such a society was as the defender of the
people and champion of the king. Such a warrior would
hold a high rank in society, and be expected to represent his
people in battle – either in a personal duel or as a leading
figure on the battlefield. The tales of Cuchulain explicitly
show this. Outside of war, a man of Cuchulain's character
would have been equally well received – unlike peacetime
soldiers in so many other ancient and modern societies – for
his wisdom, pride and courage.

Ptolemy, in the second century, even recorded the Latinized
names of the political groups (or, as many would write, 'tribes')
of second century Ireland as he perceived it to be; these
political groups, described geographically, were as follows:

> North west: Vennicnii, Erpeditani, and Nagnatae
> North east: Robogdii, Darini and Voluntii
> Central west: Auteini, and Gangani
> Central east: Eblani, and Cauci
> South west: Vellabori, and Iverni
> South east: Manapii, Coriondi, and Brigantes
> South central: Usdiae
> (source: Ryan, 1991)

A Bronze Age Cuchulain?

Cuchulain is often attributed to the Celtic Iron Age, as the cultural aspects of the tales match that which we have long considered to be true of this period of European history. However, recent research has shown that the preceding era – the Bronze Age – may have been as equally violent and heroic, despite the common view of this period in north-west Europe as being one of peace. Among the many arguments for the lifestyle and culture described in the tales of Cuchulain is that of the similarity of the Irish heroes to those of Homer's *The Iliad* and *The Odyssey*.

Many bronze weapons have been found deposited as votive offerings to now forgotten Bronze Age gods. Quite commonly, the leaf-bladed bronze swords and thin spearheads characteristic of this period have been found with damage caused through combat (these can be distinguished easily from the many weapons that seem to have been ritually broken before deposition). Swords were used for slashing at enemies, and both thrusting spears and javelins are in evidence through excavated metal spearheads. Wooden and leather shields have been found, including one from Oxfordshire which appears to have been pierced by a spearhead (Osgood, 1999).

Skeletal evidence also contains traces of violent death. A number of skeletons from the Bronze Age have been found with injuries caused by weapons – shattered bones being amongst the most common, although a body excavated at Tormarton still had a spearhead impaled in its spine (Osgood, 1999).

323

Warriors

However, chariots are unknown in Britain during this period
(Osgood, 1999), so if a real life Cuchulain did really live and fight in the
Bronze Age, the addition of chariots to his stories would have been a
later insertion by Iron Age Celtic bards.

Hill forts and high status domestic sites feature highly in
Iron Age Celtic archaeology, as do individual farmsteads.
More common than hill forts in Ireland are ring forts,
great defensive ramparts thrown up on the generally flatter
land that occurs there compared to mainland Britain. The
crannog was known in Celtic Ireland, and also in Wales
and Scotland; this was a man-made island sitting in a lake,
usually accessible only by boat. Navan is the best known
royal site of Iron Age Ireland, although similar high status
sites are also known at Tara, Dun Ailinne, and Cruachain;
the earthworks of all these sites may still be seen today. Hill
forts, ring forts and crannogs all offered a degree of defence
to their inhabitants (varying depending upon the size and
style of fortification thrown up), but perhaps more
importantly, these sites exuded ostentation and power,
symbolic of the high status rulers who dwelt within them or
owned them.

Navan itself has been tentatively identified by John
Matthews and Bob Stewart as Conchobar's court (1993: 14),
which excavation has led to suggest saw the end of its
occupied life around 90 BC. There is no firm evidence to
support their theory, and, like Hissarlik's identification as

Troy (Chapter Three), there must have been a number of notable sites in Ireland at this time – some of which we may no longer have any record of. Matthews and Stewart also suggest that the latest that Cuchulain could have lived was in the late first century BC, which, as discussed in the first paragraph of this section, is credible; they suggest that the myth of Cuchulain may have built in a similar way to that of Arthur, where a historical hero became incorporated into myth. It is unlikely that we will ever gather enough specific evidence about Iron Age Ireland to prove or disprove this theory, but at least we are able to identify the role and manner of a King's Champion – or Hero of All Ireland – through the generalized evidence available.

In Battle

B attle in Ireland in the Iron Age was endemic. Much of what we know of Celtic battles comes from classical writers such as Julius Caesar and Tacitus. Such writers portrayed the Celts in barbaric splendour, in a less than subtle display of propaganda against the enemies of Rome.

Iron Age Celts have the modern day reputation of being fearsome warriors; however, perhaps disappointingly to the modern reader, the average Celt at this time was a farmer first and foremost, and only took up arms in times of true crisis. Examples of whole clans rising in war are fairly rare and often took place only against a great enemy – such as Rome. However, a warrior elite existed – very much the distant ancestor of the warbands of Beowulf or Arthur – comprising of minor nobles, relations of the chieftain, and others whose skills had been well demonstrated in battle. As battle could determine the fall of one clan and the rise of another, a chieftain would have been very narrow minded to surround himself only with those of similar breeding at the expense of martial prowess – it is likely that lower class warriors who proved themselves in battle stood a chance of being elected to a chieftain's warband.

Celtic society appears to have been a highly structured culture based on social standing and upbringing. Whilst the ordinary folk toiled their earth, grew crops and bred animals (all of which, it must be said, the Celts were very successful at), the social elite lived an almost unrecognizable life of warfare, raiding and feasting. Indeed, one of the few times that the two sides of Celtic culture occupied their time in similar ways would have been when the clan was roused for war – be it against another Celtic tribe or the threatening power of Greece, Carthage, or Rome.

The legend surrounding Cuchulain makes it clear that one of the warrior elite's main pastimes – aside from fighting one another for prestige and reputation – was raiding rival clans. The Irish economy was dependent upon gold and cattle, and these items – notably cattle – were targeted by raiders. Organizing raids into neighbouring clans is a feature of primitive warfare even today, and provides those involved with the chance to test their skills, without resorting to all out war – which is often considered a very much more dangerous way to 'earn one's spurs'.

Cuchulain: The Hound of Ulster

The splendid, vivid images of the Celt at war left by classical writers presents a fearsome, violent and unforgiving image. Proudly parading, sometimes appearing to fight naked in an open show of aggression and disdain for one's enemies, and making a huge noise with both war horns and battle cries, a Celtic warband would have had quite an adverse effect on the majority of opponents. The Ritchies described the impact of the combined Celtic battle panoply upon Classical observers thus:

> The ancient writers dwelt upon the terrifying effect an army of Celts had on their opponents; their great stature, their wild cries, their gesticulations and prancing, the clashing of arms and blowing of trumpets – all combined to terrify and confuse the enemy. (1985: 25–26)

A lower class clansmen would have arrayed himself on the battlefield armed with a shield, a spear (possibly supplemented by javelins) and perhaps a sword. Bare from the chest up (or clad in a tunic in the temperate climates of the north), and usually wearing trousers on his lower half, such a warrior would have relied on his individual fighting skills for survival, as opposed to any well-rehearsed cohesive tactics involving his fellow clan members.

Such warriors, en masse, formed up into roughly linear formations, and upon a given signal (or sometimes before they were supposed to), charged headlong at their enemies. Such a charge could break a foe at first contact – the very

The Battle of Mons Graupius, AD 84

One of the most vivid descriptions of the Iron Age Celts at war in the
British Isles comes from Tacitus's account of Agricola's campaign
against the Caledonians in modern-day Scotland, culminating in the
Battle of Mons Graupius in AD 84. Aside from Tacitus, the only
surviving account of this campaign was written by Cassius Dio, who
recorded that Agricola 'overran the whole of the enemy's territory'.
This has led one or two modern commentators to suggest that the
battle may never even have taken place, but was written as a piece
of propaganda by Tacitus, promoting the abilities of his father-in-law
Agricola.

Tacitus's account begins with Agricola marching his army of 20,000
to 30,000 men north into the foothills of the Grampian Mountains.
Building a fortified base camp at the bottom of the rising highlands
(possibly at Durno, near Aberdeen), the Roman army was presently
confronted by the 30,000-strong Caledonian army led by the warlord
Galgacus. Galgacus's army arrayed itself on the moorland at the foot of
the slopes, with chariots, horsemen and foot skirmishers armed with
missile weapons to the fore, supported by densely packed foot warriors.

Against this wild and flamboyant host, Agricola deployed 8000
auxiliaries (Roman soldiers recruited from previously conquered
regions, and considered to be inferior in battle to the famous legions)
and 1500 cavalry on each wing. Two thousand cavalrymen were held in
reserve, and the legions remained behind specially prepared ditched
defences. To bolster the confidence of his men, Agricola reputedly sent
away the cavalrymen, and joined the legionaries personally, to direct

the battle from among them; this insight reflects the powerful psychological effect a fully arrayed Celtic battle host could have on even the most experienced opponents.

The battle began at a distance, with skirmish missile fire; the Roman pila and javelins had little effect on the more agile Celtic formations. Agricola ordered five cohorts of his Batavian and Tungrian auxiliaries to engage the enemy, which they did with aplomb; the long swords and small shields of their Celtic foes were not well suited to such a tightly packed melée, and the Caledonians were pushed back across the battlefield. The remaining auxiliaries and the Roman cavalry also engaged at this stage, and the retreat of the Caledonian foot soldiers became a rout. The Caledonian chariots and horses crashed into the pursuing Romans as the rout occurred, and forced the Roman cavalry to back away. Eventually, however, the Celtic mounted warriors and their companions in chariots lost impetuous and became caught and outfought at the legion's ditch.

The remainder of the Caledonian army watched from the slopes, and, seeing an opportunity to engage the Roman left flank, charged down the hill to make contact. This wild charge scattered the Roman horses on this flank, but a counter-charge by the Roman reserve cavalry overcame and defeated this threat.

As this action on the Roman left flank was concluded, the Celts who had so eagerly charged down the hillside now retreated away just as eagerly, opening up a gap for the Roman reserve cavalry to wheel through and completely surround the remainder of the Caledonian army still engaged on the moor. The Caledonians lost all cohesion, and attempted to flee. Hundreds of fierce running battles took place, as individuals and small groups attempted to escape the battlefield. Other Caledonians stood their ground and fought fanatically against the

Romans until they were cut down where they stood. Many other less
fanatical Caledonians were taken prisoner, but apparently escaped in
the confusion of the battle.

As night fell, Tacitus informs us, the Romans grew weary of the
pursuit, and the battle gradually fizzled out. The ground was thick with
the dead and their broken weapons. An estimated 10,000 Celts lay
slain, compared to only 340 Romans (as recorded by Tacitus – and we
cannot be sure that this figure includes non-Roman auxiliaries).

much later battle of Killiecrankie (1689) saw an English
Regiment of the Line break before a wild Celtic charge,
despite the English advantages of firepower, drill and
training. There appear to have been no complex tactics, just
a headlong and headstrong rush into the enemy; of course, if
the enemy line did not break at first contact, the charging
mob would be at an immediate disadvantage (a disordered
charge naturally leads to a disrupted formation, and the rapid
fatigue of the troops involved). Thus, a battle involving
Cuchulain's Celts could be won or lost in the first five
minutes.

We have little evidence of other Celtic tactics from the
Iron Age period – indeed the tactics of Imperial Rome's
early enemies are fairly difficult to fathom beyond simple yet
ferocious charges. In AD 9, German forest tribesmen in
northern Europe completely surprised and annihilated an
invading Roman force; the ambushers crouched and lay in
the dense woodland awaiting the Roman force's advance. As

the Roman column came close, unready for attack and unable to form into the usual close-packed formation for which Roman infantry were renowned, the Germans rose from their hides and the Roman column collapsed before their initial onslaught.

Young, unproven warriors are often assumed to have fought as skirmishers ahead of or to the side of, the main battle line. Javelins, slingshot, and arrows would all have been directed at the enemy, in an attempt to disorder them and to produce the occasional casualty. Missile weapons at that time in Europe did not hold the power of the later longbow, for example, and should be considered to have only really held any value as a nuisance weapon. It does not seem that many Celts in the British Isles used the bow for warfare; the most common missile weapon appears to have been the sling, which itself is mentioned in some of Cuchulain's battles. This strap of leather was whirled around the user's head whilst holding a small shot (either stone or metal), conjuring up speed and velocity, and, when the slingshot inside reached a peak of force, one end of the strap was released, hurling the shot out with tremendous force – and, with practice, unerring accuracy.

Richer warriors fought in a similar way yet with more protection, and more practised weapon-handling skills. Helmets and mail may have been reserved for the nobility and upper class warbands. The famous Battersea Shield and Waterloo Bridge helmet, dredged from the River Thames in London, show Celtic military craftsmanship at its best, shining gold and with elaborate decoration; however, it is unlikely that these protective items were ever used in battle, and are far more likely to have been ceremonial dress. As Rolleston noted, writing early in the twentieth century:

> The Celtic warrior loved display. Everything that gave brilliance and the sense of drama of life appealed to him. His weapons were richly ornamented, his horse-trappings were wrought in bronze and enamel... his raiment was embroidered with gold.
> (1994: 40)

Another unique helmet from Romania had a huge, flying bronze bird on its crest; many other less ostentatious head gear is also known of – including 'jockey' helmets (as the name suggests, similar in style to a modern jockey's helmet), and conical helmets with top knobs on them. Other helmets were of similar design to Roman patterns, although these may have been less common in areas outside of Roman influence. Body armour may have comprised occasionally of bronze, iron or leather breast plates, but, in the later Celtic period at least, chainmail, which was almost certainly a Celtic invention in itself; as noted above, only the richer warriors would have been able to afford such armour – Pausanias telling us that the vast majority of Celts had no protection apart from their large shields.

The shields that the Celts used were often described as being colourful, and long or oblong in design; most measured about 3½ feet long by 2 feet wide at the middle. Made largely from wood, leather or wicker, all that often remains of such shields to be found by the modern archaeologist are the iron bosses that were centrally mounted to protect the user's hand. The Arc de Triomphe in Orange, France, includes carvings of Celtic shield patterns, these being intricate patterns closely related to the patterns from other Celtic craft work; we have less idea of colours. Wooden shields were susceptible to piercing by stabbing weapons, rendering them useless after a pointed weapon penetrated and became impaled in the wood. A project carried out in the twentieth century by experimental archaeologist John Coles showed that a leather shield was more useful in deflecting blows and protecting the user than an ostentatious, yet only thinly metalled shield; perhaps the thin metal shields were mounted on a hardened leather backing for battle?

Two types of spear were known to the Celt – the light, throwing spear or javelin, and the heavier, and broad-bladed thrusting spear used in close combat. A great many spearheads have survived from the Celtic period, varying from 4 inches in length to nearly 20 inches in length. Ash wood traces may sometimes be found in the socket, and two complete spears discovered at La Tène were just over 8 feet in total length.

Despite the standard of Celtic craftsmanship Polybius recorded that Celtic blades bent in battle and blunted quickly. Tacitus described British swords as being overly long and unsuited to swirling, close quarter melée. The whole weight of a warrior could be thrown into a blow with such a weapon, allowing a death-giving blow to be dealt. A number of typological groups have been established by archaeologists for the identification of different sword types; early swords often measured around 2½ feet long, whereas later swords – such as those of the Britons at the time of the Roman invasion – could exceed 3 feet in length and were often narrower than early blades. This suggests that early swords were used as thrusting or stabbing weapons, and that the later types of sword had developed into a slashing long sword.

Chariots were famously recorded amongst the Britons' forces that opposed Julius Caesar's army; it is widely assumed that all Celts used such vehicles, where in fact the chariot was

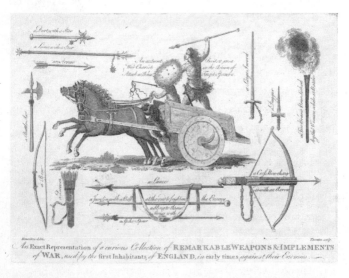

This hand-coloured engraving, c 1790, purports to show a selection of ancient British weapons. In fact, many of the weapons can be dated to the medieval period, although the engraving certainly demonstrates the theory of the Ancient Briton as a Noble Savage. (Author's collection)

Cuchulain: The Hound of Ulster

an antiquated weapon of war on the European mainland at
this time. A number of chariot burials have been excavated,
but common sense would suggest that chariots were only
utilized in areas of flat plains – a chariot would be severely
disadvantaged in a battle on broken or hilly land. The legends
surrounding Cuchulain frequently mention chariots. The
social standing of those using the chariots – and their drivers
– is clearly implied. The driver was very much the chauffeur
to the aristocratic warrior; although the social standing of the
driver is not explicitly outlined in Irish myth, enough is
implied to suggest that the driver was of a lower class than his
passenger, yet still highly considered in society. The warrior
transported by chariot is always a professional warrior in Irish
myth, and the level of martial skill displayed from the account
of Julius Caesar supports this idea. Julius Caesar gave an
account of the British neighbours of Ireland after his
campaigns of the mid first century BC. He was particularly
taken by the Britons' continued use of now obsolete chariots:

> At first they ride along the whole line and hurl javelins;
> the terror inspired by the horses and the noise of the
> wheels generally throw the enemy ranks into
> confusion. Then when they have worked their way
> between the lines of their own cavalry, they jump down
> from the chariots and fight on foot. Meanwhile the
> drivers withdraw a little from the field and place the
> chariots so that their masters, if hard pressed by the
> enemy, have an easy retreat to their ranks.
> (quoted in Ritchie & Ritchie, 1985:32)

Caesar continues by explaining that the chariot-riding Celts were so skilled in their vehicles that they could control their horse-led chariots over steeply falling slopes, and could turn them on a very sharp curve.

Chariot warriors could also run along the chariot's pole, between the horses whilst they galloped, and stand on the yoke without falling. Britain and Ireland seem to have been fairly poorly equipped with troops mounted just on horseback; Gallic cavalry and earlier Celts were renowned as horsemen, yet for some reason the British Isles steadfastly stood by their chariotry – perhaps this should be seen as implying the Isles were a political and cultural backwater; however, it may well be that the Britons chose to stick to what they knew best – rather like the continuation of the longbow in English armies well into the age of gunpowder.

Iron Age Celtic shields. The shield above is from John Hewitt's *Ancient Armour*, 1860. The shield opposite is from *L'Art Pour Tous, Encyclopedie de l'Art Industriel et Decoratif.*

Cuchulain: The Hound of Ulster

Perhaps one of the most surprising elements of Irish myth to the modern reader is the assertion that women were sometimes accomplished warriors. Despite the attempts by Classical writers to claim that the only thing more fearsome than the warlike Celt was his warlike and even more brutish wife, references to women warriors are relatively rare – but exist in sufficient numbers to lend the theory credence. The name that springs most rapidly to mind when the mention of women as warriors is made is that of Boudicca. Boudicca was the Queen of the Iceni, based in modern day East Anglia, who rose with her people against the early Roman governors of first-century AD Britannia. Her revolt was bloody and short lived, yet the warriors of her own and neighbouring tribes thought nothing wrong in being under the military control of a woman.

Strabo, the Classical writer, recorded that the Celts took the heads of their enemies from the battlefield, tied to their horses' necks; other Classical writers horrified their audiences with similar stories. Cuchulain drove back to Ulster from a

raid into Connaught with the heads of his enemies dangling
from his chariot car. To the Gauls, and presumably to other
Celts who continued this practice, head taking held a mystical
or religious significance. A variation on head taking can be
seen in the tale of Cuchulain, when a mysterious stranger
challenges a number of Irish Champions to a beheading
competition – each champion may swing an undefended
blow at the stranger, as long as they agree that the stranger
may take his own swing afterwards (also see Chapter One,
feature on Gawain and the Green Knight).

Irish myth has never failed itself for creating larger than
life characters, and warriors capable of superhuman
deeds on the battlefield. Yet Cuchulain stands out as the
greatest of all these warriors. Competing against challengers
for the renown of being the greatest warrior in all Ireland,
the legend of Cuchulain has always been told in the spirit of
traditional Irish folklore, and the social system and culture
outlined in myth fits well with what we know of Iron Age
Ireland. Thus it would appear that although Cuchulain fights
mystical beasts and battles against magicians, the background
in which he exists is of greater use when considering Celtic
lifestyle than one may first assume. The historical fighting
styles of Cuchulain's Celts also fits well with what we know
from legend – the elite appear to have fought from chariots,
supported in times of strife by a gathering of the entire tribe
on foot, armed with swords, spears, slings and shields. The
historical Celt at war seems to have been just as formidable
as Cuchulain and his fellow heroes of Ulster.

10

WILLIAM WALLACE
Scotland's Braveheart

The legend of William Wallace – Braveheart – is an excellent example of a modern myth in the making and the manner in which different chroniclers add their own political and historical bias to the legend. In the case of Wallace, the latest spin has been created by the Oscar-winning 1995 film starring Mel Gibson; *Braveheart* the movie is itself based upon a medieval manuscript detailing the exploits of the outlaw turned Guardian of Scotland, William Wallace. *Braveheart* follows the original story fairly well, but does not fully adhere to the traditional or historical story – despite this, and perhaps unsurprisingly, the *Braveheart* legend is the most well known story relating to Wallace. Hollywood turned a minor Scottish noble who was wanted primarily for outlawry into a crusading hero, fighting the evil King Edward Longshanks of England.

The movie begins with beautiful images of the Scottish highlands – beautiful countryside indeed. The narrator, after a brief note stating that we are now in Scotland, 1280, opens the tale:

Warriors

Narrator: 'I shall tell you of William Wallace. Historians from England will say I'm a liar. But history is written by those who have hanged heroes. The King of Scotland had died without a son, and the King of England, a cruel pagan known as Edward the "Long Shanks", claimed the throne of Scotland for himself. Scotland's nobles fought him and fought each other over the crown.'

Accordingly, Longshanks called a truce, inviting all of the Scottish nobles to meet him unarmed and accompanied by one page only. The young child Wallace stumbled upon the hanging bodies of all those invited in a barn – Wallace therefore became rudely introduced to English brutality at an early age.

After this English atrocity, the local Scots, including Wallace's father, decided to make a stand against the English, and went to war. Edward's ploy had robbed the area of most of its noble men, so the farmers took to battle themselves; it was a battle that would make the young Wallace an orphan, as his father died at the hands of the English. Before setting out to fight, Wallace's father left him with words of wisdom that were to influence the young boy for the rest of his life, telling him that it was wits, not warfare, that made men great.

After the death of his father, Wallace went to live with his learned, clerical uncle, Argyle. Argyle educated the boy as a scholar and a warrior, instilling virtuous ways into the boy's mind. In a dream, Wallace saw his father, who declared to him:

William Wallace: Scotland's Braveheart

'Your heart is free – have the courage to follow it.'

Many years later, Edward Longshanks – still king yet now older – arranged the marriage of his son to the rival king of France's daughter; this was a political marriage, as Prince Edward already had a male lover. Perhaps, it implies, Longshanks wanted the French Isabella for himself. Still intent on ruling Scotland – disorder on one's borders was a sign of weakness – Longshanks saw the key to conquest being the nobility of both England and Scotland. The Scottish nobles were to be offered lands and titles in England, removing them from their troublesome homelands and denying them national support; the English nobles were to be offered lands and titles in Scotland, integrating English ways with those of the Scots.

> Edward Longshanks: 'The trouble with Scotland is that it is full of Scots,'

And the ruthless Longshanks intended to overcome this by breeding the Scottish blood out of the natives; he declared that English nobles would be granted the right of *Prima Nocta* on their land in Scotland – the sexual right to any newly married Scottish woman on the first night of her marriage.

> Edward Longshanks: 'If we can't get them out, we'll breed them out.'

The Fishing Fight

Of the many folk tales that sprang up in Scotland about William Wallace in his early career as an outlawed fugitive, one of the better stories recalls the day upon which Wallace went to fish at the River Irvine. He was accompanied by a child who carried his net for him, and, expecting no trouble, Wallace had decided to venture out without his sword.

Happily catching fish for ten hours, Wallace was disturbed by the approach of Lord Percy, captain of Ayr. Part of his retinue detached themselves from his party and rode down to the river to confront the Scotsman. They demanded his fish, to which Wallace calmly replied that he would let them take some, but not all, of his catch. The English men at arms did not take kindly to being told what they may do by a lowly Scot, and charged at Wallace, swords drawn.

Wallace hurled his fishing net at the first to attack him, and wrestled the sword from the stunned Englishman's hand, using it to cut the aggressor's throat. Two of the other Englishmen he also slew, and the other two fled on horseback. When Lord Percy heard the story of the fight, he laughed aloud and exclaimed to the frightened survivors:

> 'May foul things befall you, since one has put all of you to
> confusion. Whoever means it most, may the Devil of hell
> drown him! In faith for me this day he will not be sought.'
> (Quoted by Walter Scheps in Ohlgren, 1998: 260)

William Wallace: Scotland's Braveheart

As William Wallace grew, his hatred of the occupying English was compounded by the many atrocities that he witnessed. The arrogant swagger and chilled brutality of the English nobles and their feudal followers made the anger swell in all red-blooded Scotsmen. In Edinburgh, the Scottish nobility – including Robert Bruce, the heir to one of the most powerful native claims to the Scottish throne – gathered, to discuss what to do about the English garrisons and the degrading English right of *Prima Nocta*. Robert Bruce's father (a leper in *Braveheart*), believed that Edward Longshanks would have to be placated until the Scots were strong enough to fight back, patiently and peacefully resisting to gain independence and maintain their land rights and titles. His son Robert, he felt, should have been allowed to speak for the whole for the Scottish nation.

Whilst such fruitless meetings were going nowhere, an older, wiser William Wallace returned to his home town of Lanark from the guardianship of his uncle. Immediately challenged to a rock-throwing duel, he won it with guile and cunning; speaking with wisdom beyond his years, Wallace announced that:

> 'A test of a soldier is not in his arm, it's here.' [pointing to his head]

Wallace then witnessed the local English lord brutally claiming his right of *Prima Nocta* with a local woman. Even so, Wallace contended to gain the heart of his childhood sweetheart, whom he quickly married in secret under a

343

Celtic cross. Things were not to remain happy though, as a group of three English soldiers attempted to rape Wallace's wife; putting his strength and wits to good use, Wallace attacked and defeated all three, and evaded the garrison's clumsy attempts to arrest him by escaping in an English uniform. Wallace's bride was not so lucky however, being tied to a post and having her throat slit by the garrison commander, who proclaimed that:

> 'An assault on the king's soldiers is an insult on the king himself.'

Wallace quickly learned of the brutal, cold-blooded murder of his bride, and returned to Lanark with a group of disgruntled local Scotsmen. He single handedly killed four English soldiers, and then, with the help of his followers routed the rest of the garrison and put the commander – who killed his bride – to death by slitting his throat.

The locals called upon Wallace to lead them in an uprising against the oppressive English, and other local clans flocked to Wallace's army to go to war against the hated English. Success followed success – Wallace's men, disguised in the Lanark garrison's uniforms, stormed the local lord's castle and exacted their revenge on his foul abuse of *Prima Nocta*. Other members of this English force were sent home to England with the message 'Scotland is free'.

Meanwhile, news of Wallace's minor victories had reached the ear of the ruthless Longshanks in England. Leaving to attend to duties in France, the king ordered his son Prince

William Wallace: Scotland's Braveheart

Edward to sort out his Scottish problem. Prince Edward commanded his northern garrisons to brutally burn Scottish farms and terrorize the native communities. Even so, Wallace continued his uprising, outwitting and surprising every English force that had the misfortune to meet with his small yet growing army of common folk.

As yet, the Scottish nobility had not become involved in Wallace's fight. Weakened by infighting, and the fear of losing their lands when Scotland's eventual but inescapable defeat occurred, they were not keen to side with the peasant outlaws. Robert Bruce wished to support Wallace's movement, but was prevented from doing so by his pragmatic father, who wished to maintain a public cordiality towards the English to preserve the family's lands and titles. A compromise was reached though, as the elder Bruce allowed his son to raise their northern lands in revolt whilst

The siege of Carlisle, 1315, showing the English garrison repelling a Scottish attack including a siege engine and scaling ladders. Drawing based on a medieval manuscript. (Author's collection)

remaining neutral in the southern lands which were watched by the English; the elder Bruce wryly commented that it was a time to survive and protect the Bruce claim to the throne.

Meanwhile, Wallace's mustered leaders discussed how they may have been able to stand in an open battle against English heavy cavalry, for they knew that such troops would be sent north soon. Most of Wallace's companions favoured the idea of simply melting away into the forests and hills rather than fight a set piece battle, and conduct a guerrilla war only. This, they told Wallace, was the traditional Highland way of coping with invasion. Wallace, though, had other ideas – he suggested that the Scottish warriors should carry long spears (pikes) to keep the horsemen at bay.

As Wallace's force awaited its next challenge, Wallace went hunting alone in the forest. A plot to assassinate him – perhaps by Edward Longshanks or perhaps by the Scottish nobles who considered him a liability – was foiled by one of the Irish warriors who had flocked to his side. Their country, like Wallace's own, had been invaded by Longshanks, and many were keen to strike a blow – be it in Ireland or Scotland.

A strong northern English army marched into Scotland, making their way north towards Stirling. At the same time, the Highlanders – not usually known for their interference in lowland politics – marched to join Wallace (perhaps under the persuasive influence of Robert Bruce, although Bruce himself did not commit openly to Wallace's cause). The main Scottish army, led by a committee of bickering Scots nobles, was outnumbered three to one, and its warriors were mostly inexperienced in battle, yet the two forces came to stand either side of a field at Stirling, facing one another. The ordinary Scottish folk looked to desert their cause whilst their social betters argued who would take command, but Wallace turned up with his own army – covered in Gaelic war paint and making a speech about national pride, not politics:

> Wallace: 'You've come to fight as free men and free men you are.'

Spoken to in terms they related to, the Scottish foot soldiers decided to stay and fight under Wallace's command, paying homage to Scotland's pride, not it's landed nobility or those with money. Rousing them into a frenzy, Wallace declared:

> 'They'll take our lives but they'll never take our freedom!'

Passing out the long pikes devised by himself, Wallace organized the foot soldiers and the noble cavalrymen alike; the cavalry, he decreed, would feign flight and work their way around the English flank to ride down the archers. The footmen would stand with Wallace, and entrap the English cavalry on their pike heads. After enduring a deadly arrow shower, the Scottish cavalry feigned flight, and the English cavalry surged forward – to become impaled on the pike heads of the lowly Scottish infantry. The Scottish infantry then charged forward into their English enemies, their wild highland charge routing most of the invading army. The

Scottish nobles appeared in the English rear, encircling and
riding down the remaining Englishmen, and Wallace's great
victory was complete.

As the remnants of the English army retreated from
Scotland, Wallace was knighted and declared the Guardian of
Scotland. The nobility were not happy – Wallace was of
common blood – but gave their consent in order to keep the
populace on their side. Whilst the nobility argued amongst
themselves as to who should become king, Wallace announced
a plan to invade northern England – taking the fight to the
enemy rather than waiting for them to return to Scotland.

Wallace's invasion went well: storming into northern
England, he laid siege to York – the finest city in the north.
Using battering rams to smash down the gates, the garrison
was put to the sword – including its commander,
Longshanks' nephew. Longshanks himself had just returned
from France, to be greeted by this news; unsurprisingly for
one so cruel, he killed his son's boyfriend in a fit of rage at
the Prince's inadequacies, and set about organising a truce.
Longshanks intended to buy himself time – organizing a
meeting between Wallace and Longshanks' ambassador
(Prince Edward's bride, Isabella). Isabella was sent north,
unaware of her use as a decoy, to meet with the Scottish
warlord, offering him gold and other rewards in return for
peace. Wallace, of course, refused, as he was a man of
principal not greed. Intrigued by the Scotsman, and
concerned for his safety against Longshanks' rage, Isabella
returned to the king, telling him that Wallace had refused the
bribe and waited for the king at York, to meet in battle.

William Wallace: Scotland's Braveheart

Delighted by the time gained through Isabella's mission, Longshanks announced that he now had men advancing on Edinburgh from all directions, from England, Wales, Ireland and France, and that Wallace, still at York, could do nothing to prevent this. Isabella sent warning to Wallace of the plan, and the Guardian of Scotland retreated with all speed to his own country. The Scottish nobility had been organizing a treaty, fearing for their lands if invaded, but Wallace dismissed them as cowards and being unworthy to be named as Scots. Robert Bruce was keen to join with Wallace, yet his father prevented him from doing so; the elder Bruce told Robert to bide his time, for the sake of his country. Indeed, this was sage advice, and Robert was to later achieve his own victories.

The Scottish army mustered at Falkirk to meet the invading army led by Edward Longshanks in person. Longshanks – a callous man – decided not to waste his archer's arrows (which cost money), but to first send the Irish auxiliaries against the Scots. As the Irish advanced, they joined with the Scots, deserting to their fellow Celt's cause. The Scottish archers then sent fire arrows screaming towards the land over which the English cavalry advanced – land upon which the Scots had prepared tar pits the night before the battle. Many of the English horsemen burnt to death, whilst others became engulfed in the headlong Celtic charge of Wallace and his men that immediately followed. As the battle hung in the balance, the Scottish nobility decided to flee the battlefield – they were not keen to openly fight against the King of England. Longshanks, it transpired, had presented them with lands in England in return for leaving

Wallace to his own fate. English archers fired into the swirling fracas on the command of Longshanks – he was happy for his own men to die under a hail of their own missile if it decimated the Scottish army too. Outnumbered and surrounded, the Scots finally succumbed, and a decisive English victory was won.

William Wallace, wounded by English arrows, was very nearly captured, but escaped with the help of Robert Bruce (whose father had forced him to fight on Edward's side in exchange for land and power). Robert Bruce was like Wallace in many ways though, and felt that he had betrayed his countrymen, vowing:

'I will never be on the wrong side again.'

After this defeat, Wallace and his surviving followers lived off the country, and Wallace devoted his time to hunting down the Scottish nobles whom he felt had left him to die at Falkirk. They were to meet brutally violent deaths, deserved by their greed-filled betrayal of their fellow countrymen. Longshanks was fully aware of Wallace's survival, however, and hunted him down across Scotland. All attempts to capture him failed, including one plot that sent Isabella as the bait. Instead of capturing Wallace, the princess met him in secret and made love to the man with whom she had become so enamoured.

Eventually, a group of Scottish nobles summoned Wallace to Edinburgh, wanting him to unite and lead them against the English. Wallace's loyal followers thought this to be a trap

Drawing based on a manuscript illustration of a Scottish footman at the time of William Wallace's campaigns. (Author's collection)

– Wallace himself thought this too – but, in the hope that he could rid his beloved country of the English, felt it would be worth attempting. A trap it was, and Wallace was taken into English custody.

Tried as a traitor to the English crown, Wallace refused to renounce himself and swear allegiance to Longshanks:

> Wallace: 'If I swear to him, then all that I am is dead already.'

Isabella begged her husband, Prince Edward, and his father Longshanks (who now lay seriously ill in bed) to spare Wallace; the prince's reply on his father's behalf was definite in its intent, however:

> Prince Edward: 'Before he lost the powers of speech, he told me his one comfort was that he would live to know Wallace was dead.'

Contentedly Longshanks could die, then, as Wallace was hanged, drawn and quartered in front of a baying English crowd, refusing to swear allegiance to Longshanks or England throughout his gruesome torture. Before finally dying, Wallace beheld a vision of his wife, remembering the true love that had drawn him into conflict with the English in the first place.

Wallace's body was quartered and each part sent to a different corner of the country, to discourage further rebellion. However, in 1314, when the patriotic Bruce (no longer hindered by his leprous father) led his Scottish army to victory at Bannockburn, he reminded his men of William Wallace and what it was to be a true Scotsman:

'You have bled with Wallace, now bleed with me!'

In History

The history of conflict between the English and Scots is a long one, beginning with the evolution of the early Anglo-Saxon kingdoms in the seventh century AD, continuing throughout the medieval period, and sporadically until (and twice after) the Union in 1707. A key element of the conflicts between these two countries was the division in Scotland between those who wished to ally themselves with their English neighbours, and those who wished to remain fiercely independent.

In 1286, Alexander III of Scotland died in an accident; his only heir was his granddaughter Margaret, daughter of Alexander's own daughter and Erik of Norway; thirteen other claimants were to contest the throne. Alexander's English contemporary was Edward I – probably the greatest war leader of all medieval England; Edward had defeated the rebellion of Llywelyn ap Gruffydd between 1277 and 1282, and saw in Alexander's death a chance to take control of Scotland too. Edward proposed marriage between the Scottish queen and his own son, Edward. This peaceful solution to English control of Scotland was foiled by

Margaret's premature death. Edward of England then placed John Balliol on the throne, after obtaining oaths of loyalty from the other contenders (the future hero of Scotland Robert the Bruce was the stronger claimant under Scottish tradition, though). Balliol was middle-aged, and often described as being a weak-willed and weak-minded man, and stood as Edward's puppet ruler.

In an uncharacteristic change of mind, Balliol revolted against the English, and Edward despatched an army to the north in March 1296 (he had other troubles to contend with in person – war with France in Gascony and a rebellion in north Wales). The English arrived at the border town of Berwick, which was under Scottish control, and proceeded to capture it in a few short minutes, and filled the rest of their day slaughtering the inhabitants. Such atrocities were not uncommon in the medieval world, and the pillage of enemy towns bolstered the pay of the common soldiers of the army. With Berwick captured, Edward sent one of his most trusted lieutenants, John de Warenne, to render Dunbar in the same manner. The force sent to capture Dunbar included the best heavy cavalry available, Welsh bowmen under the pay of the King of England, and a strong force of infantrymen of the northern levies. De Warenne's force was confronted just outside the town, and inflicted a heavy defeat on the Scots, who lost over 10,000 men and had a handful of earls captured. Edward's force continued into Scotland, showing their strength by pushing further into the country than any southern invader had since the Romans over 1000 years before. Balliol was forced to abdicate.

William Wallace: Scotland's Braveheart

William Wallace first appears in the pages of history soon after, in the spring of 1297. The English occupation had not ended after Balliol's defeat, which caused a great deal of tension and hatred amongst many Scots; although others of their nation, certain members of the nobility, benefited from working alongside the English and gained in power. Early in 1297, the tension overflowed into violence and the majority of Scotland was in a state of undeclared war. At Lanark, Wallace announced himself to history through his massacre of the entire English garrison, in revenge for the death of his fiancée at the hands of an English nobleman. All was not quite so black and white as at first seems, though, as the noble in question, Hazelrig, the Sheriff of Lanark, had killed Wallace's fiancée in revenge for Wallace's earlier surprise attack on an English patrol at Loudon Hill.

The Great Seal of Edward I, showing the arms and armour of a noble at the time of Wallace's challenge to Edward's authority. (From Hewitt's *Ancient Armour and Weapons in Europe*, 1855)

The Anglo-Scottish Wars after Wallace

With the brief highlight of Robert Bruce's success at Bannockburn in 1314, the history of warfare between England and Scotland after Wallace's death reads as an almost unbroken string of dismal defeats for the Scots.

At Halidon Hill in 1333, Scottish losses were noted as 10,000 compared to an English casualty list of around 100 men. Neville's Cross in 1346 was a closer run battle, although it still ended in an English victory.

Otterburn, fought in 1388, is recorded as a Scottish victory, although both sides were badly bloodied; this defeat for the northern English army was avenged a few years later at the battle of Homildon Hill in 1402. After limited campaigning, scaled down throughout the fifteenth century due to English campaigns in France and their own Wars of the Roses, further victories occurred at Flodden in 1513 and Pinkie in 1547. The success of English armies in these battles came about through the superiority of a combined cavalry and longbow army fighting against a pike-based army. In general, the Scots were shot down before they reached the English battle line, leaving them disordered when the impact of hand-to-hand combat occurred. Surprisingly, the Scots never tried to update their battle tactics or learn from their previous defeats. This had a knock-on effect on the English, who did not see the need to upgrade from longbows to gunpowder until long after most of the other major European powers in the sixteenth century.

William Wallace: Scotland's Braveheart

Wallace was the son of a minor knight, Sir Malcolm Wallace the Laird of Elderslie (now a district of Paisley). His surname suggests that he was originally of northern British descent, 'Wallace' being a corruption of 'Welsh'. For at least a while in his youth, he lived with his uncle, a cleric at Cambuskenneth Abbey near to Stirling. Reputedly a huge man – some accounts describe him as 6 foot 2 inches – he had a fiery temper, as the English were later to learn. After his slaughter of the garrison, he took to the countryside as an outlaw, his small band of followers gradually rising to the size of a small army. They travelled huge distances across the open hills of Scotland, striking at ill-prepared English strongholds across the occupied areas of the country. This was Wallace at his best – a strong leader of men and a shrewd guerrilla fighter. His reputation grew, which is unsurprising when he was known to kill every Englishmen that he could; his intimidation and inspiration of the common folk made it difficult for Hugh de Cressingham, the English treasurer of Scotland, to raise taxes. In short, Wallace was a problem for the English, partly through his physical actions of violence, but perhaps more threateningly as a folk hero for the Scots to be inspired to rise up by. Wallace was the spirit of Scottish resistance.

At the time of Wallace's rising reputation, John de Warenne – by then appointed Warden of the North – was preparing for a further punitive expedition into Scotland. He did not predict any strong Scottish resistance; indeed from the evidence he witnessed first hand the previous year, he probably expected to march straight into the heart of the land without any difficulty at all. De Warenne marched into

Scotland, aware that Wallace was laying siege to Dundee
Castle; de Warenne would probably have been quite
unconcerned by this – Wallace was not a proven general,
having won nothing more than a few skirmishes by de
Warenne's reckoning. In addition, Wallace did not have a
siege train, and stood little chance of storming the castle;
Wallace knew this too and changed his tactics when he
learned of the English army entering the country. As de
Warenne marched further into Scotland, Wallace led his men
away from Dundee and deployed his army astride the road
that led north from Stirling; this was a strong defensive
position and Wallace intended to contest the Warden of the
North's march into the newly liberated area of Scotland
north of the Firth of Forth.

The point that Wallace had chosen to defend was a good
one. His army sat about a mile north of the River Forth,
where the bridge could only be approached over a long
causeway flanked by meadows. Wallace had some 5000 men
under his command; de Warenne's force consisted of 300
men-at-arms and a few thousand English and Welsh infantry.
On 11 September 1297, de Warenne drew up his force on the
southern bank of the river, and sent his mounted knights and
men-at-arms thundering over the bridge to confront the
Scots. De Warenne had not scouted the far bank well enough,
though, and the flower of his invasion force rode straight into
boggy ground, unable to move in the deep mud. This was
Wallace's finest moment: he had deceived the English into
trapping themselves, and his own men did not fail him.
Scottish horns blew and the Scottish infantry charged forward

to butcher the English force divided by the bridge. The
English on the south side of the bridge watched on helplessly
as the elite of their army was cut to pieces; discretion being
the better part of valour, the English footmen fled to Berwick;
de Warenne was disgraced and fled to York. The battle of
Stirling Bridge ended in a decisive victory for the Scots.

In March 1298, Wallace was appointed Guardian of
Scotland, king in all but name. He declared that he was to
take this role to rule in the name of the exiled king. As the
defiant Scots rejoiced their victory and Wallace's
appointment, Edward of England made his own plans to
march to Scotland; matters had now gone far enough that
the King of England had to take personal control of the
Scottish war. He organized the largest force to march into
Scotland since Agricola's Roman army. It consisted of
around 2500 armoured cavalry and 2900 infantry. Edward
was accompanied by eight notable earls; each of these
brought along their own retinue of knights and infantry.

This new threat demanded new tactics by Wallace, who
was now officially responsible for the defence of Scotland –
much to the annoyance of many Scotsmen of higher birth
than him. As Edward's great force lurched into the lowlands
of southern Scotland, Wallace pursued a policy of 'scorched
earth', removing or laying waste to all food and resources in
his wake. This was a shrewd move, showing much of the
guile that Wallace had gained as an outlaw. He knew that
Edward's force was too large to be supported by its own
stores: supplying armies was a very basic affair until well into
the nineteenth century. Bringing Wallace's army to battle

proved difficult for the English; their men were hungry, they knew the countryside less well than their quarry, and morale was at its lowest ebb. Desertion was a problem, and tensions between the English and Welsh contingents resulted in fighting (one must remember that the Welsh had only been subdued by Edward during the previous ten years).

Wallace knew that he would not be able to evade his enemy forever, and his ravaging of the land would not have been popular with the common folk upon whose support he relied. Additionally, this policy was an expensive waste for the Scottish nobles who owned the land; many would have been as happy to pay feudal dues to the King of England as they were to pay the Guardian of Scotland. On 21 July 1298, Wallace led his army forward to meet the English. Through the early light of the next morning, scouts from the opposing armies reported their enemy's positions, and two of medieval Britain's most famous and feared warriors met in battle at Falkirk.

Wallace knew that he would have to defeat the English heavy cavalry at Falkirk as he had at Stirling Bridge, and intended to do this with a 'schiltron' (a formation of tightly packed pikemen, who would keep horsemen at bay). Wallace was a veteran of many skirmishes and had led an army to victory in the previous year; Edward, on the other hand, had defeated the French, the Welsh, the Irish and the Saracens in on-going campaigns. He was probably the most capable military leader that medieval England had seen up to that time. Edward also entered the battle with new tactics, placing more reliance on his Welsh bowmen than his knights. The

William Wallace: Scotland's Braveheart

Welsh archers poured showers of arrows into the stationary Scottish spearmen, concentrating all of their firepower onto one schiltron at a time. The battle ended in Scottish slaughter, and Wallace, defeated by superior tactics and generalship, fled into the wood of Callander with a few followers.

After the battle of Falkirk, Wallace resigned his title as Guardian of Scotland. We do not know if he did this of his own free will, or whether the Scottish nobility forced him out. Two men were chosen to replace him – Robert Bruce and John Comyn. Wallace was left to continue his fight against the English in his own way, although from now on, there were to be no more great victories for him.

Edward did not follow up his victory to any great effect, instead retiring to Carlisle; perhaps this was as a consequence of his age (he was in his sixties). In the spring of 1300, whilst Wallace was still at large in the countryside, Edward planned yet another invasion of Scotland, which broke up the centre of resistance in south-west Scotland's Galloway; the Scottish army of the Earl of Buchan was defeated at Twynholm.

Also in 1300, there is some evidence that Wallace attempted to seek the support of the French king, Philip IV. He sailed to France, and also made a pilgrimage to Rome to visit the Pope. Wallace may have been offered lands in France by Philip IV, and was certainly given financial support.

The following year, two more invasions took place; Wallace was still conducting guerrilla operations, but the English concentrated their efforts on unsuccessfully hunting for Robert Bruce, a newly emerging Scottish leader. By 1303, the nobility of Scotland began to sue for peace with Edward and his

occupying forces; many had never been fully behind Wallace –
perhaps through jealousy of his position due to his (relatively)
lowly birth – and left him to continue his fight against the
English alone. The last recorded battle that Wallace fought was
in 1304, against Aymer de Valence at Black Earnside, inflicting
a minor defeat upon the English. Whilst continuing his
struggle by fighting small scale skirmishes much as those early
in his career, Wallace was eventually betrayed on either 3 or 5
August 1305. Taken to Dumbarton Castle, he was handed over
to Aymer de Valence and Sir Robert Clifford. They took him
to Carlisle, and from there went to London, where Edward I
refused to see him. On 23 August 1305, he was hung, drawn
and quartered, and his decapitated head was displayed on
London Bridge. The disembowelled quarters of his body were
sent to the four major cities of the north (Newcastle, Stirling,
Perth and Berwick) as a warning to others that would stand in
the way of English expansion to the north.

Beyond the basic historical story of Wallace, a few glaring
inconsistencies exist between the *Braveheart* Wallace and
reality. To begin with, the portrayal of Edward I as a 'cruel
pagan' is a little unusual – Edward journeyed to the Holy
Land to fight for his faith against non-Christians.
Additionally, in 1280, when *Braveheart* begins, England and
Scotland were in a rare lull between wars, and Alexander III
did not die until six years after this. After his death, the Scots
had requested the respected Edward I to act as the arbitrator
of the nobles' opposing claims. Perhaps the most significant
political omission from *Braveheart* is the complete absence of
John Balliol; removing him entirely allowed the scriptwriters

to present Wallace as the only true patriot and freedom fighter, as opposed to being a claimant alongside Balliol. In a similar way, the Bruce family have been misrepresented in *Braveheart*, and there appears to be no evidence that Robert Bruce's father had leprosy.

The opening scene, where Wallace finds the Scottish nobles hanging in a barn, was based on a contemporarily recorded event, which occurred in 1297 at the height of Anglo-Scottish warfare; this perhaps makes the actions more understandable (as they occurred in war and not peacetime), and could therefore not have influenced Wallace as a child. In *Braveheart*, Wallace follows up his victory at Stirling Bridge with an invasion of northern England; this did occur, but only as small scale raiding, and at no time did Wallace (or indeed any other medieval Scottish warlord) attempt to storm York as shown in the film. In reality, Wallace failed even to capture Carlisle – a far less well fortified town than York – due to the lack of siege machinery in the Scottish army.

In the film, Isabella, who is sent by Edward Longshanks to act as a spy against Wallace, falls in love with 'the hero'. Prince Edward is portrayed as a homosexual, and later in *Braveheart*, we see Isabella and Wallace making love. This, we can safely guess, aided by Isabella's words to her husband and father-in-law, infers that Wallace was the father of the future Edward III – England's most successful military leader of the fourteenth century! Sadly for those to whom this idea appeals, Isabella was only one year old in 1297, and did not marry Edward until the age of twelve, three years after Wallace's death. Paul V Walsh has succinctly summed these scenes of *Braveheart* up as 'Patriotism and Queer-bashing all rolled into one.' (1998: 15).

Intriguingly, for a film in which the battle scenes were so well choreographed and shot, the actual geography and tactics of the historical battles seem to have been ignored completely. The outcome of Stirling Bridge was significantly altered by the location of the battle – a looped, unfordable river with a solitary bridge to cross – but this is not reflected in the movie. Falkirk is better represented, yet the inclusion of Irish troops in the English army is unwarranted, as is the scene of desertion to the Scottish cause. There was some anxiety between the English and Welsh elements of Edward's army (the Welsh having been conquered only in the 1280s and 1290s), but this took place in camp, not on the battlefield. Indeed, the Irish would have been unlikely to have aided the lowland Scots – the bloody fourteenth-century involvement of the Bruce family in Ireland typified the lack of Celtic brotherhood between the two nations at this time.

Overall, many of the changes between history and *Braveheart* have been made to allow a modern audience to feel that they can understand the complicated nature of medieval politics – the purpose of *Braveheart* was, of course, to make money and create an enjoyable film, not to increase world knowledge of medieval Scottish history; the easiest way to achieve this is to turn any tale into a simple battle between Good (in this case Wallace and his Scots) and Evil (which Patrick McGoogan acts so well to incarnate as Edward Longshanks). This does not make *Braveheart* a poor movie to watch – indeed it is very good as an action film –

but what is seen on screen should not be immediately accepted as 'the truth'. In so many ways, *Braveheart* is a classic example of myth being regurgitated as history.

Scotland's freedom fighter was dead, but his struggle was to continue for centuries to come: first through Robert Bruce, and later by other noted Scots such as Rob Roy and Bonnie Prince Charlie. Arguably, none of those who followed William Wallace evoked such a romantic folk tale. Even since the union of the two countries in 1707, rivalry has existed between the English and Scots, although the two nations have continued to be united against enemies, and modern rivalries are mostly restricted to sporting events. Even so, 800 years after the uprising of William Wallace, many Scots still share his idealism of independence, as noted in Danny Boyle's 1996 movie, *Trainspotting*:

> Renton: 'Some people hate the English;… [we] Can't even find a decent culture to be colonized by.'

In Battle

John Hewitt, writing in the mid nineteenth century, described medieval Scottish armies as follows:

> In Scotland, two leading influences were at work. The highlanders adhered to their old habits and their old arms with a pertinacy which has not been extinguished even in our own day. The round shield ornamented with

knot-work subsisted to the field of Culloden, and the
dagger with its hilt of the same pattern, is still in vogue.
[In the Crimean War, Highlanders in the British army
went to war in kilts, their rifled muskets accompanied by
claymore swords.] But in the south of Scotland the
fashions of France and England had made great in roads;
especially advanced by the crowds of discontented nobles
of Saxon and Norman blood, who sought in the court
of the Scottish king solace for their misfortunes, or
revenge for their wrongs.
(1996: 106)

As we have seen, warfare between the English and Scots was
not a new development at the time of Wallace's battles.
However, William Wallace himself is often given credit for a
new development on the battlefield – rightly or wrongly –
which at first appeared to be a formidable weapon: the
schiltron, or pike hedge. In this formation, the Scottish
common folk stood, armed with long pikes (about 12 feet in
height), shields, and if lucky and more wealthy, some form of
body armour. Such formations were to constitute the
mainstay of Scottish armies from the time of Wallace in the
late thirteenth century, through to perhaps the most decisive
defeat of the Scots at Flodden by Henry VIII's army in 1513.

The schiltron had much in common with the pike
phalanxes of Alexander the Great's Macedonians, and indeed
with the famous Swiss pikemen of later years. However, a
much closer comparison can be drawn with the spearmen of
north Wales, who, on the rare occasions that they could be

William Wallace: Scotland's Braveheart

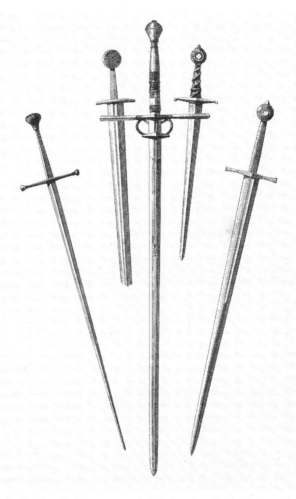

A collection of medieval European swords, including a large two-handed sword in the centre, not unlike that wielded by Mel Gibson in the Hollywood movie *Braveheart*. (From *L'Art Pour Tous, Encyclopedie de l'Art Industriel et Decoratif*)

drawn into a set battle, fought in similar 'hedgehog'
formations. Formations of closely formed pikes or spears
were long associated with 'common' armies, which relied on
the massed manpower of the common folk as opposed to
the skilled fighting techniques of the military elite (who
were often nobility).

Unlike the portrayal of Wallace in the movie *Braveheart* as
a highland warrior, he would have dressed little differently to
other minor nobles of the time, taking to the field of battle
armed as a feudal knight. The arms and equipment of such a
warrior would have included a chainmail suit from head to
foot, with, at this time, the beginnings of plate armour to
reinforce vulnerable points:

> After 1250, the development of plate armour was a
> general process and many tomb decorations from the
> end of the thirteenth and beginning of the fourteenth
> centuries depict plates for leg (*gauntlets*), throat (*gorgets*)
> and arm (*vambraces*) protection.
> (Vuksic & Grbasic, 1993: 80)

The head was protected by a Great Basin or bowl-shaped
helmet, and a heart-shaped shield was carried on the left arm
– decorated with the knight's coat of arms. Mounted on a
trained war-horse, the knight carried a 10- or 12-foot long
lance, which could be cut down to fight on foot; this weapon
was accompanied by a well constructed sword of between
3 and 6 feet in length (wielded in one or both hands
depending upon length), a steel headed mace or battle axe, or

William Wallace: Scotland's Braveheart

a morning star (a heavy ball mounted on a chained handle). There is no contemporary record of Wallace's coat of arms, but earlier and later records note that they were red with a white lion Argent (rearing). Greatly influenced by the courts of England and France, Scottish nobles fought in a similar style to their English counterparts. The richest knights would have been similarly attired to their English equivalents, as shown in the seals of Scottish kings such as Alexander III. Lower class nobles may not have been so well equipped, wearing slightly dated armour and riding less well protected horses. However, the Scottish heavy cavalry were essentially mail- and plate-armoured horsemen, riding heavy, trained destrier war-horses, charging home with couched lances.

The armoured heavy cavalryman had but one tactic in Europe – the charge. During the Crusades, a shocked and, as one may imagine, rather disgruntled Saracen, commented that a charging Frank (a generic term for all north-west Europeans) could smash through a wall if he so desired. Vulnerable when exhausted or surrounded, yet almost untouchable in any other straight battlefield situation, the mail-armoured knight of the late thirteenth and early fourteenth centuries was the equivalent of a Main Battle Tank in the Second World War.

Perhaps a greater difference existed between the upper and lower class warriors of a Scots Common army than between the social strata of any other Celtic nation at this time. The Scottish nobility had exchanged intrigue with English nobles for a time before and during the Norman

Conquest; the rise and fall of MacBeth was inextricably linked with English interference, for example. Many historians have commented that the Scottish nobles were more like French lords than Celtic chieftains – and the French and Scots were frequently allied during the medieval period and beyond. Perhaps of some significance for this less Celticized outlook may be laid at the feet of the Norman horsemen employed in Scotland, pre-dating the famous invasion of 1066. Also, with the emergence of Norman power in England, many Anglo-Saxon nobles fled to exile in Scotland, diluting the Celtic nature of the Scottish nobility.

Matthew Paris, an important mid thirteenth-century chronicler, recorded the fighting attitude of a Scottish army in 1244, writing that it was:

> ...very numerous and powerful, consisting of a thousand armed knights, well mounted, although not on Spanish or Italian, or other costly horses, and well protected by armour of steel or linen; and about a hundred thousand foot soldiers, who were all of one mind, and who, having made confession, and been encouraged by the consoling assurance of their preachers, that the cause in which they were engaged was a just one and for their country's good, had very little fear of death.
> (quoted in Hewitt, 1996: 217)

It seems most likely that Matthew Paris may have exaggerated the number of Scottish footmen present, but he does shrewdly make the point that they made dangerous opponents due to

their high morale, and differentiates between the lower quality
Scottish knights and the best equipped continental and
English knights that were the flower of European chivalry.

The definitive warrior of medieval Scotland is often
believed to have been the pikeman. In the later, larger battles
of this period, this is true, but it has to be remembered that
many moments of conflict arose as the result of raiding,
where the pike would have been an impractical weapon.
William Wallace is often credited with the invention of the
schiltron, which appears to have been a circular or oblong
phalanx of close order pikemen – a hedgehog of spear points,
bristling to impale a petulant charge. The tactic is mentioned
from the late thirteenth century onwards, although it may
well have been used in some form before this. The schiltron
was a mostly immovable formation (some sources speak of
small schiltron formations advancing towards the enemy, but
never of larger scale manoeuvres), and after the initial
successes of Stirling and Bannockburn, it became highly
vulnerable to combined attacks by bowmen and knights.

From the mid or late thirteenth century, pikemen
dominated Scottish armies. Before this, men-at-arms and
skirmishers made up the bulk of Scottish armies. The typical
armament of the pre-pike Scottish warrior would have been a
spear and shield, or a two-handed axe. Swords were fairly
commonplace in the medieval period, and most warriors
would carry a weapon of last resort – be it a dagger or a hand
axe. Contemporary illustrations of lowland Scottish warriors
show them in a similar fashion to any other European
footman of the time – with heater shields, kettle helmets, and

quilted jackets for protection. The highland Gaelic warriors were different, of course, but did not often enter into the affairs of the south; they were too busy in their own deadly affairs of politics in the Highlands and Isles. Paul V Walsh (1998) argues for the use of the schiltron before Wallace's time (however, not significantly earlier); before this tactic became widespread Scottish practice though, as explained above, it is likely that Scottish footmen went to war with axes, spears, and swords, in a style similar to that of English men-at-arms.

War Paint and Wallace

Mel Gibson portrays Wallace as a Gaelic warrior complete with blue war paint in the 1995 movie *Braveheart*. As noted in the text, Wallace was actually a minor noble, and would almost certainly have fought in a befitting style on horseback with a lance or axe. Indeed, by the time of his death, Wallace had his own coat of arms. But would any of Wallace's men have donned war paint to go into battle?

The last Roman mention of decorated Pictish warriors appears to be an early fifth-century AD panegyric. By the time the *Anglo-Saxon Chronicle* mentions contact with the Picts, there is no mention of tattooing or war paint – and this would almost certainly have been too good an opportunity for the overtly religious sentiments so often recorded by Anglo-Saxon chroniclers at this time to have not picked up on, taking the war of God upon a painted, unholy northern culture.

William Wallace: Scotland's Braveheart

Despite the initial success of the schiltron, where perhaps the bravery and organization of the Scottish pikemen surprised the English nobility, its triumph was short lived. In the years after the greatest Scottish victory of the entire period, at Bannockburn (1314), the English refined tactics that had first been used by Edward's commanders against the Welsh at Orewin Bridge in 1282 and to inflict the defeat over Wallace's Scots at Falkirk. By a combination of archery and heavy cavalry charges, the English learnt to overpower the tightly packed Scottish pikes. Not well equipped to protect themselves from missiles (pikemen often only having small, buckler shields), the English bowmen rained showers of deadly arrows into their ranks; when depleted to the point of disorder, the Scots were then charged by the flower of English chivalry. This tactic, similar to the Norman victory over the Anglo-Saxons at Hastings, was remarkably effective against the inflexible and stationary Scottish schiltrons. Throughout the fourteenth and into the early fifteenth century, Scottish armies fell to the same English tactic of firepower and cavalry, despite the two initial Scottish successes at Falkirk and Bannockburn.

Other evidence tells us of more lightly armed infantrymen, and that some use of bowmen also occurred. The composition of a Scottish army, like that of most armies at this time, depended upon factors such as who had raised the army, what role it was fulfilling, and (notably for highland armies) what terrain it had chosen to fight on. In many ways, this final point made the Scots more flexible than their English opponents, whose army had individual types of soldier equipped to fulfil specific roles than that role alone.

Warriors

The 'small folk' of medieval Scottish armies should not be
forgotten; peasants in arms, who although not usually an
effective battle force, came into their own when following
up a beaten enemy. Armed with farm implements, old
battered war relics, or the occasional good quality weapon,
the small folk followed the main army to the battlefield
without armour or suitable provisions for a long campaign.
Although of limited value as a fighting force, the lure of
looting the injured and dead made them a useful 'mopping-
up' force, and such small folk were recorded on occasion as
following up a broken enemy with vigour.

The tartans now considered traditional in Scotland were not
worn at this period; Celtic clothing had long favoured woven
chequered and linear patterns, but these were mostly in dulled
natural tints; the modern tartans mostly originated in the
nineteenth century. Ian Heath suggests that medieval tartans
were 'merely a brightly coloured woollen cloth' (1989: 94), but
as most natural dyes give a muted tone (either immediately or
over time), this may not have been the case. Heath also tells us
that Scottish clothing was spotted, striped, or patterned
(derived from the Gaelic word for tartan: *breacan*).

Wallace's greatest moment was undoubtedly the battle of
Stirling Bridge. Wallace's force consisted of around 5000
men, almost entirely infantrymen armed with pikes. The
opposing English force comprised of 300 heavy cavalrymen
and several thousand supporting infantrymen. Wallace chose
his position well – a loop in the River Forth, approachable
by one road only, along a causeway flanked by meadows. Sir
Richard Lundie, a Scottish knight in English service,

apparently tried to warn the English commander, John de Warenne, of the danger of fighting Wallace in this situation:

> 'My Lords, if we cross that bridge now, we are all dead men. For we can only go over two abreast, and the enemy are already formed up: they can charge down on us whenever they wish.'
> (quoted in Guest & Guest, 1996: 28)

Instead, Lundie advised crossing 2 miles upstream at a ford; the impatient de Warenne was keen to get the battle over with and defeat the Scottish force there and then, however, and advanced his force. As the vanguard crossed the bridge, the Scots poured down towards them, and crashed into the forward-most English troops. The English rear surged forward in support, and the bridge creaked, groaned, and broke under their weight. The English vanguard were entrapped across the river from their colleagues, surrounded on marshy land by the jubilant Scots, with little room to manoeuvre and no hope of reinforcement. They were cut down where they stood with the brutality that often accompanied battle between the English and Scots. Across the river, and powerless to send aid, de Warenne could do little more than watch as his vanguard were swamped over and hacked to pieces. A few unarmoured English and Welsh soldiers swam back across the river, but a great many more either drowned or were butchered on dry land on the Scottish bank. The mail-clad knights could not try to cross the river, and over 100 were dragged from their saddles,

fighting desperately to the end. In the aftermath of the
battle, de Warenne fled to Berwick and Wallace was knighted
and proclaimed the Guardian of Scotland. The English king
Edward I decided that next time, he would not send one of
his men to defeat Wallace, but would go in person, applying
all the skill and strategy he could muster from his many
year's experience of fighting victoriously in battle.

After the unsolicited success of Wallace at Stirling Bridge,
his followers were probably confident of another such
success when Wallace met with Edward I's army at Falkirk in
July 1298. The mid nineteenth-century antiquarian John
Hewitt analyzed the battle in typically vivid prose:

> In 1298 Wallace contending against Edward I in person,
> formed his pikemen, who were the strength of his
> army, into four circular bodies, connected together by a
> number of archers from the Forest of Selkirk. Before
> them he planted a defence of palisades: behind them,
> the cavalry was stationed. In front of all was a morass,
> dividing them from the English. The latter, having
> passed the night on the bare heath, in the morning
> advanced to attack. Their first division, commanded by
> the Earl Marshal, from its ignorance of the ground,
> soon became entangled in the morass. The second, led
> by the Bishop of Durham, wheeled around the swamp
> and came in sight of the Scottish cavalry, when the
> prelate ordered his men to await the arrival of other
> bodies. "To thy mass, bishop!" exclaimed one of his
> knights, and rushed on the enemy. They gave way at the

first charge; the bowmen were trampled under foot, but
the four bodies of pikemen opposed on all sides an
impenetrable front. The bravest resistance, however,
could not restore the fortune of the day. Edward
advanced his archers, supporting them with his military
engines, an opening was made in each circle, the men-
at-arms dashed in among the disordered pikemen, and
the battle was won.
(1996: 217–18)

Hewitt, with a cautionary note that should still be echoed
today, makes mention that writers contemporary to the battle
could not be trusted on the number of casualties caused;
Trivet, he tells us, 'reports the loss of the Scotch at twenty
thousand; Matthew of Westminster raises it to forty thousand'
(1996: 218). Edward I's tactics at Falkirk seem to have been
inherited from those of his commander John Giffard at
Orewin Bridge in 1282, where a spear-armed Welsh force was
cut to pieces by a similar combination of cavalry and archery.

Siege warfare is often considered to have been a standard
feature of campaigns in medieval Europe; although a low-
risk method of cordoning off and making impotent an
enemy force, sieges were not often used in the Anglo-
Scottish wars. The Scottish army, by its very nature (a force
mostly consisting of commoners), did not contain a strong
siege train, although later medieval Scottish armies were
amongst the earliest users of gunpowder in western Europe.
A medieval illustration of the Siege of Carlisle gives a good
idea of Anglo-Scottish siege warfare – although a few

engines may have been used (Edward I's famous War Wolf may have been the most exceptional, if mysterious, of these), tactics seem to have mostly revolved around scaling walls with ladders, and mining operations. Both could be costly in manpower, of limited effectiveness against an average or better defender. Scottish armies, when raiding, were more likely to avoid large English garrisons and fortifications, preferring easier targets on the open land – much like any other raiding force throughout history.

Treatment of prisoners in the essentially guerrilla war between Scotland and England varied greatly. The English of Edward I, reportedly believing that they were involved in a holy war against their Celtic enemies, would offer no mercy; Scottish leaders apparently acted more chivalrously towards their English captives, but the war crimes of William Wallace tell us a different story on his part at least.

Army sizes varied according to the campaign. The Scottish force at Dunbar in 1296 absorbed 10,000 casualties, whereas Wallace's initial forces consisted of a handful of brigands only. At Stirling Bridge, Wallace had some 5000 men under his command; de Warenne's force consisted of 300 men-at-arms and several thousand English and Welsh infantry. After the defeat at Stirling, Edward marched into Scotland with the largest force since the Romans, 1000 years before. It consisted over around 2500 armoured cavalry and 2900 infantry. Eight notable earls accompanied Edward; each of these brought along their own retinue of professional knights and infantry. The great Scottish raids that crossed into England in the early fourteenth century consisted of several thousand men; not all of these would be prepared to stand in a set piece medieval battle, deciding that discretion (and pillage) were the better side of valour.

A noble went to war with his household troops; the excellent research carried out by John Morris at the start of the twentieth century into Edward I's well documented Welsh wars of the 1270s and 1280s gives some idea of the numbers of troops involved. Usually a noble would bring between ten and thirty lancers with him, and these would presumably be supported by a number of trained and well equipped infantrymen. The feudal levy supplemented the numbers available. Wallace himself fought with and against small forces early in his military career – he ambushed the English knight Fenwick at Loudon Hill in the Irvine valley, where he was supposed to have defeated a small English force of two hundred men with only fifty warriors himself (100 of the English were recorded to have been killed). Wallace also fought against the English garrison of Lanark, killing around 300 of the garrison.

Raiding was a constant tactic in the harrowing border wars between the English and the Scots. Raids had been going on across both sides of the border for centuries, and continued for many after Wallace's time. The most famous era of lawlessness occurred in the sixteenth century, known as the era of the Border Reiver. When Wallace marched south into England, his force laid waste to much of Cumberland, and rampaged and pillaged its way through to Cockermouth. Typical of such border warfare is the incident where Wallace learnt that many of the Northumbrian

crofters were returning home when the Scottish army had
passed by; he sent men back to slaughter them and steal their
remaining belongings. Border warfare was harsh, designed to
make one's enemies live in constant fear. War waged against
civilians has never been a pleasant campaign to describe, and
Wallace's methods were no different to any other raider's
tactics from Ancient Egypt to the Vietnam War.

Before Mel Gibson's imaginative bio-pic of William
'Braveheart' Wallace, this medieval Scottish warrior
was seldom heard mention of outside of traditional
Scottish folklore. A great deal of credit should be given to
the actors, writer and director of *Braveheart* for turning a
relatively minor brigand and warlord into a general of
international appeal. William Wallace is a historically attested
to warrior, whose actions gave rise to his portrayal as a folk
hero – traditional tales recount the events of his life, albeit in
an 'adjusted' way to make Wallace's deeds more impressive,
even to the extent that his military career took a backseat
compared to his activities as a brigand. Wallace's motley army
inflicted a number of small defeats on ill-led English
garrisons, and achieved a great victory against one of
Edward I's leaders at Stirling Bridge; however, Wallace met
his match in the formidable and very experienced English
king, and his defeat at Falkirk led to his eventual demise.
Wallace's name was remembered by later Scottish leaders,
helping them to will their soldiers on to fight both in
defence of their own lands and while invading English soil.

BIBLIOGRAPHY

Perhaps unusually, this bibliography is not divided according to chapter but by historical and legendary sources; many of the books listed below are extremely useful sources of further information for more than just one chapter.

Sources of Legend

Barber, P, *Vampires, Burial, And Death*. 1988.
Barber, R, *Living Legends*. 1980.
—*Myths and Legends of the British Isles*. 1999.
Bulfinch, T, *The Golden Age of Myth & Legend*. 1915.
Coe, J B and Young, S, *The Celtic Sources for the Arthurian Legend*. 1995.
Cooper, J C (ed.), *Brewer's Myth and Legend*. 1992.
Cotterell, Arthur (ed.), *World Mythology*. 1999.
Crystal, D (ed.), *The Cambridge Biographical Encyclopedia*, second edition. 1999.
Doel, F & Doel, G, *Robin Hood: Outlaw or Greenwood Myth*. 2000.
Ebbutt, M I, *The British*. 1910.
Evans, Alun, *Brassey's Book of War Films*. 2000.
Geoffrey of Monmouth (trans. Lewis Thorpe), *The History of the Kings of Britain*. 1982.
Gregory, Lady I A, *Cuchulain of Muirthemne*. 1902.
Guerber, H A, *The Myths of Greece and Rome*. 1907.
—*Myths & Legends of the Middle Ages*. 1919.
Haining, P, *The Dracula Scrapbook*. 1987.
Harrison, R (trans.). *The Song of Roland*. 1970.
Heaney, Seamus, *Beowulf: A New Translation*. 1999.
Holt, J C, *Robin Hood*. 1989.
Homer, *The Odyssey*.
Homer, *The Iliad*.
Longfellow, H G, *The Song of Hiawatha*. 1855.
Malory, Thomas (ed. Janet Cowen), *Le Morte D'Arthur*. 1969 (two volumes).
Marsden, J, *Northanhymbre Saga*. 1995.
Matthews, C and J, *The Arthurian Book of Days*. 1990.
Newton, Sam, *The Origins of Beowulf*. 1993.
Ousby, Ian (ed.), *The Wordsworth Companion to Literature in English*. 1994.
Piggott, Stuart, *Ancient Britons and the Antiquarian Imagination: Ideas from the Renaissance to the Regency*. 1989.
Rolleston, T W, *Celtic Myths and Legends*. This edition 1994.
Rose, H J, *A Handbook of Greek Mythology*. 1958.
Shakespeare, William. *Macbeth*. This edition edited by A W Verity 1962.
Spence, L, *Myths and Legends of the North American Indians*. 1914.
Stoker, Bram, *Dracula*. This edition 1993.
Stone, B (trans.) *Sir Gawain and the Green Knight*. 1964.
Summers, Montague, *The Vampire in Europe*. 1929.
Tennyson, A, *The Passing of Arthur*. 1869.

Sources of History

Alcock, L, *Society, Economy and Warfare Amongst the Britons and Saxons*. 1987.
—*Arthur's Britain*. 1989.
Bassett, S (ed.), *The Origins of the Anglo-Saxon Kingdoms*. 1993.
Carver, Martin (ed.), *The Age of Sutton Hoo: The Seventh Century in North-West Europe*. 1992.
Catlin, G, *Life Among the Indians*. 1875.
Chard, Chester S, 'New World Origins: A Reappraisal' *Antiquity* XXXIII, No. 129: 44–49. 1959.
Cotterell, A, *The Penguin Encyclopedia of Ancient Civilizations*. 1980.
Creasy, E S, *The Fifteen Decisive Battles of the World From Marathon To Waterloo*. 1851.
Cunliffe, B (ed.), *The Oxford Illustrated Prehistory of Europe*. 1994.
Ellis, P, *Celt and Saxon*. 1993.
Evans, Stephen S, *Lords of Battle: Image and Reality of the Comitatus in Dark-Age Britain*. 1997.
Foster, S M, *Picts, Gaels and Scots*. 1996.
Fox, R A Jr., *Archaeology, History and Custer's Last Battle*. 1993.
Foxhall, L and Davies, J K, *The Trojan War: Its Historicity and Context*. 1984.
Graham-Campbell, J, *The Viking World*. 1989.
Greene, K, *Archaeology: An Introduction*. 1983.
Griffith, P, *The Viking Art of War*. 1995.
Guest, K & Guest, D, *British Battles*. 1996.
Gush, George, *Renaissance Armies 1480–1650*. 1982.
Hakluyt, R, *The Principal Navigations, Voyages, Traffiques & Discoveries of the English Nation Made by Sea or Overland*. This edition 1907.
Halsall, Guy, *Early Medieval Cemeteries*. 1995.
Haywood, J, *Dark Age Naval Power*. 1999.
Heath, Ian, *Armies of the Dark Ages 600–1066*. Second edition 1980.
—*Armies of Feudal Europe 1066–1300*. Second edition 1980.
—*Armies of the Sixteenth Century: Volume 2: The armies of the Aztec and Inca Empires, other native peoples of the Americas, and the Conquistadores*. 1999.
Hewitt, John, *Ancient Armour and Weapons in Europe*. 1855. (Reprinted as Ancient Armour and Weapons, 1996.)
Hibbert, Christopher, *The Story of England*. 1992.

Warriors

Holmes, M, *King Arthur: A Military History*. 1996.

Hooper, N and Bennett, M, *The Cambridge Illustrated Atlas of Warfare: The Middle Ages 768–1487*. 1996.

Hope Robbins, Russel, *Encyclopedia of Witchcraft and Demonology*.

Humble, R and Scollins, R., *The Soldier*. 1986.

Jarman, A (trans.), *Aneirin: Y Gododdin*. 1988.

Karunanithy, D, 'Scone of the Bright Shields', *Slingshot* 198. 1998,

Keen, Maurice (ed.), *Medieval Warfare: A History*. 1999.

Kishlansky, M, Geary, P, O'Brien, P, *Civilization in the West: Volume A, to 1500*. 1991.

Laing, L, *Celtic Britain*. 1979.

Macdowall, S, *Late Roman Infantryman*. 1994.

—*Late Roman Cavalryman*. 1995.

Matthews, John & Stewart, Bob, *Celtic Warrior Chiefs*. 1993.

McInally, R and Florescu, R., *In Search of Dracula*. 1992.

McNamee, Colm. *The Wars of the Bruces: Scotland, England and Ireland, 1306–1328*. 1997.

Mersey, Daniel, 'Early Anglo-Saxon burial and St Neots', *SNLHM* 33. 1997.

—*Glutter of Ravens: Warfare in the Age of Arthur AD 400–700*. 1998.

—'Medieval Welsh warriors and warfare', *Slingshot* 204. 1999.

—'Between fire and sea: the armies of the Britons AD 400–450', *Slingshot* 211. 2000.

Morris, J, *The Welsh Wars of Edward I*. 1901.

Morris, J, *The Age of Arthur*. 1973.

Nagelfell, K (ed.), *North American Indian Chiefs*. 1995.

Newark, T, *Warlords: Ancient, Celtic and Medieval*.

Nicolle, D, *Arthur and the Anglo-Saxon Wars*. 1984.

—*The Age of Charlemagne*. 1984.

—*Medieval Warfare Source Book*, (two volumes). 1995.

Ohlgren, T H, *Medieval Outlaws: Ten Tales in Modern English*. 1998.

Oman, Charles, *A History of the Art of War in the Middle Ages*. 1924.

Osgood, R, *Warfare in the Late Bronze Age of North Europe*. 1998.

—'Britain in the age of warrior heroes', *British Archaeology* 46. 1999.

Page, Denys, 'The Historical Sack of Troy', *Antiquity XXXIII*, No. 129: 25–31. 1959.

Palmer, Leonard R, *Mycenaeans and Minoans*. Second edition 1965.

Parker, Geoffrey (ed.), *The Cambridge Illustrated History of Warfare*. 1995.

Perrett, Bryan, *The Battle Book*. 1992.

Philips, G and Keatman, M, *King Arthur: The True Story*. 1992

Ranitzsch, K H, 'News from Troy', *Slingshot* 203. 1999.

Remfry, P M, *Bloody Montgomery: 1223–1295*. 1998.

Renfrew, C, *Before Civilisation*. 1973.

—and Bahn, P, *Archaeology: Theories, Methods, and Practice*. 1991.

Ritchie, A, *Viking Scotland*. 1993.

Ritchie, W F & Ritchie, J N G, *Celtic Warriors*. 1985.

Roberts, J M, *The Shorter History of the World*. 1993.

Rodrigues, Louis J, *Three Anglo-Saxon Battle Poems*. 1996.

Rothero, Christopher, *The Scottish and Welsh Wars 1250–1400*. 1989.

Ryan, M (ed.), *The Illustrated Archaeology of Ireland*. 1991.

Saul, Nigel, *The Batsford Companion to Medieval England*. 1983.

Savage, Anne (trans.), *The Anglo-Saxon Chronicles*. 1997.

Saxtorph, N M, *Warriors and Weapons of Early Times*. 1972.

Shadrake, Dan & Shadrake, Susanna, *Barbarian Warriors: Saxons, Vikings, Normans*. 1997.

Sherley-Price, L (trans.), *Bede: A History of the English Church and People*. 1955.

Skene, W, (ed. D Bryce), *Arthur and the Britons in Wales and Scotland*. 1988.

Smurthwaite, D, *The Complete Guide to the Battlefields of Britain*. 1984.

Snyder, Christopher A, *An Age of Tyrants: Britain and the Britons AD 400–600*. 1998.

Southern, Pat & Dixon, Karen R, *The Roman Cavalry*. 1992.

—*The Late Roman Army*. 1996.

Stoicescu, N, *Vlad Tepes*.

Taylor, C F and Sturtevant, W C, *The Native Americans: The Indigenous People of North America*. 1991.

Thorpe, L (trans.), *Gerald of Wales: The Journey Through Wales / The Description of Wales*. 1978.

Underwood, Richard, *Anglo-Saxon Weapons and Warfare*. 1999.

Warry, John, *Warfare in the Classical World*. 1980.

Watson, Fiona, *Under the Hammer: Edward I and Scotland 1286–1307*. 1998.

Webster, L and Brown, M (eds.), *The Transformation of the Roman World AD 400–900*. 1997.

Welch, M, *Highdown and its Saxon Cemetery*. 1976.

—*English Heritage Book of Anglo-Saxon England*. 1992.

Walsh, Paul V, 'Braveheart: History or Myth?', *Slingshot* 196. 1998.

Wood, M, *In Search of the Trojan Wars*. 1985.

Vuksic, V & Grbasic, Z, *Cavalry: The History of a Fighting Elite*. 1993.

INDEX

Warriors